The Folk-Literature of Bengal

(Being Lectures delivered to the Calcutta University in 1917, as Ramtanu Lahiri Research Fellow in the History of Bengali Language and Literature)

Author
Rai Saheb Dineshchandra Sen, B.A.

Foreword by
W.R. Gourlay, Esq., M.A., C.I.E., I.C.S.

GYAN PUBLISHING HOUSE
NEW DELHI-110002

The Folk-Literature of Bengal

ISBN: 81-212-0911-0

Published in 2006 in India by
Gyan Publishing House,
5, Ansari Road, Daryaganj, New Delhi-110002
E-mail: books@gyanbooks.com

Laser Typesetting at: Vinayak Printers, Delhi
Printed at: Salasar Imaging System, Delhi

To

THE HON'BLE SIR ASUTOSH MOOKERJEE,
Kt., C.S.I., M.A., D.L., D.Sc., Ph.D.

these pages are dedicated

as an humble token of

the Author's deep sense of gratitude

for

the epoch-making step he has taken

by initiating and organising the new department of

Indian Vernaculars in our University,

a movement that is fraught with vast possibilities

for the development of Indian National Life,

based on a clear consciousness of

India's distinctive greatness

and homogeneous cultural progress.

FOREWORD

There are few people who have not been subjected to the command, "Tell me a story," and those who, on such occasions, find pleasure in trying to make children happy, rack their brains to find something new to tell. They desire that their story should contain nothing but thoughts full of good-will and encouragement to follow good examples. In the telling of the story it is natural to picture the details of the scene according to the story-teller's own experience. Such is the incentive from which the folk-tale is born.

To those of us who come from the West, it comes as a pleasing surprise to find in the folk-tales of India scenes and incidents which are familiar to us from our early reading of Grimm's Fairy Tales and Hans Anderson's Fairy Tales. This similarity early attracted the attention of scholars and there have been controversies as to the original sources of tales common to East and West : Sir William Jones and the early Sanskrit scholars who worked with him, found two collections of these tales so complete as to leave no further doubt that the origin was, as had been surmised, in the East. This discovery made it clear that those tales, with which we are all so familiar, had their origin not later than the early days of the Christian era: and there were many who saw in the incidents and the teaching of the tales the influence of the life and teaching of the Lord Buddha and his disciples. For long it was supposed, therefore, that the tales had had their origin in the ancient kingdom of Magadha and that they might have been composed by the followers of the Lord Buddha himself. More recently, however, the Jataka collection of the Buddhist stories was discovered and amongst the carvings on the railings round the Bharhut stupa—scenes from these stories were recognised. As the carving dates from 250 to 200 B.C., the origin of the tales is now believed to be not later than the time when Buddha lived about the 5th century, B.C., and it is recognised that the features which seemed to prove a Buddhist origin are really alterations made to suit the Buddhist doctrine. It is not likely that materials will come to light to enable us to trace the origin still further back, but who can say when these tales were first conceived?

The attempts to trace the source of the tales have brought to light hidden knowledge. The history of the Indian people in these ancient days is but imperfectly known, but the tales are a mirror of the customs and the thoughts of the people and, as such, are of far greater value to us than the dates and the names of a few individuals—the dry bones of history. It needs but a glance at the pictures of the Bharhut carvings in the book of Jataka stories edited by Francis and Thomas to enable us to picture the life of the people in those times—and from these little carvings, we can create a mental picture of the incidents in the other tales; and the picture is so very like the scenes we see every day. Human nature changes little, and the primitive emotions are depicted on men's faces now as they were then. In India there has been little change in the environment of village life for thousands of years and often little change in the fashion of the simple dress of the villager. In the West, on the other hand, the environment of to-day is so different from that of ages gone by that our pictures of folk tales have often grotesque appearance almost entirely absent in India. The monkey, the elephant, the fighting ram of the Bharhut carvings have in no way changed, and their environment is the same.

In these lectures, Mr. Dineshchandra Sen gives us an interesting account of the history of some of these fables and he puts forward a fascinating suggestion that possibly the tales of the Middle Kingdom were carried by means of the ships which sailed from the coasts of Bengal to the ports of the Persian Gulf and that thus they travelled, with those who transported the merchandise, to far away ports of Europe—long before any translations of the Panchatantra or Hitopadeṣa or translations like our fables of Pilpai were known.

In the following lectures, our attention is directed in particular to Bengal, and the examples given afford a delightful picture of village life in that Province. When I read in the first lecture the author's enthusiastic appreciation of Bengal folk tales, the thought crossed my mind that possibly the Rai Sahib's patriotism had affected his judgment: but after I had read the translation of the beautiful story of Malanchamala, I went back to the first lecture and I knew that what he said was true.

Everyone who reads this Bengali folk-tale will endorse what he says. It is a tale of which a nation might well be proud: it has all the attributes of a beautiful lyric: it contains a conception of purity and love which evince a high state of civilization. The rural scenes are full of the joy of life. One cannot but feel the fresh air of the morning when the King rides out to the mango grove: one shudders at the scene round the funeral pyre: the forest is gloomy in the darkness but fresh and smiling in the sunshine. Nothing could be more simple or charming than the account of the life in the cottage of the flower woman: I have never read anything which lead me to such an understanding of the sublimity of the conception of the ideal Hindu wife, as I have obtained from the reading of the story of Malanchamala. The interest never flags. No one who begins the story can rest till he has reached the end. The teaching too is sublime.

I hope Rai Sahib Dineshchandra Sen will be able to do a further service to literature by making a collection of Bengali folk tales. Such a collection would help the people of the West to get nearer to the people of Bengal. There are so many barriers. Good will is often present, but good will must be supported by knowledge. It is easy to obtain some knowledge by studying the history and the literature of the country and by reading novels such as those of Bankim Chandra, but here is a door that has been little more than pushed ajar by Lalbihari De, and from the evidence we have in these lectures, I feel sure the author could open it for us. Our childhood is spent under very different conditions of environment. When we read tales such as Malanchamala it brings us much nearer to understanding, and if we could only learn to know each other's childhood, there would be less anxiety regarding our understanding later on.

I am grateful to the author for having asked me to write this introduction. I hope it may have the effect of bringing the lectures to the notice of some who might not otherwise have been led to a knowledge of the Folk Tales of Bengal.

W. R. GOURLAY.

The 18th January, 1920.

PREFACE

My first course of lectures as Ramtanu Lahiri Research Fellow of the Calcutta University in the history of Bengali Language and Literature, delivered in 1914, was published under the title of *Chaitanya and his Companions* in 1917. The present volume contains my Fellowship lectures delivered in 1917. From 1914 to 1919, I delivered six courses of such lectures; each course, complete in 12 lectures, forms a volume of the size of this book. As most of these lectures have not yet been published and as there is no certainty about the time of their publication, I owe it to the public to refresh their memory about what they heard long ago, by mentioning the subjects treated in them.

1. Chaitanya and his Companions, delivered in 1914.

2. The second course of my lectures delivered in 1915 treats of the following subjects :

(*a*) Glimpses of Bengal History from old Bengali Literature.

(*b*) Songs and Ballads of the Buddhistic period.

(*c*) Chandidāsa.

(*d*) Desertion of Nadia by Chaitanya.

(*e*) Humour in old Bengali poetry.

3. The Bengali Rāmāyaṇas. In these lectures, delivered in 1916, I tried to prove that some of the legends and stories about Rāma, Rāvana, and Hanumāna, now found incorporated in the various versions of the Bengali Rāmāyaṇas by different authors, are of a prehistoric origin, probably anterior to Vālmīki's epic. It is evident that these Bengali authors did not follow too closely the foot-steps of Vālmīki, but introduced indigenous elements in them not contained in the Sanskrit epic.

4. The Folk Literature of Bengal—delivered in 1917.

5. The forces that developed our early literature—delivered in 1918.

6. Chaitanya and his Age—1919.

I have to offer a word of explanation for the publication of my fourth course of lectures delivered in 1917 before the preceding courses of such lectures, delivered in 1915 and in 1916 respectively, have seen the light. An active research is going on in the field of old Bengali Literature and new materials are being made available to us every year. The history of our language and literature no longer presents a fossilized form, but by the powerful impetus, given to it by Sir Asutosh Mookerjee, it is fast invading "fresh fields and pastures new" and changing shapes. Some portions of my previous lectures have had to be revised and re-written in the light of the latest discoveries. Hence those lectures that are found ready at the moment are made over to the press while others have to be held up.

In the present treatise I have for the first time brought to the notice of scholars considerable materials about Bengali folk-tales chiefly those current amongst the Mahomedans of the lower Gangetic valley. It has been a surprise to us to find that stories of Rūpamālā, Kānchanmālā, Madhumālā, Pushpamālā, etc., are not only the heritage of Hindu children but also of their Moslem cousins who have been listening to these nursery and fairy tales, recited to them by their grand-mothers, from a very remote historical period which I have tried to prove to be much anterior to the Islamic conquest. The Hindu and Buddhistic converts who gave up their faith in the older religions did not forego their attachment to these folk-tales in which legends of Buddhist and Hindu gods are sometimes closely intermixed. The incantation and *mantras* used by Moslem Fakirs and physicians for curing diseases and the hymns of Lakshmi—the harvest-goddess—recited by a class of Mahomedan mendicants—are full of references to gods of the Hindu and Buddhistic pantheons, and I have tried to trace the continuity of this folklore and folk-wisdom current amongst Mahomedans, from a remote time when they had not yet accepted Islam but had been Buddhists or Hindus.

These lectures on the Folk Literature of Bengal are by no means exhaustive. I have not touched the pastoral poetry and boatmen's songs with which the whole air of rural Bengal is still resonant—not her cities and towns, but her backward villages, still lovely with the dark-blue foliage of mango-groves and rich in her summer bloom, where the fierce rays of materialistic civilization have not yet entered to dispel the charm of rural poetry. These songs and pastoral poetry open a vista showing the perspective of ages long gone by. If I find an opportunity I will deal with this fascinating subject in a future course of lectures.

A further enquiry on the lines of these lectures made by me has brought to light several very important facts in regard to the Bengali folk tales. There is a mere hint in this work that some of our old folk stories are interspersed with bits of poetical lines rendered into prose, which have been evidently current amongst our woman-folk from a remote antiquity. I have proved in another course of my lectures that some of the old stories are so fully replete with these poetical bits, cleverly strung together and put in the midst of a prose style, that the work of the goddess of Parnessus lies, as it were, hidden from our view, until the scrutinising eye of a scholar detects them. The language of these half-verses is generally very ancient and reminds one of the discovery made by Dr. E. W. Hopkins of the existence of Vedic hymnology in the great epic of the Mahābhārata.

I can scarcely suppress a feeling of joy that inspires me in my research work at the present moment. Hitherto I had felt myself alone in the task of writing the annals of the Bengali language and literature, though I do not imply by this any lack of regard for the work of some of my colleagues in the field who have in the midst of their multifarious and scholarly tasks, made important contributions to it from time to time. But a whole-hearted devotion to this cause was wanting in the young generation of Bengalees, and to-day this longfelt want seems to be removed by the daily growing number of those who are wishing to take up Bengali as a subject for the M.A. Examination and by the enthusiasm displayed by these earnest students in the cause of their hitherto neglected literature. They appear to me to be the heralds of a new age, that will, let us confidently hope, ere long dawn on us. In the march towards this goal our confidence is accentuated by the fact that the man at the helm has a never-failing steady foresight and sees the vision of our future glory, as no one else in the country has the power to see. The boat is launched and the pilot will steer it on to the shore of the ideal land, let us hope.

I take this opportunity to thank Mr. W. R. Gourlay, M.A., C.I.E., I.C.S., Private Secretary to H E. the Governor of Bengal, for writing the Foreword. Mr. Gourlay has been in Bengal for more than 20 years and is well known as a diligent student of the life and civilisation of our people. In his address delivered at a meeting of the Indian section of the Royal Society of Arts held in London on the 6th of March, 1919, he indicated the various stages of our national history and suggested a practical scheme of an up-to-date comprehensive history of Bengal with a scholarship and breadth of outlook that evoked the admiration of such eminent men as Sir S. Bayley, Mr. C. E. Buckland, Mr. Skrine and Lord Carmichael. The appreciation of the story of Mālañchamālā as contained in his Foreword, though he had at first hesitated to accept my views expressed in pp. 44-47 will give to the reader a glimpse of the characteristic sympathy and genuine goodness of the heart with which he has always tried to understand India and her people.

I have to thank Dr. G. Howells, Dr. H. Stephen and Dr. H. C. Mookerjee for revising some of the proofs of this book. Mr. A. C. Ghatak, Superintendent of the University

Press, has also helped me in such matters—but I am sorry to say that there are still many printing mistakes in the book. This has been inevitable because I am not a good proof-reader myself and I could not make satisfactory arrangement for getting this very tiresome work done from the beginning to the end.

BEHALA,
NEAR CALCUTTA;
The 21st January, 1920.

DINESH CHANDRA SEN.

Contents

CHAPTER I

CHAPTER II

CHAPTER III

CHAPTER IV

Muhammadan folk-tales in Bengal, pp. 98-145.

The three main divisions, p. 98; Class I, 'Satya Pīr,' pp. 99-113; Wazed Ali's story of Satya Pir, p. 103; Sundara in charge of Sumati and Kumati—they try to plan his assassination—restored to life by Satya Pīr—assassination a second time—Sundara goes to Kanur by means of the magic tree—Sundara returns home—transformed into a bird—the princess comes to Chandan Nagar—return of the elder brother—Sundara gets back his human shape—the joy of union—the punishment, pp. 103-113; Manik Pir, Pizuruddin's version, p. 113; Dhuda Bibi's pride and misfortunes—defiant attitude and the punishment—Manik sold to a merchant—a mean suspicion and Manik thrown into fire—rescued by Gebrial and turns a Fakir—Ranjanā's punishment and eventual restoration to good fortunes by the grace of the Pīr—the Ghosh family—the mother does an wicked act—Kānu stung by a cobra—restored to life—they lose and regain their fortunes, pp. 113-122; historical side totally obscured by legends, p. 123. Class II—Pioneers of Islamite faith, p. 123; the story of Mallikā, p. 124; Hanif goes on an expedition against Rajā Varuṇa—the princess not only handsome but possessed of great physical strength—how

CHAPTER V.

Four kinds of folk-tales, pp. 232-344.

Folk Literature of Bengal

CHAPTER I

Striking coincidences between some of the Bengali and European Folk-tales

WE need not enter into the vexed question of the origin of folk-tales. We may imagine that long before the introduction of the art of printing, primitive peoples sat by their blazing hearths in wintry nights at the close of their day's labour, reciting nursery tales to their children. The songs and tales became transmitted from generation to generation, and long after a nation had scaled the height of civilization, this invaluable heritage of their primitive stage, recording the earliest conditions of their social life, still supplied fountains of pleasure and sorrow to children, and taught them moral lessons—of virtue predominating over vice in the long run. For, every story, however crude its form, has an object-lesson to teach to the

The early origin of folk-tales and the moral lessons they convey.

young. In it "justice always prevails, active talent is everywhere successful, the amiable and generous qualities are brought forward to excite the sympathies of the reader, and in the end are constantly rewarded by triumph over lawless power".[1]

The Greek legends as folk-tales.

The early European tales are full of adventurous spirit, of fights of legendary heroes with dragons and monsters for the acquisition of rare prizes. The tale of Perseus who carried the head of the Gorgon Medusa in a magic wallet,—of Herakles who secured the golden apples from the garden of Hesperides and made his escape from the giant Atlas with the prize,—of Bellerophon who killed the Chimaira with the help of the ærial steed Pegasos,—of the encounter of Theseus with the Minotaur, and of the former killing the dragon with the help of Ariadne,—of Jason who fought with and killed the terrible dragon that guarded the Golden Fleece, with the council of Medeia, the enchantress,—these and other Greek legends, full of enterprize, physical daring and valour, were the fables that European children were accustomed to hear from their grandsires when civilization dawned on the West. These are typical stories of early Europe and have scarcely any oriental flavour in them.

[1] Grimms' Popular Stories. Oxford University Press, 1909, Preface, p. X.

But even in these early Greek tales, we occasionally come across one or two which savour of an exotic origin. The story of the miraculous milk-pitcher, which had the marvellous quality of being never empty, obtained by Philemen and his wife Baukis is so like some of the Indian stories, that we may not be very wrong in finding a faint trace of Eastern origin in the fable. The story of Kirke, the enchantress, who could transform princes to animals by her sorcery, has many a parallel in our Indian, notably Bengali, fables.

Europe indebted to India for its Medieval literature of fairy tales and fables.

In many of the stories prevalent in different countries of Europe, we find animals supporting the leading characters. Western scholars are of opinion that these "strongly bear the impress of a remote Eastern original".[1] There is no doubt that many of the nursery tales travelled from their eastern homes to Europe in the middle ages. We know for certain that the Indian fables in the Panchatantra and in the Hitopodeça made a triumphant march to the West and "exercised very great influence in shaping the literature of the Middle ages of Europe".[2] Europe imported these fables into her shores chiefly through their Arabic translations. Many of the stories are now as

---

[1] Grimms' Popular Stories, Oxford University Press, 1909, Preface p. X.

[2] Macdonell's History of Sanskrit Literature, Ed. 1899, p. 421.

familiar in European countries as they have been in India. Among a considerably large number of these we may mention here the story of the milk-maid "who while carrying a pail of milk on her head to the market, and building all kinds of castles in the air with the future proceeds of the sale of the milk, gives a jump of joy at the prospect of her approaching fortune and thereby shatters the pail to pieces on the ground." This story, first related in the Panchatantra, was made familiar in Europe by La Fontaine in his charming book of fables in 1678 A.D. The Persian writers copied it with slight alteration in the story of Young Alanaschar's dreams. Another familiar story in the Panchatantra is that of the avaricious jackal, whose calculations and too economic wisdom ended in his tragical death by the bow of the hunter starting asunder and piercing his head. The well known line অত্যভক্ষ্য ধনুগুর্ণঃ has now passed into a common saying in this country. La Fontaine popularised this story in Europe. Dr. Macdonell in his History of Sanskrit Literature tells us "Europe was thus undoubtedly indebted to India for its Mediæval literature of fairy tales and fables".[1] The Persians and the Arabs are also indebted to India for acquiring the art of story-telling. We quote the same authority on this point.[2]

[1] Ed. 1899, p. 420.
[2] " " p. 369.

"The style of narration was borrowed from India by the neighbouring oriental peoples of Persia and Arabia, who employed it in composing independent works. The most notable instance is, of course, the Arabian Nights." That some of the stories of the Arabian Nights were taken from Indian tales will be mentioned later on. But how could the folk-tales of Bengal current amongst her peasant folk and her women break through the mud-walls of the rustic homes and the seclusion of the female apartments to find an audience in the world outside? The Jātaka stories, the Panchatantra, the Hitopadeça and even the Kathāsaritsāgara certainly obtained a world-wide celebrity in the past. Most of these were written in courts by royal order and commanded circulation all over the world by authoritative translations into foreign languages.

How did the unwritten folk-tales of Bengal travel to Europe?

But the folk-tales of Bengal, told by village-women and mostly composed by them, in the quiet environment of shady mangoe-groves amidst which stood their straw-roofed mud-huts, —like the coy Mālati flowers that bloomed in the evening there—did not venture to peep out and show themselves to strangers. What conveyances could carry these our family-treasures to Europe in the remote past? These stories passed from mouth to mouth and were never written in Bengal itself, till the middle of the 16th century, when only one of them is known to us to have been recast and written out in a verse form by Fakir Rām Kavibhushana. The rest, so far as we know, were never written till only recent times. How could these travel to Europe? How could the whispers of our own woodlands be heard on the shores of the Baltic, of the Mediterranian and the English Channel? This could only be possible by the humbler classes of Indian people coming in contact with European men. No printing press could give publicity to what was never written and was chiefly confined within the four walls of the Zenana. We have it on the authority of Firdausi, that Sankhal, the king of Kanauj "sent 10,000 men and female *Luris* recruited from different parts of Northern India, who could play upon the lute" to the Persian king Behram Gor in 420 A.D. at his request. These *Luris* travelled to Europe and settled in various parts of it and became known as Gypsies. Their language bears a close affinity to Hindi and other Aryan dialects of India. And the latest of these Gypsy settlements took place in Hungary in 1470 A.D. It may be that these people brought their folk-tales to Europe. Or who knows but that the hulls and ships which landed the cotton fabrics known as the Dacca Muslin on the European shores also landed our folk-stories there! The Arab merchants conveyed much of oriental, notably Indian, wisdom to European countries. The connection between Europe and Asia by means of trade has been one of hoary antiquity. Gujarat, Bengal and the picturesque shores of South Orissa had a considerable number of ports that sent their ships all over the world and were famous for their maritime activities in ancient times. It may not be wrong to suppose that our nursery tales travelled to other countries in boatmen's songs and in their half-broken narrations to foreign peoples whose dialects they could have but imperfectly acquired. Thus it will be seen that though the European versions of some these imported tales bear an undoubted stamp of Indian—probably Bengali origin, the details are worked out in different methods, proving that the outlines of our stories, rather than their finer shades, were gathered from imperfect verbal narrations of story-tellers not thoroughly acquainted with the speeches of the people before whom they were narrated. Some of the European scholars have proved that a close communication between the European and Asiatic races was established during the days of the Crusade when the folk-tales and the legends of the one country passed to the other.

We will now show by illustrations that some of the folk-tales that are even now narrated in the lower Gangetic valley have their exact counter-parts in those which delight the young in European countries. The story of "Faithful John" collected by the Brothers Grimm[1] is one such for instance. The Rev. Lal Behary Dey calls this the story of 'Fakirchānd.' But the story has got other names also. It was known to us in our younger days as the story of the Princess Rūpamālā. We need not however trouble ourselves with the name which is a very trivial point. The chief actors in these stories were three birds who had the power to see into the future and whose sayings were always of a prophetic nature. Let us now show the leading points of similarity between the European and the Bengali versions. Faithful John attended his new King, to whom he was devotedly attached on his journey back to his capital. John was seated on the prow of the ship, and was playing on his flute. The king and his consort were very happy at the time. John saw three ravens flying in the air towards him. Then he left off playing and listened to what they said to each other, for he understood their tongue. The first said "There he (the new king) goes; he surely has her, for she is sitting by his side in the ship." Then the first began again, and cried out "what boots it him? See you not that when they

The story of Faithful John and of Fakirchānd or Rūpamālā.

[1] Grimms' Popular Stories, Oxford University Press, Ed. 1909, p. 194.

come to land, a horse of a fox-red colour will spring towards him ; and then he will try to get upon it and if he does, it will spring away with him into the air, so that he will never see his love again." "True ! true !" said the second, "but is there no help ?" "Oh yes, yes," said the first, "if he who sits upon the horse takes the dagger which is stuck in the saddle and strikes him dead, the king is saved, but who knows that, and who will tell him, that he who thus saves the king's life will turn to stone from the toes of his feet to his knee." Then the second said : "True ! true ! but I know more still, though the horse be dead, the king loses his bride ; when they go together into the palace, there lies the bridal dress on the couch, and looks as if it were woven of gold and silver but it is all brimstone and pitch ; and he puts it on, it will burn him marrow and bones." "Alas ! Alas ! is there no help ?" said the third. "Oh yes, yes," said the second, "if someone draws near and throws it into the fire, the young king will be saved. But what boots that ? who knows and will tell him, that, if he does, his body from the knee to the heart will be turned into stone ?" "More ! more ! I know more," said the third, "were the dress burnt still the king loses his bride. After the wedding, when the dance begins and the young queen dances on, she will turn pale, and fall as though she were dead, and if someone does not draw near and lift her up and take from her right breast three drops of blood, she will surely die. But if anyone knew this, he would tell him, that if he does do so, his body will turn to stone, from the crown of his head to the tip of his toe." Then the ravens flew away. Faithful John did fulfil all the conditions to save the young king and his consort from their impending perils, and then turned to a stone image. For he was obliged to state the reasons for his conduct which had appeared highly offensive, though he had to do so at the sacrifice of his life. The only condition on the fulfilment of which John could be brought back to life was that the king should cut off the head of his baby as soon as it was born, and sprinkle its blood over John's image. Though it was the severest trial for the parents to undergo, the king and the queen did it for the sake of faithful John. The sequel of the story is that John was restored to life and the baby also revived by the will of Providence.

In the old story from Bengal, the minister's son plays the part of faithful John. The young prince with his fair bride is on his way back home. It is night and the married couple sleep under a tree finding no human habitation near. The minister's son keeps watch in order, to prevent any danger. He overhears the following conversation between Bihangamā and

Bihangamī, two prophetic birds perched on a bough of that tree.[1]

Bihangamā (the male bird)—The minister's son will find it difficult to save the prince at last.

Bihangamī (the female bird).—Why so?

Bihangamā—Many dangers await the king's son; the prince's father, when he hears of the approach of his son, will send for him an elephant, some horses and attendants. When the king's son rides on the elephant, he will fall down and die.

Bihangamī.—But suppose some one prevents the king's son from riding on the elephant and makes him ride on horse-back, will he not in that case be saved?

Bihangamā.—Yes, he will in that case escape that particular danger, but a fresh danger awaits him. When the king's son is in sight of his father's palace, and when he is in the act of passing through its lion-gate, the lion-gate will fall upon him and crush him to death.

Bihangamī.—But suppose some one destroys the lion-gate before the king's son goes up to it; will not the king's son in that case be saved?

Bihangamā.—Yes, in that case he will escape that particular danger: but a fresh danger awaits him. When the king's son reaches the

[1] Folk-tales of Bengal by Lal Behary Dey, Macmillan & Co., 1911, pp. 40-42.

palace and sits at a feast prepared for him, and when he takes into his mouth the head of a fish cooked for him, the head of the fish will stick in his throat and choke him to death.

Bihangamī.—But suppose some one sitting at the feast snatched the head of the fish from the prince's plate and thus prevents him putting it into his mouth, will not the king's son in that case be saved ?

Bihangamā.—Yes, in that case the life of the king's son will be saved ; but a fresh danger awaits him. When the prince and the princess retire into their sleeping apartment, and they lie together in bed, a terrible cobra will come into the room and bite the king's son to death.

Bihangamī.—But suppose some one lying in wait in the room cut the snake into pieces, will not the king's son in that case be saved ?

Bihangamā.—Yes, in that case the life of the king's son will be saved. But if the man who kills the snake repeats to the prince, the conversation between you and me, that man will be turned into a marble stone.

Bihangamī.—But is there no means of restoring the marble statue to life ?

Bihangamā.—Yes, the marble statue may be restored to life if it is washed by the life-blood of the infant which the princess will give, birth to, immediately after it is ushered into the world."

The risks are undertaken and all the conditions duly fulfilled. In the case of the Bengali tale the Wazir's son is obliged to state the reasons for his conduct which had appeared highly offensive though he had told the king repeatedly that if he did so, he would turn to stone. The baby here is restored to life by the grace of Kālī. In the Christian version this part of the tale is slightly altered. One need not, however, put any undue emphasis on the dissimiliarity between the details of the prophesies of the ravens and of Bihangamā and Bihangamī. There is no doubt that the western hearer of the Oriental story introduced such alterations in the details as suited best the conditions of Western life. The talk of Bihangamā and Bihangamī and their prophecy form a familiar incident in many of the Bengali folk-tales. All of us have heard of such things in our childhood. I heard this story under the name of Rupamālā, the young bride, more than forty years ago from an aged uncle of mine who had in his turn heard it in his childhood from his grandfather on the banks of the Dhaleçwarī, as Lal Behary Dey heard the story under the name of Fakirchānd on the banks of the Ganges. The story is one of great antiquity and its Eastern origin is acknowledged by European scholars. The story of Faithful John, "Der Getreue Johannes" passed from Zwehrn and Paderborn to many other countries of Europe.

The Oxford University Press, which undertook an English translation of Grimms' tales first published in 1823, made the following observation regarding the story of Faithful John :—"The tale is a singular one, and contains so much of Orientalism that the reader would almost suppose himself in the Arabian Night's Entertainments". But a careful student of Oriental literature will see that this story is not of the nature of Arabian fables, characterised by flights of unrestrained fancy, chiefly aiming at amusing the young. The Indian fables have, on the other hand, a deep ethical and moral lesson underlying all creations of fancy. The idea of *Sakhya*, of dedicating oneself to the service of his friend, at all costs and sacrifices, to open the mouth knowing its consequence to be turning into a marble statue, this ideal friendship in a folk-story marks it out as preeminently Indian. Nay, I am inclined to trace the home of this story to Bengal, the land of Bihangamās and Bihangamīs, the birds of prophetic sayings in hundreds of our folktales.

It seems to be a Bengali tale and holds up the Hindu ideal of *Sakhya*.

In the songs of Maynāmatī, written in the 12th century of the Christian era, we find an account of the old queen Maynāmatī's pursuing in a curious manner Godā Yama, the messenger of the king of Death, who had taken away the life of her royal husband, Mānika Chandra.

"Godā Yama became bewildered at this, and changed himself into a carp. The queen changed herself into a water-fowl and began to beat the carp with her wings. Thereupon Godā Yama changed himself into a shrimp, and the queen became a gander and searched out the shrimp under the water. Godā Yama next flew up in the air in the shape of a dove, but the queen changed herself into a hawk and pursued the dove."[1]

Queen Maynāmatī's pursuit of Godā Yama.

The pursuit is continued for long, till Godā Yama turns himself into a Vaiṣṇava saint and sits in an assembly of holy mendicants of that Order. The queen, changing herself into a fly, sits on the head of the saint. Here Godā Yama is caught by the queen Maynāmatī and becomes her captive.

We find nearly an exact parallel of such change of shapes and pursuit of the foe in some of the western folk-tales and legends traced to about the same point of time. Here is an extract from one of such tales:

"Caridwen went forth after Gwin Bach, running. And he saw her and changed himself into a hare and fled. But she changed herself into a greyhound and turned him. And

Caridwen's pursuit of Gwin Bach.

[1] Typical Selections from old Bengali Literature, Part I, Calcutta University, Ed. 1914.

he ran towards a river and became a fish. And she in the form of an otter-bitch chased him under the water, until he was fain to turn himself into a bird of the air. Then she, as a hawk, followed him and gave him no rest in the sky. And just as she was about to stoop upon him, and he was in fear of death, he espied a heap of winnowed wheat on the floor of a barn, and he dropped amongst the wheat and turned himself into one of the grains. Then she transformed herself into a high-crested black hen and went to the wheat and scratched it with her feet and found him out".[1]

Of similar pursuit and change of shapes we have many instances in our folk-tales, an interesting example of which will be found in the story of Sonār-Kāṭhi and Rupār-Kāṭhi in Mr. Dakshina Majumdar's *Ṭhākurmār Jhuli* (pp. 193-196). Many of these folk-tales are however, still unwritten. I remember to have heard in my childhood a similar story where the pursued does not indeed turn himself into a grain of wheat but to a mustard-seed. In the Gaelic legends we have again a similar example in the account of the sons of Tuirenn carrying the three apples from the garden of the Hesperides. "The king of the country" says the legend, "had three daughters who were skilled in witchcraft. By

The sons of Tuirenn pursued by the princesses of Hesperides.

[1] Mabinogion, Vol. III. Taliesin p. 359.

sorcery they changed themselves into three ospreys, and pursued the three hawks"—the shapes taken by the three sons of Tuirenn. "But the latter reached the shore first, and changing themselves into swans, dived into the sea."[1]

Bhasma-lochana, the Indian Balor.

Many of the incidents, described in our Bengali Rāmāyaṇas and Mahābhāratas, were gathered from local folklore. These do not form a part of the original Sanskrit epics. Such for instance are the legends of Bhasmalochana's fight in the Laṅkā-kāṇḍa of the Rāmāyaṇa and of Çrīvatsa and Chintā in the Bengali Mahābhārata. Pandit Ramgati Nyāyaratna tells us in his 'Bangabhāshā Sāhitya Vishayaka Prastāva' that he had consulted all the Sanskrit Purāṇas, not to speak of the original epic of Vyāsa, in order to trace the source from which the Bengali writers of Mahābhārata got the story of Çrīvatsa and Chintā but that he could not find a clue to it. This story is evidently a folk-tale. The carrying off of Chintā by a merchant whose ship floated in the water by her touch, the garden of a flower-woman long lying like a piece of waste-land, but suddenly smiling with flowers and green leaves at the approach

Çrīvatsa and Chintā.

[1] Celtic Myth and Legend by Charles Squire, Gresham Publishing Co. p. 99.

of Chintā, the vow taken by the heroine for performing a religious rite with the object of gaining one year's time in order to make inquiries about her lord, and many other incidents of the story show its kinship with hundreds of folk-tales prevalent in Bengali; and the Rev. Lal Behary Dey was right in calling this story a folk-tale and incorporating it as such in his work on folk-literature. It was absurd to attempt to trace its source in Sanskrit works. But let us turn to that episode of the Bengali Rāmāyaṇa in which Bhasmalochana appears in the battle field, to fight against Rāma. This episode, as I have just stated, is a purely indigenous tale. Here is an extract from the Rāmāyaṇa :—

"His chariot was covered with animal-skin, and he wore on his eyes leather-spectacles. Thus equipped Bhasmalochana, the dreaded hero, appeared before Rāma in the battle field. Rāma was in the company of Bibhishana and Sugrīva. And Bibhīshana gave the alarm and said to Rāma, "Look there, Oh lord, the hero Bhasmalochana is before us. Now protect us from him. He, on whom his gaze will fall, will turn into a heap of ashes. You see his chariot covered with animal-skin, within it lies the dreaded one—he is like Death. In his early youth he had practised austerities for a thousand years. Brahmā, the creator, was pleased with him for this, and appearing before him, said: "What boon Oh Rākshasa, would you have from me?" Our hero said: "Make me immortal, Oh creator of the universe." But the god said—"You will destroy my creation if I do that; seek some other boon." "Then do I pray unto you to grant me this boon that my eyes be possessed of such power of destruction that they slay all on whom their look may fall." Brahmā granted him the boon and said: "Now it is all right, your gaze will wither all whom you may happen to see, wear a pair of leather-spectacles and shut yourself up in a room of your house." The Rākshasa hero was greatly delighted to have this power and with a view to experiment it, he gazed at his own followers who instantly withered as soon as the look of his eyes fell upon them. His own children and wife have a dread for him and none of them dares approach this unfortunate monster. Such is the foe, Oh lord, that has come to fight with you; take care lest all of us are destroyed by his venomous gaze."

Balor, the terrible monster-god of the Gaels is said to have been a son of Buarainech, *i.e.*, 'cow-faced.' "Though he had two eyes, one was always kept shut, for it was so venomous that it slew anyone on whom its look fell. Neither god nor gaint seems to have been exempt from its danger; so that Balor was only allowed to live on condition that he kept his terrible eye shut. On days of battle he was placed opposite to the enemy, the lid of the destroying eye was lifted up with a hook, and its gaze withered all who stood before it."[1]

In the story of "the giant with three golden hairs" in the collection of tales by the Brothers Grimm, a young man, whom the king of the country wished to murder, was entrusted by him with a letter to the queen in which it was written "As soon as the bearer of this arrives, let him be killed and immediately buried." The young man, who had no idea of the contents of this fatal letter, lost his way and took shelter in a hut which belonged to the robbers. They opened the letter when the young man was asleep and read the contents. Then their leader wrote a fresh letter in the king's name desiring the queen, as soon as the young man arrived, to marry him to the princess. Meantime they let him sleep on till morning broke, and then showed him the right way to the queen's palace; where as soon as she had read the letter, she had all possible preparations made for the wedding; and as the young man was very beautiful, the princess took him willingly for her husband.

The story of Chandra-hāsa and that of "the giant with three hairs."

---

[1] Celtic Myth and Legend by Charles Squire. p. 49.

This story will naturally remind one of that of Chandrahāsa told in the Mahābhārata. While both these stories have some strikingly common features in them, the one in the Mahābhārata possesses a more romantic interest. The king, in this story, sends young Chandrahāsa to the palace desiring his queen to put him to death immediately by means of poison. His mandate ran thus: "give him poison, as soon as he arrives at the palace". Now the word for poison in Sanskrit and Bengali is 'Visha.' The queen had an only daughter of matchless beauty and just grown into wamanhood. Her name was 'Vishayā" Chandrahāsa, like the young man of Grimms' tale, lost his way and entered a garden, reserved for the use of the princess. It was a cool evening and the fatigue of the journey made the young man sleepy, so that he fell fast asleep under a shady tree. The princess with her attending maids came to that spot and was instantly smitten with love for the beautiful youth. She saw that in his turban a letter was stuck, which she at once took for one from her royal father. She carefully opened the letter and read its cruel contents. Her love was the more stimulated by a feeling of deep compassion and she took a reed from her garden and wrote with the black paint which adorned her eyes one single letter য়া (yā) after the word Visha. This changed the spirit of the letter, for instead of

"Give him 'Visha' immediately" it now read "Give him Vishayā immediately". So the queen, as soon as she read the letter, forthwith got Chandrahāsa married to the fair princess Vishayā.

The story of Hans in luck and that of the trading fox.

There is a well known nursery tale which every Bengali boy knows, and which seems to be a very old one from the language of some of the doggerel verses that are in it. In this, a fox makes a curious trade. Once a barber, while trying to extract a thorn from Reynard's nose, cuts it with his razor. To escape from a criminal suit, which the fox threatened to bring against him, the barber presented him with his razor by way of compromise. The next stage in this trade was that the fox changed his razor for a cooking pot. The cooking pot was given away to a man who gave the fox a tinsel crown meant for a bridegroom. This the fox gave to a bridegroom; but what was the great calamity of the latter when he was obliged to give his bride to the fox as price of the crown! The fox made over the bride to a drum-player, who gave him his drum. The fox now played upon the drum and song as follows, "I got a razor for my nose, *ṭāg ḍūbā ḍūb ḍūb*, for the razor I got a cooking pot, *ṭāg ḍūbā ḍūb ḍūb*. For the cooking pot I got a tinsel crown *ṭāg ḍūbā ḍūb ḍūb*. With the crown I made a bargain for a bride, *ṭāg ḍūbā ḍūb ḍūb*. The bride I changed for this drum, *ṭāg ḍūbā ḍūb ḍūb*. *Ṭāg ḍūbā ḍūb ḍūb* is the sound of the drum at the interval of each line of the song and shows how jubilant was Reynard over this trafficking of his.

The story of Hans in luck, which is of popu lar currency and first appeared in the *Wuenschelruthe*, a periodical publication, in 1818, relates to the trade of Hans, who changed "A piece of silver as big as his head"—the earnings of his seven years' service—for a worthless pony, which he again changed for a cow; his next bargain was to change his cow for a pig; the pig he gave to a man who gave him a goose, and the goose he changed for a common rough grinding stone. This he could not carry a long way, and he felt himself greatly relieved when the stone fell into a pond, which he had approached for drinking water. Hans' answers to the grinder's questions have an unmistakable ring of the fox's song. The grinder asked "Where did you get that beautiful goose?" "I did not buy it but changed a pig for it" "And where did you get the pig?" "I gave a cow for it" "And the cow?" "I gave a horse for it" "And the horse?" "I gave a piece of silver as big as my head for that". The '*ṭāg ḍūbā ḍūb ḍūb*' is only wanting in the speech to make closer the affinity between the two stories. In Indian tales the beasts play an important part and the

European imitators may not always like to preserve such friendly relation with the lower animals in their tales.

In the story of Shīt-Basanta in the Rev. Lal Behary Dey's folk-tales we read of the marvellous qualities of a fish. "If any one eats it" said the fisherman who caught it, "When he laughs *māniks* (diamonds) will drop from his mouth." Golām Kāder [1] gives us a version of the same story; he tells us that the brothers Shīt-Basanta espied two birds on the bough of a tree. One of them said to Basanta "If any one kills me and cuts open my heart and eats it, diamonds and pearls will come out of his mouth as often as he will wish it." In the story called the Salad in the Grimm Brothers' collection, a little old woman who was a fairy, came up to the merry young huntsman—the hero of the tale—and directed him to shoot a bird, saying "when it will fall dead, cut and open the dead bird and take out its heart and keep it and you will find a piece of gold under your pillow every morning when you rise."[2] It is needless to make any comment on the above, the similarity is striking, suggesting a

The heart of a bird that yielded diamonds to its eater.

[1] Çita-Basanta Punthi by Golām Kāder Sāheb, published by Afazaddin Ahammad from 335 Upper Chitpore Road, Garānhāṭā, Calcutta, 1873, p. 18.

[2] Grimms' Popular Tales, Oxford University Press, 1909, p. 310.

common source of the stories or one's indebtedness to the other. We are inclined to suppose that the very extravagance of the idea proves its Oriental origin. The Western narrator has tried to improve on the crudeness of the fable by saying that a piece of gold would be found under the pillow, instead of a precious stone dropping from the mouth of the eater of the bird's heart, each time that he laughed.

The story of the three sluggards in the collection of the Brothers Grimm seems to have been also derived from some Oriental source. "The king of a country," thus goes on the tale, "a long way off, had three sons. He liked one as well as another, and did not know which to leave his kingdom to, after his death, so when he was dying, he called them all to him, and said, "Dear children, the laziest sluggard of the three shall be king after me." "Then" said the eldest, "the kingdom is mine; for I am so lazy that when I lie down to sleep, if any thing were to fall into my eyes so that I could not shut them, I should still go on sleeping." The second said "Father, the kingdom belongs to me; for I am so lazy that when I sit by the fire to warm myself, I would sooner have my toes burnt than take the trouble to draw my legs back." The third said, "Father, the kingdom is mine, for I am so lazy that if I were going to be hanged with the rope

The story of the sluggards.

round my neck, and some body were to put a sharp knife into my hands to cut it, I had rather be hanged than raise my hand to do it." When the father heard this, he said "You shall be the king ; for you are the fittest man."[1]

The idea of absolute inertness and suspension of all physical energy in this story seems to suggest its Eastern origin. In Bengal we have our own story of four sluggards with which I trust all of you are familiar. It is not analogous to the above tale in its detail, but is certainly so in spirit. Though most of you have heard it no doubt, yet I give it below for the purpose of comparison.

Once a king took it into his head to maintain the idle people of his kingdom by allowing them to live in a bungalow near his palace and making provision for their sustenance. When such easy living could be obtained, it proved a great attraction to many people of the kingdom, and they enlisted themselves as sluggards and lived in the king's bungalow without being required to do any work. The number of these people rose to a good many, so that several new houses had to be erected for accommodating them. At one time when the king passed by that part of his capital, he was struck by the sight of the large number of idlers who lived upon him. He now resolved to allow only the genuine

[1] Grimms' Popular Tales, Oxford University Press, 1909, p. 349.

sluggards to live there, and dismiss the rest, and accordingly took recourse to a device. He ordered his people to set fire to all these bungalows, which were roofed with straw. As soon as fire broke out, these idle people all came out of their rooms and fled in precipitous haste, except only four who remained in their room without showing the slightest sign of concern or activity. One of them who did not open his eyes, yet saw a great blaze through his half-closed eyes, said to his comrades, "How many suns have risen, brother?" The man whom he addressed, said, "Who cares to open his eyes and see what it is?" The third who felt the heat of fire on his back said "*Pi-po*" which is an unmeaning abbreviation of the word "*piṭh poṛé*" (my back burns), for he was so idle that he would not utter the full sentence but only '*pi*' of '*piṭh*' and '*po*' of '*poṛé*.' The fourth advised "*phi-sho*" which in the like manner is an abbreviation of the sentence "*phiré sho*" (turn your back and sleep). The king, who overheard their conversation, had them instantly removed from the room, and when the fire was extinguished allowed these four men only to live in the sluggard's quarters, after having dismissed the rest.

As I have already stated, Bihangamā and Bihangami are the most important figures in the Bengali folk-tales. When the hero or the heroine falls into difficulties or dangers, the birds are often found to come to the rescue by offering advice or saying prophetic things which are sure to be fulfilled. Their frequent appearance is such a characteristic element in our folk-tales that we are inclined to regard these prophetic birds to be indigenous creations of rural Bengal's fancy. The bringing in of animals as characters of popular tales, side by side with the human, is a special feature of Asiatic, particularly Indian popular fictions; but the prophesies of birds, with sympathies for the heroes and heroines, helping their achievement of the marvellous and the strange, seem to be a distinctive feature of the Bengali fables, and curiously we find birds playing the same part in some of the European stories as they do in Bengali nursery-tales. Such for instance are the stories of the "Crows and the soldier", "The Robber bridegroom" and "Faithful John". The former of these is a Mecklenburgh story; that it had an Asiatic origin seems to be hinted by the M. Grimm brothers by their assertion that there is a similar tale by the Persian poet Nisami.

Prophesies of birds.

In the story of "Jorinda and Joringel" which is popular in the Schwalmgegend, we have the old woman, a very popular character in old Bengali folk-tales, who could change princes and sons of noble men to beasts by her spell. The stories of

Sorcery.

'Sakhi-sonā', to which reference will be made again in course of my lectures, and of 'Puṣpa-mālā' give us some characters of malignant women skilled in witch-craft The sorceress Kirke, sister of King Æetes, had a similar power; her spell was baffled by Ulysses as we read in the Greek legend. In the story "The grateful beasts" which we also get from the Schwalmgegend, there are many points similar to those of a tale current among the Calmuck Tartars in which a benevolent Brahmin receives the graetful assistance of a mouse, a bear, and a monkey, whom he has severally rescued from the hands of their tormentors.

The Rose-bud and other stories giving accounts of sleeping cities.

In the Western folk-tales we have accounts of a whole city that fell asleep under the spell of magic. This we find in the story of the Rose-bud. We read in it how "the king and the queen and all their court fell asleep, and the horses slept in the stable, and the dogs in the court, the pigeons on the house-top, and the flies on the walls. Even the fire on the hearth left off blazing and went to sleep; and the meat that was roasting stood still, and the cook who was at that time pulling the kitchen-boy by the hair to give him a box on the ear for something he had done amiss, let him go, and both fell asleep; and so everything stood still and slept soundly." An exact parallel of this we find in the accounts of a sleeping city in our Dharma-mangal poems. The spell is cast by Indā, the thief, over Mainägar, the city of Lousen. Here is an account of how the spell worked.

"The potter slept over the cooking-pot he had made, and his sister Kāthā rolled in the dust by its side in profound sleep. The old weaver-woman Jayā fell dozing over her loom. The carpenter's wife was blowing fire into the hearth, her head lay near the opening of the hearth as she became senseless in sleep. The porter fell into the drain seized by sleep and his load was scattered in the street.[1]"

The earliest Dharma-maṉgal poems are coeval with the songs of Manik Chandra and should be referred to the 11th or the 12th century of the Christian era. The story of "*ghumanta-purī*" or a sleeping city in D. R. Majumdar's collection has so many points of similarity with those of "The Rose-bud" that they seem evidently to have been derived from the same source. In my childhood I heard from an aged uncle of mine a folk-tale called. "The Bejān Shahar" The name at least shows the Persian origin of the story. In it I heard for the first time the account of a whole city falling asleep under a magic spell, an account that I have since found repeated in many Eastern and Western folk-tales.

---

[1] Typical selections from old Bengali Literature, Calcutta University, p. 473 (Part I.)

Thus reading these Western folk-stories I have been often reminded of those that I heard recited to me in my childhood in my native country. The tale of Rumpel-Stilts-Kin, where naming a spirit is made a condition for escaping from a danger, is analogous to the story of Tāpāi, the ghost, that I heard from an aged relation of mine when I was a mere boy. The spirits in both the cases stand betrayed by their own carelessness. The Bengali story runs thus:—Once on a time an old Brahmin was travelling through a large marshy tract. It was winter and he saw at some distance a fire sending a glimmering light. As he was quaking in every limb owing to the severe cold, he thought of warming himself a little by the fire, and reaching it in all haste, he cried "tāpāi," "tāpāi" ("let me enjoy a little heat," "let me enjoy a little heat.") Now what was his wonder when he saw there a number of ghosts sitting by the fire-side and warming themselves! The name of one of these happened to be "Tāpāi." The Brahmin had ejaculated "tāpāi" signifying his desire to enjoy the heat of the fire, which the word literally meant, but the ghost who bore that name asked the Brahmin as to why he had called him by his name. The other ghosts also joined in the query, so that the Brahmin was not only frightened by the sight of this unseemly company, but for a

Rumpel-Stilts-Kin and Tāpāi, the ghost.

moment did not know what to say in reply to their strange question. His presence of mind returned, however, after a moment of consternation, and, assuming an air of indifference, he said "Why? Tāpāi's ancestors, up to the fourth generation, have all been servants in my house. What wonder that I should call him by his name?" The other ghosts turned to Tāpāi and said, "what does the Brahmin say? Is it true?" Tāpāi's anger knew no bounds and he was immediately going to kill the Brahmin, but the ghosts intervened and said "If what the Brahmin says is true, you can not kill him." "All right," said Tāpāi, "let him name my ancestors up to my great-grand-father. The condition is if he can name them, I will consent to be his servant; if he can not, I will put an end to his life without any more talk." The Brahmin said, "But my family had a number of servants in those days, how can I remember and name them all without consulting my domestic register!" "All right, I give you three days' time. On the third day in the evening you are to meet us here and name my ancestors. If you can not, woe will befall you, I will not only kill you but the rest of your family." The poor Brahmin went home with a feeling of alarm that can better be conceived than described. He knew that in three days all would be over with him. He ate nothing nor had any sleep in the night, and in reply to a hundred questions put by his wife, only sighed and hid his face with his hands to conceal his tears. The inmates of the house thought that there was something wrong in his head and consulted physicians. The second night came; in the evening of the following day the catastrophe was sure to happen, as there could be no escape from the infuriated ghost. In the night the Brahmin resolved to commit suicide. He thought if he did so, the cruel fate to which other members of his family were to be subjected might be averted as the anger of the ghost would be, to a certain extent, appeased by seeing his corpse. But he could find no place in his house, where he could apply a halter to his neck without being observed. So he walked a little distance and reached a forest on the northern side of the house. There he selected a spot to hang himself on a tree. But just as he caught hold of a bough to tie the rope with, he heard a conversation in a nasal tone peculiar to the ghosts and stood a moment to listen to it. One said "What is it that I hear from some of the ghosts? A Brahmin has claimed the whole of your ancestors to have been born-slaves to his family!" The other said, "Nonsense! the Brahmin said whatever came to his lips in a moment of fear. I will kill him and his whole family in the evening to-day. I have laid an impossible condition on him." "What is that ?" "To name my ancestors up to the fourth generation" "But what, if he is able to name them ?" "Absurd ! how can he do that ? No one knows it except myself and some very old ghosts". The conversation was of course between Tāpāi and his wife who lived on the top of that tree. The wife then wanted to hear the names of Tāpāi's forefathers, and Tāpāi once or twice saying "No", at last yielded to her entreaties, and said "Hārmoo's son was Sārmoo, Sārmoo's son was Āpāi, and Āpāi's son is Tāpāi." The Brahmin of course heard this genealogy which was a perfect God-send to him. He committed it to memory and returning home wrote it a hundred times in his note-book ; he looked extremely jubilant and his wife and others could not understsnd how such a cloud was removed from his looks and how it became all sun-shime in a day. We need not follow this story further. This story bears, as I have said, some analogy to that of Rumpel-Stilts-Kin in M. Grimm's collections. The spirit in that tale was heard to sing a song in which at a careless moment, he gave out his name himself. The queen of this story escaped a great scrape by this revelation. The song runs thus :—

"Merrily the feast I'll make.
To-day I'll brew, to morrow bake,

Merrily I'll dance and sing,
For next day will a stranger bring,
Little does my lady dream,
Rumpel-Stilts-Kin is my name."

The stories of Sukhu-Dukhu and Mother Holle

If we turn over the pages of Grimm's tales we cannot help being struck by a great many of them bearing a wonderful likeness to the stories current in this country from olden times. The tale of "*Sukhu ār Dhukhu*" in the Thakurmār Jhuli has an almost exact parallel in that of "Mother Holle" in Grimm brother's collections, while the tale of Ashputtel also in the latter is to some extent analogous to the same Bengali tale.

The poor girl Dhukhu in the Bengali tale is entrusted by her mother to put some cotton before the sun for drying it up. The wind suddenly blows and the cotton is carried away. Dhukhu begins to weep, whereupon the wind says," "Come with me Dhukhu, do not cry, I will return your cotton." Dhukhu follows the wind, weeping. In the way a cow says to Dhukhu, "Dear girl, come and remove my dung from this shed." The girl feels sympathy for the animal and does as she is bid. Then she again follows the wind. A banana plant calls her and says, "Dear girl, see, these weeds and creepers have covered my trunk, be kind to remove these." The girl stops again and lends her helping hand. Then she follows the wind as fast as she can go, but stops to listen to the call of a *shawra* plant which asks her to remove the dirt that has gathered at its root. Doing that she goes again following the course of the wind, but a horse calls her in the way to give it a little grass. She does so, and then the wind brings her to a very fine house, where she meets an old woman sitting by the door. She asks Dhukhu to go into a room of the house and get from it dress and other things for her toilet. She goes and finds the room glittering with golden robes and toilet-articles of the highest value. She takes for herself those that are of the humblest quality and price. She is asked to bathe in the tank which she does, and no sooner does she dip into the water, than she finds her person grown wonderfully handsome and shining with ornaments that are only worn by a princess. The old woman then asks her to enter a room full of trunks and chests of various sizes and quality and tells her to take any one from them. Our Dhukhu takes one that is the smallest and of the lowest value. Then she goes back home. In the way the cow, the banana, the *shawra* plant and the horse whom she has severally served give her many rich and beautiful things. After, returning home she shows all these to her cousin Shukhu who was in affluent circumstances, wishing her to partake in all that she has got, jointly with her. But Shukhu disdainfully rejects her offer. The next day Dhukhu opened the small chest, from which lo! a prince came out, and, taking her by the hand made her his wife.

That day Sukhu put some cotton in the sun and then when the wind carried it off, followed the wind, wishing to be in possession of a fortune like her relation. Sukhu met the cow, the banana, the *shawra* plants and the horse. They wanted her help, but she said in a haughty tone, "I am going to the old woman for riches, away, you fools, do'nt interrupt me." Then when she saw the old woman spinning at the door of the house, she said, "Old hag, you have given lots of things to that dog-faced Dhukhu; keep away your spindle and cotton, and give me all things, or I will break your spindle and all." The toilet-room was shown her and she took away the best dress, the best looking-glass and the most valuable things. Then as she bathed in the tank, she found herself deformed, her body became full of eczema and itch, and she could not speak except in a shrill nasal tone. She was asked to choose a box like her cousin, and she took the biggest one, and with it ran back homewards. The cow pursued her with its horns; the banana and the *shawra* plants threw their boughs over her head, and the horse gave her a kick. Coming home she opened the chest ; but lo ! a cobra came out and ate her up.

The poor girl of the tale—" Mother Holle" went to seek her spindle that had fallen into a well and came to a pretty cottage by the side of a wood ; and when she went in, she saw an oven full of new bread baking, and the bread said " Pull me out, pull me out or I shall be burnt, for I am done quite enough." So she stepped up quickly, and took it out. Then she went on further and came to a tree that was full of fine rosy cheeked apples, and the tree said to her " Shake me ! shake me ! we are quite ripe." So she shook the tree, and the apples fell down like a shower, until there were no more upon the tree. Then she went on again, and at length came to a small cottage where an old woman was sitting at the door. She behaved so well that the old woman was highly pleased with her; and when she expressed her desire to go back home, the old woman took her by the hand and led her behind her cottage "and as the girl stood underneath, there fell a heavy shower of gold, so that the girl held out her apron and caught a great deal of it." And the old woman, who was a fairy, put a shining golden dress over her, and said "All this you shall have, because you have behaved so well;" and she gave her back the spindle too which had fallen into the well and led her out by another door."

Now her sister, who was an ugly and wicked girl, envied her lot and sat by the well and began to spin ; she let fall her spindle into the well and seeking it followed the same path. When she came to the oven in the cottage, the bread called out as before, "Take me out, take me out, or I shall be burnt, I am done quite enough." But the lazy girl said "A pretty story indeed ! just as if I should dirty myself for you !" and went on her way. She soon came to the apple tree that cried "Shake me, shake me, for my apples are quite ripe" But she answered "I will take care how I do that, for one of you may fall on my head." So she went on. Atlength she came to the old Fairy's house; but she was soon tired of the girl and turned her off, but the lazy girl was quite pleased at that, and thought to herself "Now the golden rain will come." Then the fairy took her to the same door, but when she stood under it, instead of gold, a great kettle full of dirty pitch came showering upon her. "That is your wages" said mother Holle (the fairy) as she shut the door upon her. So she went home quite black with the pitch.

The story of Tom Thumb has many points of agreement with that of "Dér Āngulé" in Daksina Ranjan's compilation. As to some of the adventures of Tomb, a writer in the Quarterly Review (No. XLI) traces their connection with some of the mysteries of Indian mythology. The story of "Dér Āngulé" current in Bengal, details the adventures of a child born to a woodman, no bigger in size than a thumb and a half. Tom was also of the height of a thumb, and, like his Bengali cousin, was full of heroic enthusiasm and a spirit of enterprise. The woodman of the East and the West had been both childless at first and got their dwarfish issues after long prayers and patient waiting. There is another story in Grimm's collections which has a kinship with these two fables. That is the story of "The Young Giant and the Tailor." It begins with the line "A husbandman had once a son, who was no bigger than my thumb." In some of these kindred tales, Tom is represented as gradually growing in size, till he becomes a giant; his achievements are all wonderful. In England there is the story of Jack the giant-killer, a name-sake of Tom ; and in some of the countries of the north, he is called by different names, such as Tom Hycophric, the son of the Bear &c. He is a voracious eater like a tiger and Herbert in his Icelandic poetry describes him as eating "Eight salmons and an ox full-grown and all the cates on which women

'Tom Thumb' and 'Dér Āngulé.'

Jack the giant killer and the wrestler—22 men strong.

feed." And he drank three firkins of sparkling mead." But all this is child's action before the feats of Bāyis Joān (lit. the wrestler, 22 men-strong) who takes a bag containing 80 lbs. of wheat with him and, seeing a tank before him, throws the wheat into it and drinks off the whole solution. This was, however, his "*jalayoga*," light refreshment.

The folk-tales collected by some of our own men like Dakshina Ranjan Mitramajumdar, Lalbihary De, Golam Kader, Mahammed Munshi, Amiruddin Ahmad, Khondakar Jabed Ali, Munshi Afāruddin, Harinath Majumdar, Fakirram Kabibhuṣana and others have come from the country-side. They have been told in our homes times without number, from an immemorial age, before any door was opened in them for receiving rays of European or even Moslem culture.* The compilers in a few cases have given some colouring to the stories on the lines of classical scholarship and modern thought. This I will discuss in the course of my lectures. Entirely free from all such colouring are the stories in Thakur Dādār Jhuli by Babu Dakshina Ranjan, which thus possess a unique value, unfolding the true nature of some of our indigenous stories and a language in which the ring of the original country dialect still lingers.

The striking analogies, which are no chance coincidences, between these stories of the East and

West remind us of what has been acknowledged by European scholars themselves, that in the olden times the debt of enlightenment and culture was one of Europe to India, as in our times it has been quite the opposite. In India the highest culture and refinement were for ages represented by Magadha, from the ruins of which have now sprung up some of the cities and towns of Bengal, her *genteel* society inheriting the traditions and ideas that floated in the metropolitan city of the old Indian world. Owing to Lower Bengal, the Banga proper, having been one of the landing shores of enterprising foreign peoples who traded with India; it is no wonder that Bengal, or more properly Magadha, folk-literature has obtained a worldwide circulation. The north-western border-lands of Bengal where Kapilabastu stood, which with the light of Buddhism pierced the veil of darkness that had enshrouded the surrounding countries in the remote past, the south-eastern portion from which the cotton fabrics, known as the Dacca muslin went out to other parts of the world as the most valued and fashionable cloth of the ancient times, and Magadha, Champa and Banga, the great political divisions of the province in those days—were in touch with the rest of the world influencing the civilization and modes of life of millions of human beings. And what wonder that the folk-lore of this favoured land should travel to remote countries in the ships of Bengal laden with her merchandise? The Oxford University which published a translation of Grimm's tales has appended a note saying "It often seems difficult to account for the currency among the peasantry on the shores of Baltic and the forests of the Hartz, of fictions which would seem to belong to the entertainments of the Arabians, yet involved in legends referable to the highest Teutonic source." "The Thousand and One Nights" is with Occidental scholars a word to signify the Asiatic type, but should not be taken in its too literal sense. It is used here as comprehending all tales derived from Arabia, Persia, India and other Asiatic countries.

Eastern India giving her folk-tales to the world.

The similarities I shall further detail in course of my lectures. We have observed that European scholars have themselves admitted that the mediæval folk-literature of their country was founded upon Indian fables imported into their shores chiefly through Arabic translations. They have also proved that Arabic and Persian tales are in a great measure indebted to Indian folk-literature. The Indian folk-stories must therefore have some special excellence and claim to superiority which made them the models to be copied by peoples far and near. The Kathā sarit sāgara is a store house of such fables. The Panchatantra, the Hitopodeṣa and the Jātaka stories originated in Magadha, on the ruins and remnants of whose glory stands the Bengal of to-day.

Where lies the superiority of the folk-literature of Eastern India, which accounts for its world-wide circulation? Oriental scholars have pointed out that the ethical lessons contained in Indian stories form their chief attraction. These have their match in old Æsop's stories, and some of the Teutonic fables which originated in the North and have been current in England ever since the time of Hengist and Horsa and of Ebba the Saxon.

We have, however, a limited number of Bengali stories, which are not of the same nature as those that have been copied by foreign nations. These have come down to us from the Buddhist times, and their striking excellence from literary and æsthetic points of view have come upon us like a surprise. They are not to be valued merely because "they made long nights short," when we were children; no apology is needed in recommending them, on the plea of antiquity or of a primitive rustic origin. They are specimens of lyrical excellence, of superior art in style and the construction of plot that seem almost unparalleled in folk-literature. These stories show Bengal to be the true home of folk-tales in a sense in which perhaps no other country can claim such a place in the world's literature. The stories of Çankhamālā, Puṣpamālā and Mālanchamālā, composed in the rural dialect of this country, contain in them elements of purity, conception of love and moral feeling which indeed evince a high stage of civilization. Written in prose, interspersed with songs, they have all the attributes of master-pieces of lyrics, of which any nation could be proud. It will be wrong to suppose that they were meant for children ; people in that case would like to turn into babies in order to hear these marvels of poetic fiction. The smell of fresh buds is in them ; the charm of poetry—of rural life, the love of pure women, the wreath of juvenile mirth, which is of eternal delight to the old, the renunciation of saints and the devotion of martyrs—have all combined in these unassuming tales rendering them sublime and beautiful in every sense of the words. I shall dwell upon these stories towards the end of my present course of lectures. The copyists and imitators from outside have approached many of our stories in such a way as to introduce them by a change of garb into their own countries ; but the inimitable beauty of Malanchamālā's character, of Kānchanmālā's devotion and Rupalāl's remorse for rejecting a true wife, possess a unique Bengali grandeur, which can be admired, but cannot be taken away and be adapted to other climes by changing the language, any more than a Tajmahal or a Pyramid can be removed and shewn off from any other spot of the earth than where they stand now. The character of Mālanchamālā, especially, is peculiarly an Indian conception and gives us the flowering point of Hindu and Buddhistic ideals, and, like a big lily of an Indian tank, is beautiful when shewn from its congenial back-ground of this tropical country of ours. It will scarcely stand the frosty chill of North-western realism. Like Sāvitri Mālancha wins her dead husband back to life; she is devoted to him as Sita of the immortal bard of Tamasa; in her martyrdom she reaches the level of a Sikh Guru; and in endurance she can be compared only to an Indian yogi. She is the very spirit of renunciation—the essence of what Buddhist and Hindu philosophers have taught for ages. These have filtered down to the lowest stratum of our society and been assimilated by them, rendering the rural life of Bengal grand in its simplicity and sweet and resigned in its faith. The sunshine and the clouds of life, its lights and shades, laughters and tears are all in these simple folk-tales. They possess the epic grandeur of Vālmiki and the lyric beauty of Jaydeva. How fortunate the country whose men and women heard these stories in their childhood

The Gītikathās.

from the lips of their mothers and started in life with the invaluable treasure of devotion and poetry contained in them, and how unfortunate the country whose men and women, in the eagerness to play the parts of the vainglorious and the showy, have thrown away, as it were, diamonds from their ancestral treasure and often run after trinkets of no value! These superbly beautiful stories are called the Gītikathās. Their authors' names are lost, though we shall try to prove that women for the most part composed these marvellous tales. As the stream of the Ganges passes by our doors to satisfy our thirst and daily needs and we forget that it comes to us from a lofty peak, as the rays we warm ourselves with serve us the ordinary needs of life and we forget that they come from the greatest Orb of the solar regions, even so the master-minds that could conceive and produce such stories have remained unheeded and unrecognised even by those who have profited most by these unique treasures. Being within our easy reach they have been mistaken for the ordinary and the commonplace. But they are no ordinary folk-tales,—their prose style, resonant with musical sound, sometimes lapses into metrical forms which become lyrics of great beauty; their workmanship is often rich as Persian carpets that should not be confounded with Bazar mats. But we reserve the treatment of this subject for the present.

**

Magadha and Gaur the seats of some of the early Indian folk-tales.

Magadha was the seat of some of the greatest lines of Royal dynasties that ever reigned in India in bygone times. The Mauryas, the Sungas and the Guptas were sovereigns who held suzerainty over a great part of India; and the capital of Magadha, Pataliputra or Kushumpur, was during centuries not only the highest reputed seat of learning in this land, but amusements and fashions flowed from this centre to all parts of India—nay, even outside this great country. It was in this place that Visnuçarmā wrote those fables in the fourth or fifth century, which combined interest for the young with moral lessons. These fables were translated into Persian by Burzubi, the illustrious physician of the court of the Emperor Nasirban in the sixth century. The translator was helped in the compilation of this translation by an Indian Pandit named Braja Jamehar. In the ninth century the tales were translated into Arabic by Imam Hoshen Abdul Mokaka by the order of Kaliph A. Mansabji. In the tenth century Sultan Mahammad Gaji had these tales again translated into Arabic. Since then we have had many translations of this work into Hebrew, Greek, and Syrian languages. The Hebrew translation was prepared by a scholar named Dunn, and his translation served as a model for other scholars who have translated it into the modern languages of Europe. The tales of Visnuçarmā are known in England as "Pilpay's fables.".

When the glory of Magadha was extinguished Gaur rose to eminence over its ashes ; and the flower of the Magadha population for the most part migrated to Bengal. During the reign of the Pāl kings, Gaur kept up the tradition of learning and other glories that had attached to the name of Magadha ; and we find that the ballads of Pāl kings were not only sung in the Gangetic valley but in the picturesque hilly sides of Orissa, nay, so far down as the shores of the Indian ocean, in the Bombay presidency. The songs in honour of Manashā Devī, the home of which was the city of Champā in Bengal, travelled on the lyres of minstrels from Gaur to the remotest part of Aryavarta. We have discussed this point at some length in our Introduction to the Typical Selections from old Bengali Literature and tried to solve the historical question involved therein.

Bengal in the early European folk-legends.

The connection of Bengal with the rest of the world is hinted at by many legends current in other countries. In one of the folk-tales, to be found in Bosching's Volks-sagen, called "Cherry or the Frog-bride" the condition laid by the old king on his sons, all of whom wished to be the heir to his kingdom, was to bring him "one hundred ells of cloth, so fine", the king said, "that I can draw it through my golden ring."[1] This evidently refers to the Dacca muslin. King Arthur's porter vaunted of his experience and travels in this way:—"I have been heretofore in India the Great and India the Lesser."[2] I do not know if Bengal was included in those days in 'India the Great' or in 'India the Lesser.' But it must have been in one of them. If there is any substratum of truth in the Arthurian legends, the porter of that king must have been the first British visitor to Bengal.

In view of the remarkable coincidences between some of the folk-tales of Bengal and those current in the West, especially as they have all an unmistakable Eastern flavour, we may not be wrong in supposing, as we have already supposed, that some of the fables of this country passed from the banks of the Ganges and the Padmā to the shores of the Baltic and the English Channel. There are many points strikingly common, and we have but given a very few illustrations. The enquiring scholar will find heaps of evidence on this point, and re-echo the sentiments of Lalbehary De, who while discussing this subject enthusiastically said, "The swarthy and half-naked peasant

[1] Grimm's tales, Oxford edition, p. 268.

[2] Mabinogion, Vol. II, p. 255.

on the banks of the Ganges is a cousin albeit of the hundredth remove, to the fair-skinned and well-dressed Englishman on the banks of the Thames."[1]

The special features of the Arabic and Persian tales as contrasted with those of Indian.

There is one point, to which I should draw your attention, in regard to the claims of other Eastern countries than our own, on some of the folk-tales of Europe, possessing an unmistakable stamp of Oriental origin. The genuine Arabic and Persian tales have less regard for the moral side than those that are Indian. In most of the Indian stories the animals are acting characters, whereas in Arabic and Persian tales the giants and fairies play the most important parts. The tales of the Moslem world relate more to wonders performed by super-human agencies and give a far more sensuous description of love-affairs, whereas the Indian stories have a greater solicitude for giving rewards to virtue and humanity and protection to the weaker and the more amiable against the wily and the violent. The fairy of the Arabic and Persian tales is in Indian stories a nymph of Indra's heaven and the demon of the former is a Rākṣasa in the Indian tale.

---

[1] Folk-tales of Bengal, Preface, p. VIII.

CHAPTER II

Internal evidences in the early Bengali Folk-tales proving their Origin before the Hindu Renaissance

Story-telling a time-honoured profession of a class of Indians especially of women.

Story-telling was an art practised in India from immemorial times. We see in the Rāmāyaṇa that in the royal court of Kekaya, prince Bharata was one day entertained by tales told by professional story-tellers, when he was sad and gloomy on account of a bad dream that he had dreamt in the preceding night. In the Bengali Rāmāyaṇa by Chandrāvali,[1] Sitā in her private apartments is found to amuse herself with listening to tales by professional story-tellers who were women. In the folk-tales of Bengal we have it repeated again and again that the princesses and other ladies of high rank kept these professional women as companions whose business was to tell stories affording not only amusement but sound instruction as regards morality and laws of conduct. In Lal Behary Dey's collection of tales we have an account as to how these stories which were called Rūpakathās used to be told by old and expert

[1] A 16th century poetess, daughter of Dija Baṃçī, the illustrious poet of the Manasā-cult.

women to the ladies of high-rank and even to the king and to his queen.[1] In the story of Mālancha Mālā[2] compiled by Babu Dakshinaranjan we have again a reference to the Rūpakathās told by a professional woman to a princess. In fact the Hindu kings not only had such story-tellers engaged in the queen's palace but kept a number of them in their courts. Even in our own times we find this custom, which has come down from a remote antiquity, followed by some of the Rājās of this province. Late Babu Bhāratchandra Sen of Dhāmrāi in the district of Dacca, was appointed not very long ago, by Rājā Birachandra Manikya of Tippera as the story-teller of his court on a pay of Rs. 60 a month. I had an opportunity of hearing a story related by this gentleman. His intonation, gestures and manner of speaking added a wonderful poetic vividness to the story that he related. And I knew that he had learnt this art from professional story-tellers—an art that had been handed down from a very remote age.

Let us now examine the various sources of Bengali folk-tales that have been accessible to us. An examination of these will throw a light on the periods of their composition.

We shall try to prove that most of our folk-tales that the old ladies recited to their

---

[1] *Vide* the adventures of two thieves and of their sons, pp. 176-77, in the Folk-tales of Bengal (1911).

[2] Thakur Dadar Jhuli, p. 90 (1912).

children in the past, and which the women-folk in the backwoods of Bengal still do recite to the young in the evenings, belong to the period intervening between the age of the ascendancy of Buddhism and its decline in Bengal. This period may be defined roughly as covering the third to tenth century A.D. The reasons leading to this conclusion may be summed up as follows.

1. We have some definite internal proofs that most of these stories were conceived before the Hindu Renaissance and also before the advent of Islam in this country.

The early folk-tales are different from Paurānic stories.

As regards the literature of the Hindu Renaissance, the characteristic feature of this period is its abundant references to the Sanskrit epics. The Paurānic stories, which in later times took the place of folk-tales, such as the legends of Dhruba, Prahlāda, and a hundred others that derived their sources from the Bhāgavata, the Rāmāyaṇa and the Mahābhārata, are full of the propaganda of the Bhakti-cult. They offer a striking contrast to ethical laws which governed the Indian communities during the sunny days of Buddhism. In the folk-tales these ethical laws form the basis of human virtues, and seldom do we find any propagandism of the tenets of Bhakti, such as recitation of God's name, fast, vigil and austerities undergone for the sake of spiritual devotion which form the essential feature of the Paurānic stories. There is besides nowhere in the earlier folk-tales any allusion to the Rāmāyaṇic or Mahābhārata-episodes, nor to those which relate to the early life of Kṛiṣṇa as told in the Bhāgavata. The Bengaḷi poems written from the 14th century A.D. downwards are permeated by the spirit of Paurānic-lore, and as we have frequently remarked elsewhere, even low-class people such as the hunter Kālaketu and Phullarā, his wife, who were absolutely without any knowledge of letters, are found to refer to the Shāstras and Paurānic tales in their daily conversation. Wherever there is any occasion to offer advice in political, social or domestic matters, examples are freely quoted from the Sanskrit texts. So great was the craze for citing the Purāṇas, that even a country pedagogue while giving elementary lessons to boys would sometimes be found to bring down some great heroes of the Purānas to figure as chief actors in a mathematical puzzle. Sometimes Arjuna and sometimes Karṇa fling a number of arrows under complicated mathematical conditions, but more often the mighty ape-god Hanuman throws down a stone-wall into a river, the measurement of the stone, so far as it lies in its watery bed and so far as it rises above, form- the problem to outwit a student. In the earlier folk-tales, as I have said, this Paurāṇic element is absolutely wanting, which shows that they are at least older than the 13th century when the Hindu revival was an established fact in Bengal. Nay, there are evidences in these tales which show that the idea of the authors of the folk-tales about the Purānas and the Vedās was not in the lines of the Brahminic leaders of the Hindu Renaissance. In the tales of Madhūmālā and of Malanchamālā we find a mention of 12 Vedās and 8 Purāṇas which is quite against the historical and conventional notions of the Hindus. This tradition the country-folk must have derived in an earlier age from other sources than the stock-in-trade learning of the Hindu revivalists. For in the literature that sprang up after the revival, Brahminic views and ideas in such matters are clearly pronounced; even the village scribe who wrote with his reed-pen, be he so humble as a barber or a washerman, could not put down anything in black and white which did not bear the stamp of Brahminic inspiration.

12 Vedās and 8 Purānas.

2. The metaphors and similes with which the Renaissance-literature is strewn are all stereotyped and of a classical model, in the Bengali literature from the 13th to 18th century. For the beauty of a nose the poet is sure to refer by way of comparison to the *tila*-flower, for the lips to the *bāndhuli*, for manly arms to the

The Paurānik metaphors.

elephant's trunk, for the teeth to pomegranate seeds, for the face to the lotus or the moon, for the braided hair to a black snake or clouds, and so forth. Read one poet's description of a woman's beauty and then read a second, a third, a fourth, in fact as many as you like; one is as good as another. The gifted poet writes in an inspired language, the ordinary votary to Parnassus writes in plain words, but the model which both the genuine poet and the common versifier have before them, is a classical one; the Sanskrit Rhetoric, in its stereotyped form, inspires both. These descriptions of men and women in the old Bengali literature have often grown stale, flat and wearisome. When the Pandits learnt Persian, the descriptions became ingenious and subtle to the extreme; and the '*rūpa-varṇanā*' formed one of the favourite subjects of the country bards for display of all the wit and learning that their brain possessed. It is said by a poet in praise of a woman's waist, that one could hold it within the hollow of his hand, it was so slender. Even in this, he fell far short of the ideal waist of the Persian poet who said of his heroine "Her waist was like a hair nay, half of it." One might argue that this was all the ingenious nonsense of the few Pandits who wrote Sanskritic Bengali; the absence of such things in the Bengali folk-tales only proves that they were composed by the unlearned who did not know Sanskrit or Persian nor cared for any classical rules. This however is not true. For, as I have already said, from after the 13th century A.D. no Bengali poem was written till the 18th century, however humble its author, who did not introduce classical similes and figures for adorning his poem. We find the 16th century poet Madhusudan, who was a barber, literally caught in the meshes of classical metaphors.[1]

What a sense of relief do we feel while reading these old folk-tales! The long descriptions of a heroine's personal appearance, from the crown of her head to the tip of her toe, are nowhere in these folk-tales. One or two words produce a far greater impression of the beautiful one; the excellence of the tales lies in their brevity and well-chosen forcible expressions.

The folk-tales do not give a catalogue of ornaments nor a stereo typed description of beautiful women.

In the Paurāṇic literature of the later age, we not only come across descriptions of the figures of youthful heroines generally in the most monotonous verses, but also long catalogues of ornaments which form very tedious reading after all, producing often a rather grotesque effect, as these ornaments have mostly run out of fashion now-a-days. In the folk-tales mention is sometimes made of "a flame-coloured" or "blue-tinted"

[1] See Banga-Bhāsā-o-Sahitya, p. 491.

silk which like the muslin were in ancient times the marvels of Indian manufacture. In the Arthurian legends we find a lady wearing "a robe of flame-coloured silk"[1] which reminds us of আগুন পাটের সাড়ী of a princess in our own story of Sankhamālā. "Robes of flame-coloured silk" in the British isles of those days, we contend were of Indian manufacture, but the next line which says that the hair of the princess was black as ebony is significant and makes it clear enough, for the black hair belongs to and is favoured in the tropical climes. Woman's chief beauty in the folk-literature of Bengal, lies in the tender qualities of the heart. These folk-tales, though they do not give erudite and elaborate descriptions of women's physical charms, do not however fail to invest them with truly noble virtues of the soul. Reference to physical beauty, often given in a brief line, carries a far greater effect than the long tiresome accounts on classical lines.

I have said that these stories generally show an ignorance on the part of the people, of the *Çāstric* legends and of the gods and goddesses of the Hindu pantheon, which even a common farmer and artisan know now-a-days; neither do the gods come to help the mortals in their difficulties as they are found to do in the later epochs of Bengali literature. The mortals, possesed of devotion

---

[1] Mabinogion, Vol. II, p. 276.

and superior moral qualities, come out of their trials by dint of their own virtues and merit. The popular notions about gods which these tales unfold, seem strange and unfamiliar. We have read of the Godē Yama, the messenger of Death, in the Mayanāmati legends; he has no place in the Hindu pantheon. In "Mālanchamālā" we find similarly the names of Sāldut and Kāldut who are said to be the brothers of Yamadut. Vidhāta fulfils a function which show him not at all like the creator Brahma whose name he bears in these stories. The duty of the former seems to be only to write the "luck" of a new born baby on its forehead. In this arduous task he is assisted

Notions about gods are not on the lines of those of the Hindu Puraṇas.

by his two companions Dhārā and Tārā. Their work appears to be similar to that of the tabulators of a public office who put their heads together for comparing the results of their tabulations. They set down the providential decree by some mysterious scrawlings on the forehead of the infant, and seem to do it automatically under the directions of a higher power. This power appears to be the *karmic* law over which Dhārā, Tārā and Bidhātā have no hands; so that when once the letters are inscribed in an automatic process, they become the destiny of the infant—"unshunable as death."

The Viṣnudut and Çivadut,—the Vaikuntha and Kailāsa,—which are indispensable in

Brahminic stories describing a hero's death and his subsequent march to the other world, have no place whatever in these folk-tales. The Brahmin himself has seldom any function to discharge in them. In the Paurānik tales his blessings or curses bring about their inevitable result of good fortune or calamities to the characters concerned; but here nothing of the sort is met with. Witchcraft takes the place of a Brahminic curse and the Brahmin, who appears very seldom, when he comes at all, does so in the capacity of an astrologer to find out an auspicious date for a marriage or maritime journey. A Brahmin's sacred thread is not an indispensable thing always about him. It is allowed to hang on a racket like one's robes, and he wears it when he has to go out to the king's court or a nobleman's mansion. The astrologers of the folk-tales are those Scythian Brahmins who are now called Āacharyas in our country and for whom the Hindu revivalists have reserved no place in their own superior order. These Scythian Brahmins held high position during the ascendancy of the Buddhists in this land.

The Brahmin is not an important figure in the folk-tales.

All these evidences tend to prove that the folk-tales of Bengal, generally speaking, had been composed before the Paurānik tales were popularised in the country by the Renaissance-

The prohibition of Sea-voyage.

Brahmins. But these are not all. We have other proofs, quite as convincing, to illustrate and bear out our proposition. It is an established fact that one of the principal acts of Hindu revivalist was to shut the gate of commerce by sea against the members of their own community. They surely did it for their self-preservation, as, with the ruin of the political power of the Hindus, the wholesome control exercised upon the sea-faring people by Hindu sovereigns ceased to have any effect. The traders now settled in distant lands preferring free life to the political thraldom in their own country, thus creating a great drain in Indian population. And if they returned to India, they came with strange outlandish manners imitating the ways of foreigners, and fell upon their quiet homes like thunder-bolts, destroying the Hindu ideals of domestic life. The Brahminic leaders, in the absence of any political power to control the situation, prohibited sea-voyages and enacted social laws for outcasting those who would be guilty of infringing them. But whatever the cause might be, it is certain, that the commercial activity of the Hindus ceased with the downfall of the Hindu and Buddhistic political power in Bengal. The merchants' position in this country underwent a signal change from the time their naval activities ceased. The great

The position of merchants in society before the Renaissance.

mercantile community during the Buddhistic times enjoyed a social position and status which were almost on a par with those of the members of royal families. Kānchanmālā, the heroine of a folk-tale, declares to her comrades with just pride, "My father is a king and a merchant is my husband, I have played with diamonds and rubies as though they were play-things." Mahmmad Munsi, the compiler of a folk-tale, records the adventures of its hero Rūpalal, a young merchant. This youth was at once accepted as son-in-law by the Fairy king as soon as it was reported to him that the suitor for his daughter's hand was the son of a respectable merchant. A king's son and a merchant's son are always fast friends in the Bengali folk-tales, and though sometimes the Prime Minister's son, and even a kotwal's son, claim such friendship with a prince in these fables, they hold a decidedly inferior position. It is the merchant's son alone who stands on terms of perfect equality with the king's son. When a princess is to be married, she invariably elects a prince, or a merchant's son as her bridegroom. Now after the downfall of the Buddhist power, the merchants within a few centuries lost all their status in society. Most of them were outcasted. Even the Suvarna Banikas who are still notable in this country in point of wealth and whom some of our scholars have identified as scions of the royal family of Kapilavastu, were treated with contempt, and the water touched by them declared unclean. The Suvarṇa Vanikas, as their name implies, were dealers in gold, and their present low status in society is unaccountable, except as a result of Brahminic ire against the leading merchants of the Buddhistic community. This was probably due to their not having accepted the Revivalists' creed. In the story of Çankhamālā, the mother takes pride in the social status of the youthful merchant, her son, by saying "You are not a fisherman, nor one of those who deal in flowers. Don't you know that you are a merchant." Such a boast befits a person of the highest social status only. But the fisherman—the Kaivartas, and the flower-seller have now a position in society which often a merchant has not. The water touched by a class of Kaivartas is not unclean in many places of Bengal. But a considerable number of merchants, inspite of their wealth, are now struggling hard to have the privilege of offering a cup of drinking water to the higher classes. Alas! even the lowest people in our society will not accept it from their hands.

Merchants lose their high social status after the Renaissance.

The ships, their picturesque construction and names.

The folk-tales are full of glory of mercantile communities. We have descriptions of sea-going vessels which bear fascinating names having regard to their picturesque shapes. We have the "Madukaras" (the bees) which were the show-ships, and bore always a merchant with his personal staff in state. The "Mayurpankhis" and the "Çukapankhis" swam across the sea in the shapes of the birds whose names they bore. The Yuktikalpataru by the king Voja, a work of authority on the formation of ships, lays it down that the prow of the ship admits of a variety of shapes. These are enumerated as eight, of which one is the head of a bird. The "Mayurpankhis" were for long the most fashionable and favourite class of ships in Bengal. It is now an established fact that the sea-going Indians carried the bird peacock to Babylon and other Western countries, to which it was unknown, in the 6th century B.C. For a long time the bird was called in some of the European countries by its Indian name. The peacock, which thus formed one of the most important exports of the ancient Indian merchants, was given an emblematic significance in the picturesque forms adorning the prows of the ships that carried the birds to the distant shores. The Bengali folk-tales abound with descriptions of these "Mayurpankhis."

9

The Hindu-Renaissance effected a wholesale change in the tastes of people by diverting them from secular pursuits to the spiritual. The achievement of a high level of earthly prosperity had been the aim of popular ambition in the preceding age. Gold and silver, diamond and ruby were, no doubt, as precious in those times as they are now. But the Hindu Renaissance, like every great religious movement, set at naught gold and silver and called them all, 'filthy lucre.' The motto of the Renaissance became "অর্থমনর্থং ভাবয় নিত্যম্." The Brahmin prided himself in .his poverty and cared only for spiritual wealth. Men delighted during this Brahminic revival in giving their children the names of gods and goddesses of the Hindu pantheon. From the 14th century down, the names of men and women in our country have been more or less associated with the names of our popular deities. In our earlier folk-tales, however, not one name is found to be of a Hindu god or goddess, a fact which will apparently strike every student of this rural literature. Durgā, Bhavānī, Umā, and Saraswatī, names which are so familiar to us, are nowhere to be met with in the extensive field of early folk-literature. Women's names reveal a love for those things, which are liked most by the merchants.

The proper names in old folk-tales indicate the mercantile rather than Brahminical ideal.

We have "Kānchanmālā" a string of gold, "Manimālā" a string of pearls, "Çankhamālā" a string of sea-shells, etc., and the names of merchants also are significantly stamped with the same idea. Even the names of princes savour of the money-bag, and not of the temple from which, as I have said, have flown all names and titles since the days of the Brahminic Renaissance. In the story of "Kalāvati Rājkanyā, we have names of six princes, *viz.*, Hirarāja—the prince of diamonds' Mānikrāja the prince of rubies, Mātirāj the prince of pearls, Çankharāja—the prince of sea-shells and Kānchanrāja—the prince of gold. We have names of still earlier period which do not show any trace of Sanskritic elegance, but seem as unmeaning Prakrit jargon. But a closer scrutiny will discover suggestions in them indicating also a love for wealth—the characteristic trait of mercantile classes. Such for instance are "Aya Bené" (আয়বেণে) "Sāya Bené" (সায়বেণে) "Gasta Bené" (গস্তবেণে) "Masta Bené" (মস্তবেণে). "Aya Bené" may mean a merchant with large income (আয়), "Sāya Bené" is possibly an abbreviation of Sāhā Bené, the word Sāhā, which is now the family-surname of a large community of merchants, is an abbreviated form of the word sādhu, a word which in the old Bengali literature generally signifies a rich merchant. If we thus prepare a list of names, we find that it is wealth and a thought of profit and income that dominated over the mind of the people; they naturally called their babies by such things that they prized dearly in their lives. We find in the folk-tales compiled by some of our modern writers, such as the Rev. Lal Bihary Dey, that older names have now and then been changed for modern ones; this they have apparently done to suit the current taste. The names of architects and of boat-men also of the earlier folk-tales indicate the spirit of the times. In the story of Madhumālā, we have "Hirāmanik" (diamonds and precious stone) and "Shonālāl" (gold and precious stone)—the names of two architects, and in the story of Kanchanamālā the captain of the ship is called Dulāldhan (dearly prized wealth). We do not mean to say that these names are solely confined to that particular period of commercial activity in Bengal. Even in the present day we occasionally meet with such names, but in the earlier folk-tales nearly all names of chief as well as minor characters bear imports suggestive of good money. The contrast appears very striking when we find a total absence in the earlier fables of names after those of the Hindu gods and goddesses, which became so plentiful in later times. The above evidences establish one point, *viz.*, that it was during the period of great commercial activity prior to the Hindu Renaissance in Bengal that most of the earlier folk-tales were composed.

Grandeur and wealth.

The same idea is traced in the incidental descriptions of the grandeur and wealth that abound in these stories, offering a sharp contrast to the present condition of things in society. Everywhere there is that reference to a high water-mark of prosperity—the fruit of commercial success, in the homes of merchants. The number of the rich must have been great, for in the common folk-tales, allusions to prosperous life are plentiful, showing that the ordinary village-women who mostly composed the stories, spoke from their direct knowledge and observation. High-class women prided in their proficiency in the culinary art. The hearths, they used for cooking, were plated with gold; they used sandal-wood for fuel, and for the purpose of frying they generally used clarified butter in the place of oil. Such ideas of luxury have passed away from our society, not that they are out of fashion, but because the upper classes are now not so rich as to be able to afford them. We read in these tales of "spoons made of pearls," of "picturesque water-vessels made of solid gold." After the revival of Hinduism, its leaders who came from distant countries and intermarried with the local people, set a high value on their own blood and hence lineage became the chief consideration in matrimonial matters. We know that in comparatively later times, a bridegroom of high qualifications was perfectly satisfied with marrying the ugliest bride and even one who limped or was one-eyed, if she could trace her ancestry from one of the Kulin-leaders.

None but the brave deserves the fair.

The state of things unfolded by the folk-tales present a very different condition. The bride is said to be an exquisite beauty. The bridegroom must be a hero and the bride fair, proving the force of Dryden's rhymed formula declaring that none but the brave, deserve the fair. This, of course, is not only the motto of all folk-tales, but of all heroic poems of the world. We find in the folk-tales of Bengal, that the Ghatakas or the match-makers carried with them pictures of the bride and the bridegroom to be shown to the parties concerned. These were held indispensable where the bride and the bridegroom lived at a distance from one another. The pictures in the case of a wealthy couple were drawn on golden plates, trimmed with diamonds and folded within rich coverings of embroidered silk. The procession of a rich man's marriage generally consisted of a large number of *Chaturdolās*, along with many other things for display; these were temple-shaped wooden conveyances inlaid with precious stones, the

Articles of daily use, and luxury.

most picturesque one being in the middle, reserved for the bride and the bridegroom, with a roof of the form of a cupolá or minaret. This special Chaturdolā had a golden umbrella unfurled over the golden throne on the pedestal. There were, besides, the Puṣparathəs or chariots covered with floral wreaths. Pillows were sometimes made with seeds of white mustard and this was considered as a piece of luxury. For decorating the eyes with black-paint (*anjan*) artistic shaped silver-rods were used. Everywhere we find references to golden plates and cups, showing that these were in the everyday use of the merchants and other rich men. A merchant's daughter or a princess used to keep a large number of female attendants and maids who are described as waiting with oil-cakes, alkaly and towels upon their mistress when she went to her toilet-room in the afternoon. We also read of very fine robes made of cotton "that looked transparent as dew" and sandal-colouréd aprons and clothes called "the *Meghadumbur* and *Mayurpekham*." The word *Maghadumbur* may be translated as blue-tinted like a cloud, and *Mayurpekham*—of the colour of the plumes of a peacock's tail. There are also accounts of palaces whose uppermost floor was to be reached by a flight of one thousand stairs, of roofs made of white marble-plated with gold and trimmed with pendants of diamond, of the princess' crown from which big diamonds shone and cymbals of gold adorning the feet of lovely women of all castes. A merchant's treasures, we are told, consisted, amongst other valuable articles, of heaps of diamonds and rubies with seven bevelled edges and sea-shells with polished mouths of the colour and quality of pearls. The flower-women used everyday to carry baskets of "flowers that bloom in the morning and those that bloom in the dewy eve" to youthful maidens at the dawn of the day and towards its close respectively. We have glimpses into the sort of life led by a princess or a rich lady in the fascinating picture of Madhumālā who awakes from sleep by the spell cast upon her by the fairies in the middle of the night, and taking it to be the dawn of the day, thus muses within herself ;—"I wonder if it is morning, why then does not the bird *Śāri* sing its gay note in its cage as is its wont? If morning, why do not the cymbals sound on the busy feet of maid-servants? And why do the three long rows of lamps fed by clarified butter still burn in my compartments?" The princess Madhumālā is described as sleeping on a golden couch decorated with diamonds and pearls, the cushion spread over it being prepared with thirteen varieties of rich silk.

With the Brahmin revivalist, the room in which the child first sees the light is held unclean. Even in the cases of rich people, a temporary straw hut of a very miserable sort used to be raised for such purposes near their mansion and the hut remained outside the main buildings, being considered untouchable by the family. We read, however, that in the days of these rural tales such rooms used to be built with great architectural ingenuity and decorations of gold in rich men's homes. Surely it affords a striking contrast to the sort of things that have existed for over six hundred years; for who can think now, with the orthodox ideas of Hindu cleanliness in his head, of a lying-in-room being built like a parlour with artistic decorations of the most precious metal?

Natal room.

We need not enumerate other details of high-living and luxuries indulged in by the aristocratic communities of Bengal in the hey-day of her commercial activities as depicted in the rural literature. We shall, however, refer to some rites the observance of which was held indispensable for a merchant on the eve of undertaking a sea-voyage. The tradition of these lies enshrouded in obscurity owing to Indians having ceased for a long time to travel by sea. But as given in these folk-tales, some of the traditions attract us by the tender

On the eve of a sea-voyage.

associations of domestic duties which had to be fulfilled before a merchant could leave home for distant shores. The wife comes with a gold vessel full of water and washes the feet of her husband about to sail abroad, and then wipes them with her unbraided locks. The whole court-yard is decorated with *alipanā* paintings. The captain of the ship comes and asks:—"Have you, Oh master, partaken of the meal first offered to temples? Have five lights been waived and holy baths performed in the tank? Are the eight pinnacles of god's temple intact and in good condition? Is there a sufficient reserve supply in the house? Have you bowed your head down before the gods? Have you made sufficient provision for each of your family members for the time you may be absent from home? Have you taken leave of each and every one in your family? And have they gladly given such permission?" In one case, the merchant who had a dislike for his wife, did not see her before he left home. But the captain refused to set sail to the ship, until and unless his master obtained her permission. It should be said that the captain ventured to do so, because all this was held indispensable from a religious point of view. The prows of the ships had to be painted with red-powder, sandal paste and vermilion, and the whole ship oiled before starting. In the front part of the ship, amidst pearl pendants, hung five lights that burnt night and day. The merchants in later times did not always recognise honesty to be the best policy. In the 16th century, Kabikankan described Murāriçīla—a typical rogue. In earlier times also there was no want of Murari's cousins, who though not such great villains, behaved unscrupulously while selling their goods in distant countries. In the story of Çankhamālā, we get the following account of their dealings.

The merchants cease to be honest.

"Some merchants produce 'darmuj' a kind of poisonous wood, from their bags and call it cinnamon. Some sell goods worth a *kahan* for a *sikka*. Some have their baskets full of pieces of ordinary stone, and sell them as diamonds and rubies."

While taking a survey of these materials in respect of commercial transactions, we do not certainly hold these as historical evidences. The rural tales are mere products of imagination of the people of the country-side, but yet what historical facts can be a more genuine index to the state of society than these fictions, which spring from the accumulated observations and wisdom of the rural people—the true recorders of the customs and manners of their society?

The "Rūpakathās" or folk-tales, as I have already stated, used to be told in the evenings by professional story-tellers who were generally flower-women or barber-women. The women of the barber caste especially had many important functions to discharge in the houses of rich people. They were generally the *confidante* of the ladies of high rank and assisted in their toilet. The barbers, in ancient days enjoyed a quite decent position in Hindu society. The Mahābhārata lays it down that the rice cooked by barbers is good for Brahmins and other castes. The function they have still to discharge in all ceremonials of the Hindus savour of their traditional place in the social scale from a remote antiquity. Their position in our society might have, to a considerable extent, been lowered during the Mahomedan times on account of their having been obliged to shave the Mahammadans. No one in society dared to outcast them or declare their water as untouchable, when the ruling race engaged their professional services; but the barbers, since that time, seem to have ceased to do many offices which they used to perform in the homes of aristocratic Hindu families in the pre-Mahammadan period. The barber-women had ready access to the palace and to a princes'

The position of a barber in society.

dressing room. Old women of every caste acquired the art of story-telling, but it is the barber-women that learnt to do it with the greatest effect; for the flower-women and the barber-women alone adopted story-telling as the avocation of their lives.

Evidences to prove that these folk-tales were mostly composed by women.

That women composed these stories in Bengal will be easily proved by the style and manner in which they are delivered. The mannerisms, the naive and homely descriptions—their directness and tender touches all bear a testimony to that peculiar skill in manipulation which pre-eminently belongs to the softer sex. In the genuine stories collected first-hand from women, these qualities are plentifully in evidence. No one of the ruder sex could build up the tales with a rich supply of adages current in the zenana,—such as "কুঁড়ে বেঁধে কুঁড়েয় আছি। তার তলায় ও রাজার হাঁচি।" (We poor people live in huts, but lo! the king's sneeze is heard even here—which means, though so poor, we are not out of the reach of the king's oppression), "ধন রত্ন কড়ি, না বিয়লেই বুড়ী" (Money and women, if they do not breed, are worse than useless), "হাতী ঘোড়া গেল তল। ফড়িং বলে কত জল?" (The elephant and the horse are drowned, the fly wants to fathom the water). There are lots of such things in the tales and these, every one knows in Bengal, are found interspersed in the everyday conversation of the women-folk of our country. There are besides sentences which are unmeaning jargon, and may be classed with lullabies; but like the chirp of a bird, these have a singularly charming effect, especially on the young. However great the genius and poetic flight of a man may be, he is not equal to the task of writing such a language, as that which, far off from the clatter of a busy world, has developed in the inner apartments of an oriental home, fed by sentiments alone. There is one point that will at once strike the reader as a typical specimen of a woman's mode of calculation. After Khanā and Lilāvatī, the study of mathematics seems to have been given up by women particularly in this Gangetic valley. "A woman may vaunt of her many brilliant qualifications," says one of our poets, "but if she has to calculate shillings and pence, she sees no way out, except to go to her lover's house and consult him." In the folk-tales we find in several instances a peculiar mode of calculation which certainly does not illustrate the mathematical proficiency of the calculator, but proves that the mathematician is a woman.

How story-telling was practised.

In one passage the figure 265 had to be mentioned: it is put as 7 times 36 plus 13. In another, 964 was expressed by "12 times 52 and 17 times 20. In another, a period of time equal to 298 hours is indicated by the expression 12 days and 13 nights. As our women usually calculate figures by twenties and in rare cases by fifties, this is a mode peculiar to them. No man does it in this way except when he is absolutely illiterate or stupid. The high level of genius displayed in the conception of the stories from which the above quotations are made shows an odd combination of extraordinary merit with much stupidity. This could not have probably been the case, had their authors been of the ruder sex. When a Hindu woman was in confinement, which, except in the case of Brahminical and one or two high castes, is for a period of 30 days, the services of a story-teller used to be engaged in former times. These story-tellers were generally widows and sometimes old men, who had learnt the art from their grand-mothers. The stories used to be told from evening till midnight, except on the sixth night of the birth of a child, when the story-teller assisted by a chorus continued his recitations the whole night. On the sixth night the *Vidhātā puruṣa*—the god of human destiny—comes, according to Hindu notions, to write the fate of the baby on its forehead, and therefore keeping up through the whole of night, on that occasion, is an absolute necessity. The new mother feels lonely in her room during the days of confinement and for the sake of keeping her in good spirit and in a jovial mood, they adopt this means, than which nothing can be more wholesome for the occasion. The tales are interspersed with songs, and when a story is told by an old widow, two or three young women, who have good voices, form a chorus and sing the songs. The boys and girls all assemble to hear them, and between many sighs and much laughter, the soft eye-lids close like buds, sometimes when a story is yet unfinished. Such things may still be observed in our distant villages, where novel-reading and the study of Algebra and Trigonometry have not yet driven popular poetry and sentiment into the background.

CHAPTER III

Currency of older forms of belief amongst the converts to Islam in their folk-literature.

After the Muhammadan conquest of Bengal Islam found easy converts among the lay Buddhist population which was still very considerable in the country. When the Hindu community was reorganised on the basis of the old Vedic religion, and caste-rules were revised and made more stringent, the lay Buddhist people found their position very uncongenial in the country. The water touched by them was unclean and the *Bhikkus* and the *Bhikkunīs*—the Buddhist monks and nuns—who numbered by thousands in Bengal in the 13th century, were treated with contempt and called *Neḍa-neḍīs* or shaven men and women. This name, the Hindus gave them contemptuously, not only because these Buddhists represented a fallen order, from whom the Hindu revivalists had forcibly taken away all power in spiritual and even secular matters, but because of the gross immorality which a life of celibacy had brought upon the men and women living in monasteries during the days of the decline of Buddhism.

The Neḍās and Neḍis.

In an environment which was full of animosity, hatred and bitterness, these Buddhists found their position very uncomfortable, and they naturally preferred to become converts to Islam and thus associate themselves with the ruling race. In the 14th century, their lay order swelled the ranks of Muhammadan converts and the vast Islamite population of modern Bengal comprises the descendants of the Buddhist laity whom the Hindus still treat with the contemptuous epithet of *Nedās*—a title by which they used to designate the Buddhist *Bhikkus*.

But the folk-tales of Bengal were no more a monopoly of the Hindus than of the Buddhists, in the good old days immediately before the Hindu Renaissance, when both the communities had almost the same social and religious ideals. Their *tāntric* ceremonies and rites of worship were so similar that none but an adept could distinguish those of the one from the other. The Buddhist monks, who in earlier times, had strictly pursued the path of *jnan* and led an austere life of struggle to control the passions, gradually began to yield to the softer charms of the Bhakti-cult, and in the 12th and 13th centuries their temples became resonant with the sounds of the evening-bells, of tabor and of *kīrtana* songs accompanied with dance. The *dohās* of Kānupāda and other

The folk literatures of the Hindus and the Buddhists before the Renaissance — very much alike.

saintly poets were sung in the temples, and prostration, fast and vigil became the order of the day much in the same way as may be seen in the places of Hindu worship of to-day. Dr. Kern has noticed this growth of a spirit of devotion in the Buddhist temples, eventually developing into the ecstatic fervour of the latter-day Vaiṣṇavism. In fact the Mahāyāna Buddhism from the time of Nāgāryuṇa in the 1st century A.D. gradually assimilated the doctrines of the Gītā and other Hindu scriptures, till, before it finally lost its hold upon the Indian communities, it had practically demolished all barrier between Buddhism and Hinduism, bringing the former many steps nearer to the mother-cult, from which it had sprung in the 6th century B.C.

So the folk-tales told in those days in the Hindu and Buddhist families were very much alike. It was a pleasant occupation of the Bengali women to relate such stories in the evening, and it was an engaging pursuit of young children to follow the adventures of the heroes through their great perils and trials,—in the mansions of ultra-human and demoniac creatures, —in the tanks from which huge cobras sprang with jewels shining from their hoods, or, in the dark wildernesses infested with aerial beings where our heroes had lost their path in the night. But still more was the effect of the tales on the young listeners of the fair sex, who heard with beating hearts all that the heroines suffered, now from their merciless and grimly cruel sisters-in-law, now from the persistent indifference and maltreatment of princely fathers-in-law and not infrequently from their own prejudiced husbands, whom, inspite of all imaginable ills, they dearly loved.

Islam gave new faith to the Buddhists and the low-caste Hindus from whose ranks it counted its largest number of recruits. A few drops of the Iranian and Semitic blood that now run through the veins of 90 per cent. of the Bengali Muhammadans will scarcely admit of detection by scrutiny, any more than an element of the mother-tincture in a high dilution of a Homeopathic medicine. Those Bengalis who were Hindus and Buddhists at one time, but became Muhammadan converts mostly in the 14th century A.D, did not, in some cases, give up their ancestral calling, though it was connected with the religion that they had shunned. A large number of people in this country used to earn their bread by singing hymns in praise of some gods or goddesses from door to door. At the present day the *Āgamani* singers among the Sāktas do so, and the Vaiṣṇava mendicants are of course the most typical

Hindu ideas in the community of Muhammadan converts.

of this class of people. In good old days before the Muhammadan conquest, the singers of hymns in praise of Laksmī—the harvest-goddess—visited every house of the peasantry, and the women of Bengal delighted to hear from their lips the signs of a lucky woman—of the duties to be performed by the virtuous wife and the ways of the evil-eyed one—of the *hastini* "who walks with eyes fixed on the air and speaks like a trumpet," of the noble *padmīnī* "who rises with the first crowing of the crows and lights the lamp at the dusk, who does not touch any food before her husband has taken meal" and fulfils other conditions becoming a true housewife. These hymns and doggerels pertaining to domestic duties are addressed to Viṣṇu by his consort Lakṣmī. The goddess in detailing the virtues of a good wife and the vices of a bad one, thus says of their respective husbands, "The husband of a chaste wife is glorious like the summit of a mountain, but that of an unchaste one is like the prow of a rotten boat." This adulation of the virtues of a good wife by the Goddess of Harvest herself is no mean compliment, making the peasant's wife proud of her loyalty to her mate, and she fills the bag of the professional mendicant with rice, brinjal and potato, and even sometimes puts a

Singers of hymns in praise of Laksmī the harvest-goddess.

hard-earned copper-piece in the mendicant's hands. But though it is known to all in Bengal, the fact may yet sound strange to those who do not know it, that these singers of hymns on Laksmī, the goddess, are not Hindus, as it should be, but Muhammadan mendicants. It proves beyond doubt that those professional Buddhist and Hindu mendicants, whose avocation it had been to sing these songs before Muhammadan conquest in the 13th century, did not give up their calling after having embraced Islam, but have continued to sing the same songs in praise of the Hindu goddess up to now. The language in which the songs are couched have undergone no alteration and is in every respect that crude Prakritic Bengali in which the Mainā-matī songs or the Çunyapurāṇa were composed in the 11th or 12th century. The Muhammadans, inspite of their religious and iconoclastic zeal, have been tolerant so far as not to interfere with the avocations of the new recruits to their religion. The Buddhist and Hindu converts to Islam in the island of Java are allowed to perform the worship of Laksmī with all the devotion of a pious Hindu. The Muhammadans are now mostly the "*rojāhs*" or physicians of serpent-bites in Bengal. They recite incantations and *mantras* for the cure of not only those who are bitten by serpents but also of those said to be possessed by spirits. From generation to generation, these "*rojhās*," mostly Muhammadans, as I have said, have been practitioners of this art. They no doubt sprang from the Hindu and Buddhist families and did not, after they were converted to Muhammadan faith, give up a calling which had been a source of their maintenance from remote times. A manual of these incantations and *mantras* has lately been published by Mir Khoram Alí from 155-1 Masjidbari Street, Calcutta. This writer says in the Introduction to his Manual that his name stands first in the list of those physicians who cure by charms and incantations. In all cases of snake-bite, or where the patient withers away from being possessed by a spirit or under the malignant spell of a witch, the *mantras* that he knows are infallible. Hence many people seek his help in distress. But as he travels from place to place, they have often to return to their homes disappointed. "Aged am I," he says, "and know not when the final call will come upon me." So he is afraid lest the art that has been practised from generation to generation in his family, would die with him, as there is none who knows the charms so well as he does. With these preliminary remarks he introduces his subject which is full of Hindu ideas from the

The incantations for curing snake-bite.

beginning to the end. The language of these *mantras* sometimes bears a striking kinship with the Bengali style of the 10th and 11th centuries and at others with those of the 15th and the 16th. This proves that some members of the *rojhā* families were converted to Islam in the 13th century, when the Muhammadans first raided Bengal, and others in the 15th and 16th centuries. The language of these *mantras* does not seem to have changed at all from the form in which they were originally composed; for if a word is altered then the charm loses all efficacy. It may be said that the Muhammadans might have learned these *mantras* from some Hindus, just as in the country-side they learn their alphabets from Hindu *Guru Mahāçayas*. But this is not at all likely. Whole families of Muhammadans in many cases know the *mantras*, which are full of praises of Hindu gods and goddesses; the Rojhās, who cure snake bite and spirit-possession, are generally Muhammadans, at least they are the best of the doctors of such charms in the country-side. Like the singers of Lakshmī's glories, who, turning Muhammadans, did not give up the calling they practised in their 'heathen days,' these Rojhās also followed an avocation while they were 'heathen' which has not been afterwards found incompatible, as a profession, with the conditions of their new society, though from a religious point of view, such a thing could not be tolerated. Thus we conclude that long before the 13th century the ancestors of these Muhammadans had followed callings for earning their bread associated with the Hindu and Buddhist religions, and the Mollas or the Muhammadan priests relaxed their orthodoxy so far as to allow them to follow those pursuits which had been the main source of income to their families for many generations. In the Manual referred to, the compiler Khoramali invokes the aid of 64 Dākinees of the Hindu Tantras and their "60 sisters" possibly of the Buddhist Tantras. The first Mantra for snake-bite runs thus:—

The language is very antiquated like those works written in the 11th and 12th centuries.

"হস্ত সারম্, গলা সারম্, আর সারম্ মুখ।
পেট, পিট, চরণ সারম্, আর সারম্ বুক॥
পেট, পিট, চরণ গাতি মনসার বরে।
লক্ষ লক্ষ বাণ—অমুকের কি করিতে পারে॥
কাঙরের কামিখ্যা দেবী দিয়া গেল বর।
বালির বিন্দ রাজা বলে অমুক হ'ল অমর॥"

The language has evidently some Prakrit elements in it; the word সারম্ is one of such, the word কাঙর for Kamrup is one, as we find it in the early Dharma-mangala poems. We profess our ignorance in regard to the historical reference in "বালির বিন্দ রাজা দিয়া গেল বর." It is probable that a Raja of that name flourished in Bali Uttarpara, in the pre-Muhammadan days

12

who had achieved a great fame as a healer by *mantras.* The appeal to Manasā Devī shows that the *mantra* was inculcated by her followers in olden times, and Kamakṣā is certainly one of our earliest shrines. The next *mantra* is in a style which closely resembles that of the Çunyapurāṇa of Rāmāi Pundit, written in the 11th century. There are occasionally to be met with in this Manual Arabic incantations invoking the aid of the Prophet, and this is but too natural. Within more than 7 centuries of conversion to Islam, these people could not help adding some exotic element to the hymns, in accordance with the faith they had embraced, but the main portion of the book discloses purely Hindu ideas. There are references and appeals to Çiva, Kāli, Kṛiṣṇa, Garuḍa and other deities of the Hindu pantheon almost on every page. In the *mantras* relating to snake-bite, Kṛisṇa, as the vanquisher of the snake Kāliya, is frequently invoked. Hanumāna, the great ape-god, is also addressed for helping in the cure of the patient, and an appeal to Rāma and Lakṣhmana comes off as a matter of course. Kamakṣā and Kāyunr, the two-notable shrines, are mentioned and it is a curious thing that the Muhammadan prodigy in the use of spells recites "ওঁ স্বাহা ফট্" like a Hindu Brahmin. Chandi, the goddess, as daughter of a Haḍi, "হাড়ির ঝি চণ্ডী মা" is a familiar line which occurs often in the colophon. We know

Historical side-lights.

that Hāḍis, in olden times, used to perform priestly functions in some of the Kāli temples, and they even do so now in some parts of Bengal. They are also the custodians of many temples of Çītalā, the small-pox-goddess; and in Hāḍisidhyā of the Maināmatī songs, we find one of the Hāḍi caste elevated to the rank of a great sage. The Hāḍis seem to have at one time occupied a decent position in society, and it may not be improbable that their present degraded position is due to the antagonism and resistance they offered to the Brahmins of the Renaissance. This invocation of Chandi, as daughter of a Hāḍi, raises the problem of a far-reaching character as to how some of the non-Aryan deities found entrance into the temples of the Aryans. For this Chandi, who is described as daughter of a Hāḍi, and whom originally the Hāḍis worshipped as priests in temples, gradually became identical with Pārvatī, the consort of Çiva. The tradition of her origin from Haḍi parents was in course of time totally ignored or suppressed as that caste sank in the humblest social scale. There are many lines in this Manual which are full of suggestions on other lines. We find invocation in it of the god Dharma, who in the popular belief is no other than the Buddha himself. Besides there are allusions to Ballukā Sāgara. This Ballakā or Ballukā is frequently mentioned in the early Dharma Mangal poems as a Buddhist shrine.

The Manual, as I have already said, contains archaic forms of old Bengali, often reminding us of the style prevalent in the 10th and 12th centuries. There is another book, written by one Munshi Enayetulla Sircar, in which the birth and adventures of Jarāsura or the Demon of Fever, are recorded. This is evidently a record of a Hindu tradition which now seems to be lost amongst the Hindus themselves, but is still current among the Muhammadan population, transmitted from that remote time when they eschewed their belief in the older religions. Munshi Enayetulla Sircar begins with the line "শ্রীরাম গণেশায় নমঃ" ('obeisance to Rāma and Ganeça') and then goes on to tell how a rich Brahmin's beautiful daughter fell in love with a man of the Chandāla caste. This youth absconded with her, but was detected by a ferry-man in the way. The latter threatened to bring the matter to the notice of the Rājā's men, but desisted from that course on the Chandāla giving him an undertaking that he would leave the girl with the ferry-man. The woman who was *enceinte* gave birth to a child on Tuesday in the month of September :—it was the night of the new moon and the moment when the baby came to the world was

Jarāsura or the demonic god of fever.

very inauspicious. It was thrown away into the jungles on that very night by the woman with a view to escape scandal, but the foxes nourished it by their milk. In course of time this child grew to be the Demon of Fever and his adventures are related fully in the latter portion of the book. It is also mentioned how a Brahmin succeeded in gaining wealth by the help of this deified Demon, having cured a princess of persistent fever. This disease was unknown in the country before the birth of Jarāsura.

Recaptiulation of the various points at issue.

Now what we have already written proves two points, *viz.*, that the Hindus and Buddhists who had renounced their faith in their religions and turned Islamite converts, still retained some of their older religious traditions, particularly those which were associated with the callings by which they had been used to earn their bread. The vernacular hymns to Lakṣmī, which used to be sung by the Hindu or Buddhist mendicants, are now sung by their descendants—the Muhammadan Fakirs. The charms for the cure of snake-bite practised by the Hindu Rojhās (Rojhā or Ojhā, a corrupted and abbreviated form of the word Upādhyāya ; Ujjhāya and Ojhā being the gradually changed forms in Prakrit from which the Rojhā of Bengali has been derived) are still known to a class of Muhammadans—the descendants of the Hindus and Buddhist doctors of spells and charms; the traditions of the Hindus with regard to the origin of fever, at one time current among their peasantry, are now recorded by their descendants who are Muhammadans. Other evidences on this line will not be difficult to trace. The songs on Manasā Devī, on Kāli and even Kṛiṣṇa and Rādhā, sung by the Hindu and Buddhist professional singers, are still current among a large Muhammadan populace in Eastern Bengal where recruits to Islam from the ranks of lay Hindus and Buddhists have been the largest. Songs of Manasā Devī are sung by professional Muhammadan minstrels in Mymensing and other districts. The converts have not been able to give up the traditions of the older religions during the long centuries of their renouncement of 'heathen faith,' and the Bengali Muhammadan to-day, inspite of the injunctions of his Molla, who is ever busy in his efforts to root out every form of 'superstitious beliefs,' has remained true to his instinct nurtured and developed in a different atmosphere of religious and social life during long centuries.

The second point that we want to establish is that the origin of their callings and of some of the beliefs enumerated above, is to be traced to a far remoter period than the 14th or 15th century when most of the ancestors of the present

Bengali Muhammadans embraced the Islamite faith. During the 7 or 8 centuries that have passed, the Hindu or Buddhistic elements in their forms of belief have scarcely received any new light from those older religions, ever-growing under fresh social conditions and turning new leaves in the history of their gradual advancement. The Muhammadan peasantry inspite of keeping up these faiths and ideas transmitted to them from unrecorded times previous to their conversion, are now solely under the guidance of the Mollas. They have shut their gates against all fresh accretions of faiths promulgated by the new Brahmin of the Renaissance. The Purānas and the Epics which have been so popularised among the Hindu rural folk, by the new Brahmin—the creed of devotion which has been proclaimed with the sound of cymbal and tabor to the peasantry for these five hundred years,—have not made any perceptible impression on the lay Muhammadan populace. It is the older forms of faith anterior to the Hindu Renaissance, that have still some hold upon them, and the origin of these, as I have already stated, is to be traced to a period much earlier than the 14th or 15th century when the largest number of these Bengalis accepted Islam. The linguistic evidence and that of the forms of faith traced in the hymns to Lakshmī and in the Mantras and spells prove their affinity to those current amongst the Hindus and Buddhists of Bengal mostly in the 10th and the 11th centuries.

Hindu folk-tales amongst Muhammadans.

But if they do still cultivate the older forms of faith by songs, hymns and spells and by appeals to gods and goddesses of the heathen pantheon, how could their women forget those tales and fables which they had heard when girls, recited to them by their grandmothers, and which they themselves related to their children when they in their turn became grandmothers themselves ? In fact all the folk-tales current in this country during the 10th and 11th, and even earlier centuries, they still tell to their children, and in this matter the Hindu and Buddhist elements form a great factor of training of the Muhammadan child from its birth. References to the Indrasabhā, appeals to Manasā Devī and to Saraswatī, the goddess of learning, are occasionally met with in those fables ; and the Rājakumārī, the princess, and her lover the prince—his friends, the minister's son and the son of the prefect of police, are all Hindus in these tales. The grandmothers in Muhammadan harems still tell these stories, which are as old as the 10th and the 11th centuries, treasured up and transmitted to the family by elderly women, and the continuity of the strain from the time when they were pious

Hindus down to the time when they have been pious Muhammadans, has not been broken; the stories of Mālanchamālā, Bhānumatī, Sakhisonā, Amritabhāna, Chandrāvalī, Mālatikusum, Madhumāla and lots of others with which we are all so familiar, are still told in Muhammadan homes and listened to with eager attention by the young Muhammadan peasantry of Bengal. This fact was not at all known to us till recently, and the discovery has been very interesting as it shows that after the lapse of the 7 or 8 centuries of their alienation from the older religion, the sorrows of Kānchanmālā and Sakhisonā still create throbbings in the hearts of Muhammadan girls, as it does of their Hindu cousins. This proves beyond doubt the origin of the stories to be long before the Muhammadan conquest and their proselytising activities in the 14th and 15th centuries; for these Hindu and Buddhist tales could not have found entrance into the Muhammadan harems after the light of Islam had fallen on the Hindu homes. The very form in which the stories are current among Muhammadans show the earliest type, though Arabic and Persian influences have, to a certain extent, changed the original spirit of the tales.

CHAPTER IV

Classifications of Muhammadan folk-tales in Bengal.

The Muhammadan folk-tales that I have discovered may be divided into three classes, *viz.*:—

I. Those that relate to saintly men who have been given the ranks of prophets in Hindu and Muhammadan communities alike. These men are called *pīrs*, such are Mānik Pīr and Satya Pīr, who have been now raised above the level of mortals in popular legends, but were once men of the flesh, and had, by reason of their Hindu extraction, and of their catholicity of views, won the respect of both Hindus and Muhammadans, though they themselves seem to have adopted the Muhammadan faith. These legends were composed mostly during the 15th and 16th centuries.

II. The folk-tales which relate to the heroic deeds of those Muhammadan zealots who carried the religion of Islam at the point of their swords, and obtained celebrity by overthrowing the Hindu faith and breaking the Hindu temples and also by marrying some noted beauties of the Hindu Zenana, after having converted them to Islam. These stories, some of which were derived from the Persian and Arabic sources, relate to events from after the 11th century.

III. Those that have been current in Bengal from a remote period, and which the Hindu converts to Muhammadan faith have not been able to give up, though they all have direct references to Hindu and Buddhist religions. These stories all belong to a period much earlier than 1299 A.D. when Bengal was conquered.

We may still mention a fourth, *viz.*, those tales which tell us of the adventures of the heroes and prophets of Arabia and Persia, written in the vernacular of Bengal with a very large element of admixture of Arabic and Persian words. We shall not, however, concern ourselves with these, but merely touch the first and second classes of folk-tales, reserving a deservedly large space for the critical analysis of class III of these tales, which directly falls within our scope.

Class I—Satya Pīr.

The first rank in the list of prophets comprised in No. I of the above classification is occupied by Satya Pīr, whom one legend describes as son of a princess—probably the daughter of Hushen Shah, the Emperor of Gour.[1] We gather this legend from two accounts of the Pīr, one by a Muhammadan poet named Arif, and another by Sankarāchārya. The manuscript of Sankarāchārya's poem is dated 1062 of the Bengali era, *i.e.*, 1664 A.D. But there are other legends also about Satya Pīr which I shall mention hereafter. In the 16th century, the Hindu poet Fakir Rāma Kavibhuṣaṇa, who rendered some of our folk-tales into elegant Bengali verse, gave an account of Satya Pīr in animated poetry, and since then many of our poets have sung eulogies of this deified Pīr in Bengali. Gradually, however, the Muhammadan element was totally ignored or eliminated from this tale and Satya Pīr became in the hands of our Hindu poets, Satyanārayan or Viṣṇu himself, of the Hindu pantheon, deriving all his glories from the texts of the Revākhanda of the Skanda purāṇa. Some of our greatest poets have written adulatory verses in honour of this deity, who has now become a Hindu god in plain *dhuti* and *chādara* of the Bengalis, throwing off his Muhammadan's trousers and Fakir's loose mantle. And such we find him in the works of Bhāratachandra and in the magnificent poem called the Harilīla by Jayanārayaṇa Sen who flourished in the 18th century. We have come across

[1] The Bengali Encyclopædia—The Viṣwa Koṣa, Part 18, p: 159, See the words—বাঙ্গলা সাহিত্য ।

many poets in the 17th and 18th centuries writing in the strain of Fakir Rāma. But though Satyanārayaṇa enjoys a great popularity among the rural people of Bengal and though he is divested of his Muhammadan elements and is now a Hindu god in every respect, yet curiously the offering of flour and milk mixed with banana and sugar, that he recives at the hands of his worshippers, is not called *bhoga*, a name by which such offerings are generally called in the Hindu temples, but *shinni*, a name given to offerings by Muhammadan worshippers. This certainly reminds one of that exotic element which the Brahmin priests have always tried to eliminate from their religious rites and functions, but which in the present case has been allowed to remain as if by oversight.

Many of the songs in praise of Satya Pīr have been written by Muhammadans themselves. Some of these breathe a catholicity of views which doubtless accounts for their being appreciated by Hindus and Muhammadans alike. One of these poems was written some time ago by Kṛṣṇahari Dāsa, about whom nothing is known ; but it appears to me that though the writer's name is Hindu, he was a Muhammadan ; for he begins by invoking the aid of Allāh and gives an account of the Vehest and of the prophet in the devotional spirit of a devout Muhammadan. The poem is printed in the right Arabic style, beginning from where our books end and ending where our books begin. The language has also a considerable admixture of Persian and Arabic words. This work which runs over 250 pages, Royal 8vo, was printed at the Garanhata Bengal Roy press, and is generally sold in Muhammadan book-shops. The name of the book is Satya Pīr or the story of Sandhyāvatī. It begins with an account of a Rājā named Maya-Dānava, who took it into his head to imprison and oppress all Muhammadan fakirs who visited his capital. This was reported to Allah in Vehest by the angel Gabriel, and the matter engaged the earnest consideration of His Divine Majesty. It was eventually decided by the counsel of the Rasul, that Chāndbibi (who lived in Vehest) should be ordered to be born on the earth in fulfilment of a prophecy which had for long ages been current in the Vehest, that Satya Pīr would be born on the earth in the womb of Chāndbibi, in order to redress all human ills in the Kaliyuga. Chāndbibi was thus by Divine commandment born as Sandhyāvatī, and she remained a maid all her life. Satya Pīr was born of her womb by Divine will, and was nourished by a tortoise while an infant. As he grew up he gradually began to show his superhuman powers. There are many heroic achievements related of him in this intersting poem, and not the least of which is his encounter with Mansingh. This brings us to a definite historical time; and as we have already noticed another story which says that Satya pīr was the son of Hushen Shah's daughter, the two accounts practically assign the same point of time to Satya pīr's birth. It will not, therefore, be out of mark to say that the origin of the Satya pīr cult is to be looked for in the 16th century. Satya pīr in the poem of Kriṣṇahari Dās, whom we suspect to have been a Muhammadan, though he retains his Hindu name, described his deified prophet as having in his hand a long stick called the āṣā; his hair is knotted, and on his forehead is a large sandal mark; in his left hand he carries a flute; he has sacred threads on his breast and these are golden; he wears the ochre-coloured cloth of a yogi and has a chain for belt. The only Muhammadan element in this description is this chain which a fakir is often-times seen to wear round his waist.

Oazid Ali's story.

An interesting story is told of Satya pīr and of his power to help the honest people that adhere to him in times of distress, by one Oazid Ali. I give a summary of this story below.

Sundara in the charge of Sumati and Kumati.

In Chandan-nagar, in the district of Hooghly there lived a merchant named Jayadhara who had three sons. Their names were Madana, Kāmadeva and Sundara. The merchant at the time of his death called his two sons Madana and Kāmadeva to his presence, and desired them to take particular care of his youngest son Sundara. They promised to do so. On the death of their father, the two brothers started on a sea-voyage leaving Sundara in the charge of their wives Sumati and Kumati. As the three brothers had lost their mother long ago, and Sundara was a young boy and orphan, his brothers made all sorts of arrangement for his education and domestic comforts, before leaving home. The author here gives a description of the sea-voyage of the brothers detailing among other things the particulars about the route to the sea from Chandan-nagar.

The wives of the brothers, however, were no human beings, but witches. Every night they cast their spell on Sundara which made him sleep soundly till the morning, and doing this they left home and ascended a tree which by their spell moved fast in the air and carried them to Kāynur (Assam) which was their native place. Sundara knew nothing of their doings, for when he awoke in the morning, he found his sisters-in-law at home as usual; for they returned home by the same vehicle before the dawn, every day. One night when Sundara slept quietly in his bed, Satya Pīr appeared in the room and made a sign by which the spell of the witches was broken and he awoke. He found that the sisters-in-law were not at home, so he spent the rest of the night in great anxiety and fear. At the dawn of the day the witches left aside their own forms and returned home in those of human beings, Sundara took them to task for leaving the house at night and they were very much frightened lest he should report this to their husbands on their return. They were, however, shrewd enough to conceal their mental confusion and produced some pleas for explaining their absence at night. They then fed him better than on other days, and, when he fell asleep in the night, went to the river-side and worshipped Kālī with incense, flowers, and sandal. They wanted the boon of killing their brother-in-law and the power was granted to them by Kālī. They returned home vaunting between themselves that being witches of Kāynur they could put men to death and restore them to life if they so wished. They then cast their spell on the sleeping youth who vomited blood and died in their presence. Before death, he had asked of Sumati and Kumati a cup of water for quenching his thirst, but they smiled and ridiculed him in his agonies, and looked at him, all the while, with their malignant eyes. When the young Sundara, who was exceedingly handsome, died, they carried his body to a forest and left

They plan his assassination.

it there to be eaten by jackals. Now Satya Pīr, who was at that time in the company of his brother Amin, felt uneasy and perceived through his all-seeing eyes what had happened, he came to the spot and restored the dead youth to life ; for Sundara was one of his most devoted servants. The youth, on getting back his life, said, "No more shall I enter a house in which my sisters-in-law are witches. They will torture me and kill me again ; let me follow you and serve you the rest of my life. You have been my life-giver, and there can be no higher gratification of my soul than being permitted to offer my humble services to you." But Satya Pīr insisted on his return home, saying, "Take my word, if they do you any harm, I shall forthwith come to your rescue." He was thus obliged to come back; the sisters-in-law, who seeing him revived felt a thrill of horror in the heart of their hearts, outwardly showed no sign of their feelings, and received him with kindness. In the night, however, they put their heads together to devise means for killing him. This time they took a sharp knife and cut his throat with it. They then cut his body into seven parts and carried the parts in a bag to a forest, where they buried each of these in a different place. The scrutinising eyes of Satya Pīr, however,

Restored to life by Satya Pīr.

saw the foul deed through all its stages. He secured the parts and restored the murdered youth to life. The disconsolate youth could by no means be persuaded, this time, to return home; so the Pīr took him to a tree and ordered him to ascend it and keep himself concealed in one of the branches thickly overgrown with leaves. Now the witches had this time been perfectly satisfied that even the god Satya Pīr could not have possibly found out the parts of Sundara's body and restored him to life. In this hope they were confirmed by the fact that Sundara did not return home that night. They had in the meantime heard that the princess of Kāynur would elect a bridegroom from amongst her suitors that very night, and there would be consequently a great festivity in the king's palace there; so they resolved to go there and witness the ceremony, relieved as they were from all anxieties about their brother-in-law whom they now took for dead once for all. They came to the self-same tree where Sundara lay hidden, and ascending its top, cast their spell on it; the tree moved in lightning's speed through the air and reached Kāynur in the twinkling of an eye. One of the sisters had remarked on ascending the tree, "sister, why does the tree seem heavy this day?" But the other made light of it and no further notice was taken. After the

Assassination, a second time.

sisters had alighted, Sundara also got down and Satya Pīr led him to the Hall where the princes were assembled, from amongst whom the king's daughter would elect her bridegroom.

Sundara goes to Kāynur by means of the magic tree.

Sundara took his seat among the princes and Satya Pīr, whom the king's daughter also worshipped daily, privately instructed her to offer the garland of flowers reserved for the bridegroom to Sundara. The princess was right glad to do so, as Sundara was the handsomest youth in that assembly. In the night Sundara slept with the princess in the same room, but towards the last part of the night, he felt very uncomfortable at the thought that his sisters-in-law would return home by means of the flying-tree and he would be left alone in the palace of the Kāynur king; so having none of his own people there, he would be taken for a vagabond, and the princess would be ridiculed for her choice. He therefore resolved to return home with the two witches; but before he left his wife, he wrote in her apron all particulars about himself, expressing his wish that, should she feel miserable at parting with him, she might go to Chandan-nagar with her royal father's permission. He thus came back to the tree and unperceived by his sisters-in-law, hid himself in one of the leafy branches. A few moments

Sundara returns home.

after the witches also came there, and ascended the top of the tree which moved under their spell towards the city of Chandan-nagar. They alighted from the tree on reaching the city and Sundara followed them. What was their dismay, rage and vexation when they saw their brother-in-law return home in sound health and excellent spirit.

They now resolved to get rid of him by some means other than assassination. In the night they tied a charm with the hair of the youth, which effected his transformation to a Suka (a bird). This done, they took the bird to a great distance from home and let it fly in a dense jungle. When the hunters came they caught the bird and carried it to the sea-shore for selling it to some merchant. Just at that time Madana and Kāma Deva, two brothers of Sundara, were returning home with their ships laden with riches. One of the brothers said "Look there, a hunter goes with a Suka bird. I remember that my brother Sundara had asked me to get a Suka for him and it is such a beautiful bird! I shall purchase it at any cost for my dear brother." The price was settled at one thousand rupees and the brothers took the bird with them little suspecting that it was their dear brother himself transformed into that shape by the spell cast on him by their wicked wives.

Transformed into a bird.

Meantime the princess of Kāynur awoke in the morning and was greatly alarmed to find that the bridegroom was not in the room. The whole palace was in a state of agitation over the mysterious disappearance of the merchant's son. They now discovered the writings on the apron of the princess, who insisted on her royal father's giving her permission to go to Chandan-nagor in quest of her husband. Several ships were made ready by the order of the king and the princess was on board the show-ship with her maids. The ships were laden with rich dowries and it took them several days to reach Chandan-nagor, and when they did so, the witches tried to turn her out on various pretexts. But she preferred to stay at her husband's house in spite of all dissuasions; for Satya Pīr in the shape of a white fly had instructed her to stay there.

The Princess comes to Chandan-nagor.

The brothers Madana and Kāmadeva arrived at the city a few days after. They were greatly grieved to hear from their wives a story about Sundara (which they had fabricated) to the effect that Sundara's character had grown very bad after their departure; he mixed with bad women and wandered away from home for the last two months; they could not get a clue as to his whereabouts though they had tried

Return of the elder brothers.

their best; a woman had in the meantime come to their home calling herself a princess and wife of Sundara; but of this marriage they knew nothing. The brothers loved Sundara very dearly and their minds were filled with grief at this report. They joined their tears with those of the princess whom they took to be Sundara's wife inspite of the insinuations made against her by Sumati and Kumati in their report. The princess was presented with the bird Suka which the brothers had brought for Sundara. She wept as she caressed the bird affectionately thinking it to be a thing which rightly belonged to her husband. One day as she touched the head of the bird, she discovered something tied with its crest. This was the spell of the witches by which they had changed Sundara into a bird. Instantly, as the spell was removed, her husband assumed his own shape, and stood before her. He told her all about the witchcraft of his sisters-in-law which had changed him into a bird, but whispering something into her ears, asked her to tie the charm again with his forelock and not to noise about the matter. She did as she was bid and Sundara became a bird again. Next day she invited her two brothers-in-law to a dinner. She said that she would cook the meal herself to serve them. They came to dine

Sundara gets back his human shape.

at the usual hour but were surprised to find three seats and three sets of golden plates and cups with food before them. They were only two; who was the third one invited? The princess appeared before them at this stage and said "You two are here, but where is your youngest brother gone? call him to dine with you." The brothers thought that the princess' head had gone wrong owing to her grief, and they wept at what she said, and would not touch the meal. But the youngest lady of the house insisted on their calling their brother aloud and asking him to come and dine with them. Weeping they called out for their brother, only for quieting one whose brain, they thought, had gone out. But she had removed the charm from the bird's head and as soon as Sundara, who was himself again, heard the call of his brothers, he came out and joined them. Their happiness knew no bounds at meeting one whom they had given up for lost. After the dinner Sundara told the story of her sisters-in-law and convinced his brothers that they were witches by many proofs.

The invitation and union.

Upon this they ordered a big hole to be dug in their courtyard and told their wives that as robbers were reported to infest that locality, they meant to put all their riches in a secure place under-ground and they had thus made a deep hole in the

The punishment.

court-yard of their house. The two wives eagerly wanted to see the hole which would contain the wealth of the family. But as they stood near it in an inclining posture to look down into it they were pushed down from behind; and as they fell into the pit, it was immediately filled up with earth and they were thus buried alive. The two brothers next married two very accomplished and beautiful girls of Kāynur, and we need not say that in the marriage settlements the princess had taken an active part. A *sinni* on a very grand scale was offered to Satya Pīr for befriending the family in their distress.

The story of another deified saint.

Another saint who has also been deified by the Hindus and Mahomedans alike, second only to Satya Pīr in popular esteem—whose achievements and deeds have been extolled in many rural legends of Bengal—is Mānik Pīr, a Mahomedan Fakir. Among many works written about this saint we shall confine ourselves to the account given of him by Munshi Pijiruddin.

Gaza and Mānik were the twin-sons of Saha Kamaruddin by Dudh Bibi. The Saha was in prosperous circumstances, and his wife Dudh Bibi was a remarkable beauty. The twin sons were very handsome, and Hīrā, the maid-servant of the house, one day told her mistress Dudh Bibi that she should be thankful to God for giving her such lovely babies. But Dudh Bibi said "the babies are handsome because I am handsome ; don't you see they are exact copies of myself ? where do you find the grace of God in it ? If I and my dear husband live, we shall have many more children like these." Hīrā did not like this reply, but did not dare contradict this blasphemous speech. But God Almighty heard all that she said and was wroth. Gabriel, by divine command, was appointed to punish the wicked Dudh Bibi who had belittled his Divine Majesty. She got a severe fever and Saha Kamaruddin, when advised by Hīra to pray to God for her recovery, said "I shall cure the fever by my own power and by the help of the physicians." Allah heard the boast and was wroth. Gabriel by his command afflicted him also with fever. Kamaruddin went in quest of a physician and Satan led him to a wine-shop. He drank profusely at the Evil One's instigation, came home and gave some wine to his wife also. This caused an aggravation of their disease and they

Pijuruddin's version.

Dudh Bibi's pride and misfortunes.

Defiant attitude and the punishment.

gradually lost their wealth and were reduced to poverty. When verging on starvation they found themselves compelled to sell Mānik, one of their twin sons, only five years old, to a man named Badarjanda, a merchant, for ten rupees.

Manik sold to a merchant.

Now Badarjanda, making over the beautiful child to the care of his wife Surath Bibi, went to a distant country for trade, and came back home after 12 years. By this time Mānik had grown to be a handsome youth, and Badarjanda on returning home found his wife in the company of the handsome-looking young man whom he could not recognise to be the child that he had bought for ten rupees before he had left home. He called in question the propriety of his wife's conduct in receiving an unknown young man into the house with familiarity. And inspite of his wife's reminding him of his having made over the child to her charge when he was only five, and of her having nursed and brought him up ever since that time as her own son, the infuriated merchant put the youth into a wooden box and set fire to it. Mānik prayed to Almighty Allah to save him from the danger, and He took compassion on the innocent youth and sent Gabriel to render the help he needed. The fire burnt not the box

A mean suspicion and Mānik thrown into fire.

though it was fed by oil; and finally when the fire was extinguished the wooden box was found intact. But what was the astonishment of Badarjanda when on opening the box he found Mānik in good health and spirits in the attitude of prayer like a second Prahlāda of the Hindu legends. Surath Bibi, whose grief had known no bounds, for she had loved Mānik as her son, now came with open arms to receive the youth, and Badarjanda himself felt greatly repentant for his act. But Mānik said, "No more, dear parents, for, though I am not your son by birth, I have always looked upon you with the affection which only a child may feel for his parents. No more shall I stay in this world to suffer miseries from which even innocence cannot escape. The Lord has shown His mercy to me, and Gabriel has lighted the torch to guide my path of life; I belong to them and to none else." Saying so he took a staff in his hand, and put on the ochre-coloured cloth of an ascetic and saying "Blessed be the name of Allah" left the house as a mendicant. God took mercy on him and gave him supernatural powers.

Mānik rescued by Gabriel turns a Fakir.

From that time he gave many proofs of his miraculous power. He did so first of all in the house of a Rājā whose queen Ranjanā had treated him rudely. He had gone to the palace for begging alms but the queen had turned him out and when the Fakir had spoken true words without flattery, the angry queen ordered one of her maids to kill him on the spot by a stroke of her sword. The weapon however did not do any harm to the Fakir but killed the maid-servant who wielded it. The Fakir disappeared from the spot after having pronounced a curse on the queen. The curse was that the queen would wander in the forests for twelve years, forsaken by all and suffer great miseries. As a matter of course the queen suffered all that the prophet had said, and was eventually restored to her good fortunes by Mānik Pīr's kindness, whom she had propitiated by repentance and prayers. This part in the story is an exact repetition of a part of an old folk-tale which we find recorded in the story of Mālati Kusuma Mālā compiled by a Muhammadan writer and also in that of Sankha Mālā edited by Dakshinăranjan Mitra Majumdār. The only difference between the above two tales and that of Mānik Pīr, so far as this portion is concerned, is of course that the merchant's wife (in the above two stories she is not a queen but a merchant's wife) is restored to her former good fortunes by other agencies than the intervention of Mānik Pīr.

Ranjanā's punishment and eventual restoration to her good fortunes by the grace of the Pīr.

The chief act of Mānik Pīr, however, by which he revealed himself as an authorised prophet of God, is his treatment of some of the

Goālās of the city of Virāt. Here is the account (considerably abridged in translation from the original), given by Munshi Pijiruddin.

"By the command of Gabrielthe, Pīr came to the house of one Kinu Ghosh in Virat Nagar. Kinu had a brother named Kānu, and they belonged to the milkman caste. A short while before the Pīr went there, the brothers had gone to their cow-shed to bring milk. Their dairy contained a considerable stock of milk, curd and butter, and they made immense profits out of their sale; so that Kinu and Kānu were noted in the city for their great wealth by the favour of the Almighty. They had besides many cows and bullocks. One of the brothers had a son, who was handsome as a cherub. Coming to the door of the house the Pīr cried aloud, "Lāi Lāhā" and called the mother of the two traders from outside. She sat inside the house, and hearing the loud call, said to a maid-servant, "Just go and see who calls me so loudly at the door." The maid-servant approached the Pīr, and asked him as to what he wanted. The Pīr, who was accompanied by his brother Gaja, said in reply, "We are Fakirs and have not tasted any food for these seven days, if you will give us some milk and curd, we shall satisfy our appetite and bless you and go away." The maid-servant reported

The Ghosh-family.

The mother does an wicked act.

this to the old lady, but she instructed her to say that the brothers had gone to bring milk, and there was nothing at that moment in the house to offer them. Upon which Mānik Pīr told the maid servant, "The mistress of the house tells a lie ; there are 20 lbs. of milk and 40 lbs. of curd in the house at this moment." The maid-servant reported it again to her mistress, who became angry and said, "Why should we be tormented in this way early in the morning when we have not yet commenced our domestic duties. If the prophets can say what is in the house and what is not, without seeing with their own eyes, why do such big people wear rags and live by begging ?" Saying so she came out and asked "Why do you not believe my statement that there is nothing in the house to offer you ?" Mānik Pīr said, "There are 20 lbs. of milk and 40 lbs. of curd in the house. Why do you tell a lie ?" The old woman was very angry and said, "Let me see how truthful you are. There stands a cow, milk it as much as you like, and satisfy your hunger." Now the cow the old woman showed to the Fakirs was barren, having never given birth to a calf, but by the help of Gabriel and the will of Almighty God Mānik Pīr touched the nipples of the animal and profuse quantities of milk came out to the wonder of the old lady and her maid-servant. When, however, he wanted a pitcher, the old woman gave him one which leaked in a hundred places, but the Pīr filled that pitcher and several others which had similar holes at the bottom with milk, and not a drop was lost. As Mānik Pīr milked the cow, two of her nipples gave milk and two butter, and seven big pitchers were filled with these. The old woman carried them to her house and did not give a drop of them to Mānik or his brother Gaja. Sanakā, her daughter-in-law and wife of Kinu Ghosh, said, "How is it that not only did you not give any food to the Fakirs from the house, but you have taken away all the milk that they have got by their miraculous power?" The angry mother-in-law exclaimed, "You call it miracle, that is nonsense. They secretly got the milk from their house and they have produced it here. How can it be believed that a barren cow will yield so much milk and butter? The two Fakirs are great impostors." The young wife said, "If they got it from their own home, it is their property; why then have you usurped it?" The old woman said nothing, but left the place evidently annoyed with her daughter-in-law. Now Sanakā, the good wife, took with her a small quantity of milk and offered it to the Pīr and his brother. They drank milk and Mānik touched the head of the young wife and blessed her. Just at that moment the old lady came up, and very much resented the conduct of her daughter-in-law. Not satisfied with merely scolding her, she ran out of the house and met her son Kānu Ghosh, and said, "Just come, and see your wife's conduct. Two young Fakirs have come, and she is very jolly in their company." Kānu Ghosh came in all haste and struck the Pīr on the head with his stick. The Pīr threw his turban on the earth and disappeared with his brother. The turban became a cobra and it stung Kānu Ghosh who fell instantly senseless on the ground. Sanakā, the good wife, was struck with great grief, her husband being taken for dead; but the Pīr took pity on her and came there in the guise of a Brahmin who professed to be a healer of snake-bite. The old woman promised him half of her property if he could restore her son Kānu Ghosh to life. But when the Brahmin actually did so, she fainted in fear lest the physician should lay claim on one half of her property. The Brahmin, who was no other than Mānik Pīr himself, went away greatly enraged at her conduct, and, as a result, the cows and bullocks of their family-dairy died in the course of a week, and all their property was destroyed. Kānu Ghosh was in great distress; his wife Sanakā told him that all this was due to his mother's misbehaviour towards the Fakir. Kānu asked her to seek him out and propitiate

Kānu stung by a cobra.

Restored to life.

They lose and regain their fortunes.

by all means. For six days Sanakā sought him, observing fast and vigil, and on the seventh day the Pīr, who had known all about her wanderings in search of him and waited only to try her patience and devotion, appeared before her. She fell prostrate before him, and prayed him to save the family from utter ruin. The Pīr came to the house and, by his blessings, the cows and bullocks that had died long ago revived and "began to cut grass with their teeth." The Ghoshes were restored to their former prosperous condition. Kānu Ghosh was highly gratified and presented the Pīr with a cow and ten *bighas* of rent-free land. But the Pīr said, "God Almighty has made me a Fakir. What shall I do with your presents? I do, however, accept them. But return them to you." He ordered all Goālās thenceforth to offer the first milk of a cow, which would bear a calf, to the earth. His glory had now spread far and wide, and he departed from the house of the milkmen after having blessed them.

Who this Mānik Pīr was is a difficult pro blem to solve, shrouded as the account of him is in all manner of rural fiction. His own name and that of his brother are Hindu; his mother's name Dudh Bibi is also Hindu; the maid-servant of the house was Hīrā, and that is also a Hindu name. His father alone bears a Mahomedan name. From this we can only guess that he may have been of Hindu extraction ; or more probably he may have been born in a family converted from the Hindu to Islamite faith.

Historical side totally obscured by legends.

The anecdote which describes his restoring the dead cows and bullocks to life may be a legend based upon some healing power that he possessed in regard to the diseases of the sacred animals of the Hindus. This probably explains the reason of the extraordinary respect paid to him by the rural agricultural Hindus who are worshippers of cows. But all this is a mere guess. In the legendary account that we have, he does not appear as a mortal but as one whose acts are all super-human. Inspite of all these legends, however, he is not an imaginary character and must have lived as a saint or prophet in Bengal sometime after the Muhammadan conquest. We have already noticed that a portion of an old folk-tale is now found dovetailed to the account of his life in the popular legend.

Class II. Pioneers of Islamite faith.

We now come to a consideration of the second class of the folk-legends according to our classification. These relate to the pioneers of Islamite faith, who made it the mission of their lives to carry the Korān in one hand and the sword in the other as alternatives; those that declined to accept the former were put to the sharp edge of the latter. There are many such tales in the vernacular literature of Bengal, written by Muhammadans, in a style bearing in a very considerable degree an admixture of Arabic and Persian words. We give below the summary of a typical story —the legend of Hanif's victory over the Kafirs and his marriage with the accomplished daughter of Rājā Baruṇa.

The story of the Princess Mallikā.

In the city of Medina, there once lived Ali, the famous wrestler. He married a far-famed beauty named Hanifā. They got a son whom they called Hanif. This son grew to be a great wrestler and hero in his youth, so much so that no one ventured to challenge him to a fight. He waged war against the 'Kafirs' and made many of them converts to Islam.

Hanif goes on an expedition against Rājā Baruṇa.

Now one day he heard of a great Hindu king named Baruṇa. It was reported that the Rājā was invincible in war, and that he had a daughter whose beauty was unmatched in the three worlds. This report inflamed the imagination of Hanif—the wrestler. He asked permission of Ali, his father to fight the Rājā. Ali referred him to Fathema Bibi, and she again to his mother Hanifā. Fathema said that Hanifā knew everything about the Rājā, so if she granted him the permission, there could be no hindrance in the way. Hanif accordingly called on his mother and sought her permission to fight the invincible Rājā and win the hand of his handsome daughter, the princess Mallikā, after having defeated him in the open field. The mother opposed, saying that the Rājā was a very great hero and that there was every chance of Hanif being killed in the field should he try to match his strength against the Rājā. But Hanif, who was full of fire to punish the infidels, was not to be dissuaded by fear. So the mother was obliged to give him the permission.

Hanif gathered a great force. He took with him a large number of war-horses and camels outside the city of Medina and the people of that city blessed him before he departed, saying "May you succeed in the cause of the propagation of of Islam."

Not only handsome but possessed of great physical strength.

Now the Rājā's daughter Mallikā was not only the handsomest woman that lived in the world at the time, but was possessed of a herculine strength of body. She used to go a-hunting in the remotest parts of her royal father's dominions, and kill tigers with her own hands without using weapons. With her short sword that hung by her side, she would sometimes strike wild elephants across the root of their trunks which she would cut off with one blow. The animals turned from her, fell down and expired.

When she came of a fit age, her father thought of sending (match-makers) *ghatakas* all over the neighbouring countries in quest of a suitable bridegroom, whose personal qualifications and social status would be worthy of the gifted princess. But she told her father, "Not only are these qualifications required, but the prince who will seek my hand must bind himself by a promise that he will conquer me in fight. If he can do so, right glad shall I be to offer my hands to him; if not, him shall I kill with my own hands; let this be the condition, for it will preserve me from an undesirable rush of suitors." And the messengers were sent out accordingly to proclaim these conditions to the intending bridegrooms. Many a prince came and fought with Mallikā and at the end was beheaded by her hands; and when a prince struck with terror fled from her presence, she would pursue him till she caught him by the hair of his head, and would indignantly cry out "You coward of a prince, you coveted my hand, here take the reward" and saying so she struck him down with her sword and killed him on the

How the suitors were treated.

spot. So the whole of the neighbouring kingdoms were filled with a feeling of great terror, and no prince dared to approach Baruṇa as suitor for his daughter's hand.

Umhar in the Court of Rājā Baruṇa.

Now Hanif's messenger came to the capital of Rājā Baruṇa; he was called Umhar, the wrestler; he wore skin trousers, carried a shield of paper on his back and held a wooden sword in his hand; he had besides a bow with a quiver that had no arrows in it, and he limped as he walked. When he came to the great audience-hall of Raja Baruṇa, he did not bow to the king, nor observe any form of courtesy current in the court. The Rājā was angry and the courtiers hissed, saying that the unmannerly fellow should be punished for his folly. The messenger said "I am a servant of God—the one God who reigns supreme. I will not bend my head before a Kafir." Then the whole court cried out "Lo, a vile Turk has come, purify the city by sprinkling holy water over it and wash the temples with cow-dung and sandal-paste. The city is defiled by his presence." "Kill him," "Kill him" ran the cry everywhere; but nobody could see him, being made invisible by the power of the Lord in whom he believed. He remained there unseen by others. After a short while, however, he appeared to the view of the court, and, approaching the king, gave him a blow. And when the guards again tried to catch hold of him, he disappeared mysteriously as he had done before.

The king was perplexed and when Umhar, the messenger of Hanif, became visible again, he did not try to seize or molest him but asked what he wanted; upon this he delivered a letter from Hanif addressed to Raja Baruṇa. The letter ran thus—"You king Baruṇa, abandon your belief in false gods and goddesses and become a convert to Islam. And give your daughter Mallikā in marriage with me. If you do not do so I will come to your kingdom like a thunderbolt, destroying your temples and seizing your property, and I will take away Mallikā by force from the royal harem. So be advised, and, with the whole of the citizens accept Islam and secure your place in Behest and be on terms of amity with me."

Hanif's letter to Raja Baruṇa.

The letter was read aloud and hisses of indignation and cries of "Kill the upstart, the vile Turk" was heard all around. The Rājā whose face showed the deep purple of anger, exclaimed, "Messenger, tell your chieftain, the vile Turk, that if he comes with his force here, he will find his burial here, and none of his followers will be allowed to go back to his native country. With my whole city I will observe fast for three days for expiating the sin of seeing you, a *javana*, in this city." The messenger departed, and in the meantime the king said to his courtiers, "The Turks will be in this city in a short time ; they will desecrate the temples and throw cow-bones and beef in the sacred places. We cannot allow it. Let us go forth with our army to the open ground in the outskirts of our city. There shall we meet the foe." Saying so he ordered a general march of his army to a place 20 miles off from the capital. He had 10,000 trained elephants, and an immense number of foot-soldiers, besides his invincible cavalry, dreaded by the kings of other countries. An extensive field was fixed as the battle-ground where flags were raised in several spots with the name of the King Baruna inscribed on them. Hanif met him in that field. In the morning of the first day with the sound of the war-drums his soldiers marched to meet those of the Rājā. Hanif's general Umhar did great havoc in the enemy's ranks. In the evening when the drums sounded the signal to close the battle Rājā Baruṇa called his generals and ordered them to assemble together at one point the next day, with elephants carrying maces by their trunks and with chargers going ahead of them ; and thus united, to make a rush at the enemy and crush them by sheer dint of

Preparations for a march to meet the foe outside the city.

The three days' war and the flight.

their number. "Desultory fight at several points" his Majesty said "will do us no good. All, all must attack simultaneously." The next day this was done but the general for that day on the side of Hanif was Ali Akbar, whose nerves seemed to be made of steel. He made even greater havoc in the Rājā's army, than Umhar had done the day before. On the third day the Rājā himself led the army and fought with Hanif a hand to hand fight, but could not maintain his position, so that in the evening he had to make a precipitous retreat with his army and come back to his capital, losing the finest of his cavalry, a large number of elephants and foot-soldiers.

Princess Mallikā goes to fight.

But when Mallikā, the princess heard of this disaster, she trembled in anger, thinking of the insult and loss done to her country by the Turks. She armed herself then and there, and rode a horse, the speed of which could be compared to that of the wind alone.

She met Hanif in the field and cried out, "You vile Turk, do youknow that with my own hands I have beheaded many a prince, so that young men of the neighbouring aristocracy shudder at my name for fear? You have come with a vile proposal and know not my lineage and qualifications. Here do I spit at your proposal. But I will not leave this field, until I have killed you with my own hands as I have done others." Hanif smiled and said, "Better would be your place in the harem, from which I could pick you up as one plucks a flower from the garden. Your father would have been well-advised to deliver you to me; for I am really sorry for the sanguinary battle that raged here for the last three days and the loss of lives caused by it. Be advised, read the *kalma*, give up ghost-worship; you will be happy in this world, and, following Islam, you will secure permanent happiness in Behest." The princess did not wait to listen to a further eloquent discourse from the enemy, but hit him on the head with a dart which tore his turban and gave a rude shock to his head that reeled for a moment. Hanif felt in the force of the dart that his antagonist, though looking like a tender flower, really possessed a masculine strength and might prove to be more than a match for him. For the whole day they fought; they fought unceasingly with guns, arrows, spears and maces, but the hero of Medina could not conquer his lotus-eyed opponent. And when the war drum in the evening announced the close of all action for the day, Hanif returned to his camp with eyebrows knit in wild astonishment over what he had experienced during the day and for which he was not prepared. He was determined to gain the woman for his bride; and love evermore gave him strength to strike where he would fain pay the tribute of worship. The next day the fight was resumed. The princess rose from her bed first, came to the field first and was the first to challenge her antagonist. That day Hanif killed the horse of Mallikā, but she rode another horse and showed no sign of losing heart. For twenty days they fought, still Hanif could not conquer her. She looked soft like a *shirisha* flower, but at the time of battle seemed like a marble statue on whom the unceasing gust of rain-like arrows and gun-shots left no trace. On the twenty-first day Hanif said, "Look here, princess, you have fought enough and a liar shall I be, if I do not say that I have admired your strength no less than your beauty, both of which are more than what I have seen in others. To-day I offer you a challenge, which should you accept, the close of this fight might be expedited. Here do I lie on the ground with my back above and hands clasped below. If you have strength enough, fair princess, raise me up from the ground and throw me away as one would do a ball. If you cannot. place yourself in the same position and I will lift you up and throw you away." Mallikā, the undaunted woman, accepted the

The duel.

challenge. Hanif placed himself on the ground with his back above and hands clasped below his breast. And she tried all her strength to lift him up. She could not do it first time; her face reddened with toil; she tried a second time, and on her brows stood big drops of sweat, but she failed to move that body lying like a hard block of stone. And she tried thrice, she applied all her might; not an inch she could move him and she stood exhausted and ashamed failing in her attempt. Then she placed herself in the self-same position, with her back above and breasts below, and between them and the earth she clasped her both hands in firm fists. Hanif seized her body, covered with armour, and applying all his strength threw it up with such a force that for a moment she looked like a ball high in the air, and then fell. The fall would have reduced her to atoms, had not Hanif, whose love for her had not ceased but grown from day to day, caught her half-way and placed her on his knees. With a look of tender love he watched her, for she had fainted, and sprinkled scented water on her eyes. As she recovered her senses, she found herself in the embrace of a Turk, and had no other alternative left than to consent to be his bride.

In the embrace of a Turk.

Now the King Baruṇa had heard of this disaster and stood at the main gate of his capital, determined to oppose the aggressive Islamite force and to die rather than yield. Ali Akbar, the general of Hanif, after a severe fight caught hold of him and brought him before his master, bound in chains. Hanif said "I have no mind to molest you further. Much blood has been shed and I will not willingly do a cruel act to the parent of my consort. I charge you to accept Islam, to demolish the temples of evil-spirits that you have erected in your city, calling them gods. I charge you further to sanction my marriage with your daughter and tell your citizens to rēad the *kalma*, erect mosques and do as our Mollas bid. If you will do all this, I shall restore you to your kingdom and revere you as father ; or else you know by bitter experience what will befall your kingdom." And the king Baruṇa did all this, not daunted by fear, nor for saving his life, nor for any love for Islam, but for the shame that his beloved daughter had accepted a Turk for husband. The shame of this would be on him, even if he gained victory, and make him an outcast and given up by his kith and kin.

The Rājā turns a convert to Islam.

This tale so often told in the vernacular verse, has been retold by Munshi Aminuddin—a native of Kharda, though he tells us that his version is the first. Hanif's adventurous life, his heroism in the field and carrying off of handsome girls from Hindu homes, have formed the themes of many vernacular poems. We have the story of his love with Jaygun in animated Bengali verse, another with Samrita-bhāna and a third with Sonadhān. These poems show much fire of enthusiasm for the Islamite propaganda which characterised the 11th and 12th century-Moslem zealots. Love was subservient to the zeal for propagation of faith and iconoclasm. These legends and popular tales, our Muhammadan brethren derived from other sources than the indigenous, and the contrast between these and the Hindu and Buddhistic stories, which are still found current amongst Muhamadans, is obvious; the latter are characterised by quiet virtues and martyrdom at the altar of domestic duties.

Other stories illustrating the chivalry of Hanif.

Along with these tales of heroism and love-making of the pioneers of Islamite conquests, may be classed historical ballads and songs which have formed a part of the popular literature of this country. These have not reached the level of decent literature owing

Historical ballads.

to the crude language in which they are couched being composed mostly by the illiterate rural people. But some of these songs contain authentic accounts of some local historical events, or sketches of some noted village-chiefs. Such for instance is the Chaudhuri's Lārāyi, a book written in the 18th century, describing a skirmish between two zemindars of the Noakhali district.

The Choudhuri's Lārāyi.

But "Samsher Gāzir Gāna," a ballad of Samsher Gāzi, is the most remarkable of this class of songs. There is not much of exaggeration in the tale, and the author whose name I do not find in the book must have taken a good deal of notes and collected considerable historical materials before he began to write the book. It was written not long after 1752 A.D. when the Gāzi was murdered and has lately been published by my friend Maulvi Lutful Khabir from Noakhali. The book discloses a condition of the country that existed before the battle of Plassy, showing how, with the decadence of the central Moghul power at Delhi, the local chiefs tried to assert their independence in various parts of the country. But they could not often cope with the gangs of robbers and leaders of bandits who infested the land, taking advantage of the relaxation in administration—the natural sequel of the fall of a great monarchy.

The song of Samsher Gazi.

The Gāzi was the son of a poor man, who verging on the point of starvation with his family, had left his native home in the village of Kachuā, in the Tipperah district and came to a place called the Dakṣin sika—further south. Here Piru, the Gāzi's father, stole a few long gourds when he saw no way to provide food for his son and nephew Sadi. But he was caught in the act, and taken before the zemindar Nasiruddin. Here he made a confession and told the story of the extreme poverty from which his family suffered. The boys were without any food whatever for two or three days and on point of death, and seeing no way out from this peril, he had taken away seven long gourds without the permission of their owner. The pathetic story moved Nasir, who paid the owner the price of the gourds, and made provision for Piru's family.

The Gazi's father Piru driven by poverty to Nasiruddin's jurisdiction.

Nasir Mahammad, the Zemindar had *ten anna* shares in the extensive zemindary of Pargannah Dakṣin sika; the remaining six annas belonged to Ratan Chaudhury, a native of Khandal in Tipperah. Nasir's father Sada Gāzi, who was an ordinary peasant, had found

How Nasir's father got the zemindary.

valuable stones in a copper vessel under the earth when ploughing land. He took the vessel to Jagat Mānikya, King of Tipperah, and made him a present of this valuable property. Whereupon the Rājā was very much pleased with him and gave him the zemindary of Dakṣin sika. Nasir Mahammad, after his father's death, inherited this property.

The Gāzi and Sādi gradually show extraordinary physical power.

Here under the patronage of Nasir, Piru throve well. His son Samser Gāzi and nephew Sādi read in the same school with the sons of the zemindar, who treated them with affection and kindness. In this school the teachers were struck not only by the proof of the singular intellectual power and manly valour showed by the Gāzi but by the extraordinary physical strength which his cousin Sādi displayed; this appeared more than human to everyone; for, it is said, Sādi strangled a big tiger to death without using any weapon. About this time the zemindar trusted the Gāzi with the collection of rents of his landed property at Kud Ghat. Here the Gāzi found a considerable number of robber-gangs looting the property of the ryots and doing many other acts of violence upon them. He collected a force and held these gangs in check for some time; and at last his cousin—Sādi defeated them in several skirmishes and brought them fully under his control. The robbers were allowed their lives and freedom on two conditions, viz.: (1) that they would not further do any act of oppression on the ryots of Nasir Mahammad, (2) that they should pay half the amount of the wealth they might loot elsewhere, to the Gāzi and acknowledge him as their leader. They agreed to do so and the Gāzi came in possession of extensive riches by this means. He and his cousin Sādi found their position quite impregnable in that locality. And being inspired by one Goda Hossain Khondakar, whom they regarded as their religious guide and preceptor, they now aspired at far greater achievements than what the sons of poor men generally dream of. The Khondakar had prophesied that the Gāzi would one day become the King of Tipperah.

They hold the robber-gangs in check and become their head.

Nasir Mahammad, the zemindar, who had treated them with such kindness and under whom they still served, had a beautiful daughter and Sādi suggested that the Gāzi should stand a suitor for her hand. But the Gāzi said, it was impossible. Nasir's family-status was much higher, and their own status in society was low. Secondly they were picked up as street-beggars by Nasir and given education and position merely out of charitable considerations. A proposal like the one suggested would be highly offensive

The disastrous proposal of marriage.

to Nasir and prove to the world that the Gāzi and his cousin were ungrateful. But Sādi persisted, and the Gāzi, half in fear and half in anxiety to please Sādi, sent a messenger to his master proposing the marriage. Nasir took it as a regular insult and felt that the kindness he had shown to the Gāzi and his family was thrown away to ungrateful men, who might afterwards prove his deliberate enemies; a proposal like that could not, he thought, have come from one who had not harboured some further base ambition in his heart. So he instantly sent men to behead Gāzi and his cousin, so that he might "see their heads rolling in a pool of blood with his own eyes." The Gāzi had a scent of the order beforehand, and with his cousin fled from Nasir's jurisdiction and went to live in the estates of Noor Mahammad, the Talukdar of Pargannah Kachua. The latter gave him permission to build a house in his city on receipt of Rs. 500 as *nazar* from the Gāzi. Nasir Mahammad, however, pursued the Gāzi with a dogged persistence, and Sādi in his turn was determined to kill Nasir should an opportunity offer itself. The Gāzi had many hot discussions with his cousin on this point as he was not willing to be treacherous to his old master. Sādi said that not only would it be foolish to excuse one who was now their sworn enemy but

The Gazi settles at Pargannah Kachua.

it would be positively unsafe to allow him to live, should they themselves care for their own lives. In the course of a dogged pursuit on the part of each side to find an opportunity to kill the other, Sādi's spies brought the report one day, that Nasir was in an unguarded condition at a place named Banspara. Sādi sent messengers to him with many presents, again proposing the marriage of the Gāzi with Nasir's daughter. The latter was beside himself in rage when he read the letter of Sādi, which was deliberately written to provoke him. He ordered his men to throw away the presents in his presence and kick out the bearers. When this was being done, Sādi, who had also accompanied the messengers with an army and lay at some distance, came forward and attacked him all unguarded, and then and there despatched him with his sword. A pitched battle was fought between the Gāzi's army led by Sādi and those of Nasir's sons. But the latter were defeated and obliged to beat a retreat, and the Gāzi came in possession of Nasir's landed property. He made extensive charities and granted remission of rents and by these means secured the good will of the *ryats* there and became very popular. Meantime Nasir's sons had applied to the King of Tipperah for help, reporting the murder of their father and other violent acts of the Gāzi. The king was very angry and sent 3,000 soldiers with his Uzir Jaydeva at the head in order to punish the rebel. Jaydeva was assisted by his two generals—Shobhā Datta and Indra Mandal.

The appeal to the Rājā of Tipperah who sends army against the Gāzi.

The Gāzi lived at a fortified place in Chagalmuri which was surrounded by a deep ditch. The Uzir laid siege to this fort. But in the night when the Uzir lay asleep in his camp, the Gāzi with the help of some local people entered the camp like a thief and carried the Uzir off to his fort. This was done so quickly that the Rājā's army could scarcely offer any resistance. Now by the Gāzi's order, the Uzir was placed at the top of the gate of the fort, so that when the king's army attacked it, they could not shoot arrows or guns lest they hit the Uzir. The fort was besides, as already stated, surrounded by a ditch which the army could not easily cross, owing to the volley of shot the Gazi had opened. The Uzir called out to his soldiers from the top of the gate and ordered them to desist from fight. "If you shoot, there is the risk of myself being hit; if you succeed, the Gāzi will cut my head off. In either case my death seems certain; so go back and report this to the king and do as he will bid." There was therefore no alternative for his army than to retire. As soon as the king's army had gone away the Uzir's chains were removed and the

The Uzir made a captive.

Gāzi fell at his feet and gave him a *nazar* of Rs. 500. A Brahmin cook was engaged to prepare a rich meal for the minister to whom the Gāzi made many apologies for fighting against the Rājā. He attended the Uzir as a servant does his master, ministering to his comforts in every respect. He implored the Uzir to persuade the king to grant him a *sanad* for Nasir's landed estates and give him besides the lease of Chakla Roshanabad for an annual rent of Rs. 10,000. The Gāzi said "If you can make the king agree to this, here is a thousand rupees for you as my humble present to you to spend on perfumes. But if your king does not agree, I shall cut you to pieces and present the relics of your body to his Majesty." The Uzir wrote a letter to the king stating that the Gāzi behaved very well, and that he was the fit person for taking the administration of the zemindary in hand, his efficiency being undoubted. If he assumed a hostile attitude, he might prove dangerous to the State. With this remark the Uzir recommended his Majesty to grant the Gāzi his prayer. He also reminded the king of his own peculiar condition, for the Gāzi would surely kill him in the case of denial. The Rājā held an advisory council and finally decided to grant the prayer of the Gāzi. A *sanad* was issued accordingly granting

The Rājā of Tipperah grants him lease of landed estates of Nasir and of Chakla Roshanabad.

the Gāzi the lease of Chakla Roshanabad on an annual rent of Rs. 10,000. The *sanad* came to the Uzir and as soon as it was presented to the Gāzi he offered his promised reward of Rs. 1,000 to him. To the prime minister he sent a *nazar* of Rs. 300. He, besides, sent to the Dewans and Mukhshuddis of the court a sum of Rs. 400. Those messengers who had carried the *sanad* from the chief city got Rs. 10 each. He also submitted to the king a *nazar* of Rs. 1,000. The Uzir now returned to the capital and the officers of the king who had been with the Uzir thus reported, "Your Majesty has now appointed the fit man in the fit place. The Gāzi is a very powerful man with handsome features; his mind is liberal and his words are sweet; it is a blessedness to hear him talk; he always wears rich apparel and remains surrounded by his friends who all look resplendent. He is kind to those who seek his help, but rude to the rude. We were a fortnight with the Gāzi. He treated the Uzir with the respect that is due only to gods. Every day a goat was sacrificed for the Uzir's dinner and the Gāzi approached him like the humblest of his servants." The Uzir himself spoke to the king that all that the officers hadsaid was true. "The Gāzi has killed Nasir but hunters also kill birds for no fault. If that melancholy event had not taken place there would have been no chance for the only fit man of that district to come in and occupy the fit place." The Rājā's anger for the assassination of Nasir was thus removed, and he was well pleased with the Gāzi for his good treatment of the royal officers. The Gāzi next got the lease of Pergana Meherkul from the king for ten years on an annual rent of Rs. 8,000. He had in addition to pay a *nazar* of Rs. 1,000 to the king for this lease.

But the Gāzi gradually grew bolder and resolved to fight with the Rājā of Tipperah and assert his independence. With this end in view, he collected a large army, and when he thought he was sufficiently strong, stopped paying revenue to the king and declared his independence in a most defying manner. A fight ensued in which guns and cannons were freely used by both sides. It is written in the book that the Gāzi had worshipped Kali, the presiding deity of the Udaipur hills, before he declared war against the king. He had engaged a Brahmin for this purpose, and it is said that the goddess appeared to him in a dream and promised him success in his campaign. For seven days the fight continued incessantly, and on the eighth, the Rājā's army began to lose ground and towards the end of the day his Majesty left the field and made a precipitous retreat towards Manipur. The Rājā of Manipur gave him shelter in this distress. His nephew Lakṣmaṇa Mānikya

The Gāzi declares war against the Rājā of Tipperah.

was placed by the Gāzi on a mock-throne built with bamboos. The Gāzi thus became master of the field. His reign was characterised by justice, liberality and foresight, and the Emperor of Delhi gave him a *sanad* confirming him in his high position. In every department of administration his great personality made its mark. He fixed the scales of measurement and weight, and the prices of goods. We find that a grocer was obliged to take up the standard weight of a maund to be 82 shikkas; the price of oil was fixed at 3 annas per seer and that of *ghee* (clarified butter) at four annas. He placed Abdul Rajjak, one of his generals, in charge of the collection of rents on the Hill-side; the administration of Udaipur and Agartala was also entrusted to this general. The Gāzi kept to himself the monopoly of cotton in his territories, and that of salt that came by the Ganges and the Feni. He established rest-houses where guests were entertained from the royal-store, and a boarding school where he made provision for a hundred students. The principal of this institution was a blind scholar of Shondwip who taught the Koran; He was assisted by a Moulvi, brought from Hindustan, who taught Arabic and another professor from Jugdia who taught

He receives a *sanad* from the Emperor.

His administrative reforms.

Bengali. The classes remained open from 6 A.M. to 10 A.M. and from 12 A.M. to 4 P.M.

When the Gazi was at the zenith of his power, his cousin Sādi began to show a feeling of jealousy towards him. The cousin was older than the Gāzi by some years and had rendered him great help in his rising to that eminence.

Assassination of Sāḍi.

He now, however, showed chagrin and malice in every action, so that his conduct gradually became intolerable. He publicly vaunted that the Gāzi had secured his high position merely by his assistance and declared that it was wrong on the part of the Gāzi to usurp all power to himself. Not satisfied with this, he openly demanded of the Gāzi to make over the administration to him. "A nice arrangement it is that I should win your battles and you should enjoy the fruit: It is I that killed Nasir Mahammad and gained his property for you; the Rājā of Tipperah was beaten in the field by me. You have enjoyed this high position long enough, and now is the time for you to retire." Sādi after this was engaged in conspiring against the Gāzi, and the latter found it unsafe to tolerate his cousin any more. He was constantly in a state of alarm that Sādi would assassinate him. So he appointed some soldiers privately who murdered Sādi.

The Gāzi's name, as an efficient ruler, now spread far and wide; and the Nawab of Dacca, whose ancestry was high, did not feel it beneath his rank to marry the daughter of the Gāzi to his son. The Gāzi's charities were very extensive. We have many interesting anecdotes, related of his great physical power—as to how he killed tigers and wild boars without using weapons. An anecdote is mentioned of how

The barber-brothers.

two barbers Chandra and Utsava received valuable presents from him for shaving him when he was asleep. They did it so cleverly that when they cut his nails and shaved him the Gāzi's sleep was not broken.

Now the Gāzi had once gone to travel in the Chittagong-side, and there ordered fish to be caught from some big tanks. This country belonged to Alivardi Khan, Nawab of Murshidabad, whose deputies Agā Bakhar and Shekh Onich ruled the districts from a place called Nizamgunge. The Gāzi did not ask permission from them, nor give them any share of the

In Chittagong.

fish that were caught. They took umbrage and reported to the Nawab that the Gāzi had grown very powerful, and the reason of his visit to Chittagong was probably a sinister motive—to seize and occupy some of the Nawab's dominions in the eastern side. The Nawab treated this with contempt and said that the Gāzi was a reputed administrator of great abilities; he had caught fish from some of the tanks of Chittagong; that was a trifle and he blamed his generals for bringing such a petty matter to his notice. The disappointed generals now outwardly professed a great friendship towards the Gāzi and invited him to a dinner at their house. The unsuspecting Gāzi went in due time, and when the dinner was over, found himself waylaid by some assassins appointed by the generals. With his wonderful dash and physical strength he kicked two of the horse men out of his way, mounted on one of their horses and speedily passed out of sight before the others could realise their situation. He was, however, surrounded by many more soldiers of Aga Bakhar and had to hide himself in a potter's house, whence he returned home safely after an adventurous course, after many hair-breadth escapes from the pursuing enemy.

Jealousies and conspiracies amongst some of the officers of the Nawab of Murshidabad against the Gāzi.

Constantly hearing reports of the Gāzi's brave deeds, the Nawab of Murshidabad now felt that it would not be safe to encourage the growth of his power any more. So he sent a messenger asking the Gāzi to visit his capital. The Gāzi, however, was advised not to hazard such a visit. The Nawab, it is said, promised a high reward to one who would succeed in inducing the Gāzi to come to Murshidabad on a friendly visit. A Hindu *sannyasi* succeeded in doing so; for, this man had so absolutely ingratiated himself into the Gāzi's confidence that he heeded not the remonstrances of his friends and relations, but paid a visit to Murshidabad in the company of the ascetic. The Nawab received him with seeming courtesey and friendship, but one of his men, named Shamsher, killed the Gāzi when he least suspected foul-play. Thus ended the great career of Shamsher Gāzi whose name and achievements are on record in the Rajamālā—an authorised history of the Tipperah Raj—and which are very minutely described in this old rural song, published in a volume Demy 8vo. of 115 pages, by Moulvi Lutful Khabir, Sherestadar of the judge's court, Noakhali. Even up to this time the woodmen who enter the deep forest of the Udaipur hills and strike their axe on big Shal trees there, sometimes find a large number of golden coins which the Gāzi had placed inside their trunks in the course of his plundering expeditions. The treasures were preserved in this way by the help of the carpenters, whom the Gāzi, it is said, put to death immediately after they had cleverly covered the openings in the trunks with wood and bark in his presence. This he did for fear of disclosure and of the carpenters' appropriating the wealth to themselves.

The Gāzi's visit to Murshidabad and assassination.

There are many ballads and songs composed by the rural people of Bengal, Hindus and Muhammadans, which may still be found out, illuminating some of the obscure corners of the the history of Bengal. We know that the Bhātas of Sylhet used to record the leading historical and social events that transpired in this country from time to time in ballads which they had made it their profession to sing from door to door. A very stirring account of how a big zemindar was poisoned by his chief officer when the former had called upon him to submit an account of the money that he had defalcated, formed the subject of one of the Bhāta songs that we heard in our childhood. The zemindar was Babu Rājkumār Roy and his chief officer was Kishory Mahālānabis. They belonged to the village Kirtipāsā in the district of Backergunge. The song gives a vivid account of the zemindar's death in the arms of his faithful servant Baburam Bhandari, and relates to the providential retaliation that came upon the chief officer, who, trying to make his escape, fell a victim to a royal tiger of the Sundarbans. This song describes events that took place more than a hundred years hence. There are several Bhāta songs that relate to the floods which inundated particular localities of Bengal at different periods. There are besides

Rājkumār Roy and Kishory Mahālānavis.

those that describe anecdotes of some princes and other noble men of the pre-Muhammadan period. One of such that we heard long ago related the tragic death of a young and beautiful princess, who in order to escape from a tyrant, fell into a tank and drowned herself.

The scope of rural ballads.

These songs, which the Bhātas used to compose and sing in the countryside, have now grown out of fashion, and the descendants of these ministrels have long ceased to follow the profession of their ancestors for lack of encouragement. They kept afresh the memory of stirring events and historical episodes and of village politics that led to the subversion of the power of a particular line of aristocracy and the growth of power of new families in their stead. The simple village-folk did not care to know what transpired beyond the Himalayan ranges or Khaibar Pass, but they knew what were the historical events that occurred in the province of Bengal in those days when newspapers and journals did not bring a report of daily occurrences to their doors every day.

Class I—The Folk-tales.

We now come to treat the rural literature included in class I of our classification. This is by far the most important section and deserves a prominent and elaborate notice.

After the fall of Buddhism, the Hindus felt that the whole of their social organism should be remodelled according to their own ideas. With this object in view they took up the education of the masses in their own hands. Not only did they obliterate all history of Buddhism from the Purāṇas but the very legends and traditions of the country were changed, so that no trace of Buddhism might be found in her annals. In the temples the images of Buddha were still worshipped but the priests called him by the name of a Hindu God, such as Çiva or Viṣnu. In one place I found an image of the Buddha worshipped under the name of the feminine deity—Chandi. In the temple of Tilavandeçwara at Benares a very glorious image of the Buddha is called Jatāçankara or Çiva "with knotted hair." This 'Jatā' or 'knotted hair' is nothing but the historic fig tree under which the Buddha attained his Nirvāṇa. Though the Buddha is recognised by the Vaiṣnavas as the ninth incarnation of Viṣnu, the Hindus did not tolerate his worship or any thing connected with Buddhism in this country, during the early days of Renaissance. The folk-tales were of course still told in the Hindu homes conveying the lofty ideal of the Buddhistic self-control and sacrifice, but the *kathakas* introduced the stories of Dhruba, Prahllād, Harischandra, Ekalavya and

What the Hindu priests gave to the country-people in the place of folk-tales.

a hundred others from the Purāṇas, which emphasised devotion as a more potent factor in the salvation of a man than a development of his moral qualities. The Pouranic stories indicated the beauty of faith and its power more than good action and self-control on which Buddhism had laid a far greater stress. So, though the *rūpakathās* or folk-tales still found favour in the 15th and 16th centuries, they ceased to exercise the same influence in moulding the characters of men and women that they had done in a previous age. Poor Mālanchamālā and Kānchanmālā could not hold their own before Sītā, Sāvitrī and other heroines of the Pouranic tales, though the characters of the former carried an undoubted fascination and showed at least an equally high ideal of womanhood.

But the best of these folk-tales are those that have for the most part yet remained unwritten. Unfortunately, many of the folk-tales which have been printed, have lost their genuine forms, their compilers have tried to embellish them by their scholarship and pedantry. The Muhammadan half-lettered Munshi as well as the Pourāṇic exponent amongst the Hindus thought these tales to be too humble to be brought before the public in their original shape, and tried to improve upon them by introducing a high-flown classical style. The influence of Arabic and Persian, no less than that of Sanskrit, has therefore greatly marred the simple charm of these tales.

The Muhammaden laity have preserved the older popular tales amongst them.

For these seven or eight hundred years, the Mollās have not allowed the Muhammadan pesantry to accept any story or folk-tale from the Hindus, developed under Pourāṇic influences. The whole Hindu atmosphere of Bengal has rung all this time with songs and ballads based on the Purāṇas and the Epics. The Muhammadan peasant saw the *yatrā*-performances in the homes of their neighbours, but they took a superficial and momentary interest in them. The *kathakas* gave no permission to the Muhammadan rustic to enter the circle of their audience, where recitations and songs and narrations of Pourāṇic stories went on. The Bengali Muhammadans, however, amused themselves still with those folk-tales that had been transmitted to them from generation to generation, from times much anterior to the Muhammadan conquest.

We have got a number of these tales published by Muhammadans. They are evidently Hindu and Buddhistic in spirit, though the Hinduism to be found in them is different in many respects from the type developed by the Pourāṇic Renaissance. They represent the earlier forms, and this I have already indicated in a previous lecture.

A list of some of these tales.

Here lies on my table a heap of these tales by Muhammadan writers. We have the story of Kānchana mālā by Mahammad Munshi and published by Maniruddin Ahmad from No. 337, Upper Chitpore Road, Calcutta,—that of Madhumālā by Syed Shaha Khandakar Javedāli published from 155, Masjidbari Street, Calcutta,—of Mālanchamālā by Aizuddin Munshi and published from 337, Upper Chitpore Road,—of Shakhisonā by Mahammad Korban Ali, published from 11, Mechuabazar Street, Calcutta,—of Çīta Vasanta by Golam Kader, published from 335, Upper Chitpore Road, Calcutta. There are besides the stories of Mālatī Kusuma, Chandrāvalī, Lajjāvatī, and lots of others which in spirit and language are quite different from genuine Muhammadan tales.

They have been transmitted to the Muhammadan converts from a period anterior to Hindu Renaissance and Muhammadan conquest.

If it is urged that these tales, most of which are Buddhistic, have no reference to gods and goddesses of the Hindu pantheon ; but are based on moral qualities which appeal to all sects of humanity and for that reason found an access into the homes of the peasantry of Bengal after their conversion to Muhammadan faith, I should say that this could never be. Why should the Muhammadan converts whogave up their old religion and accepted Muhammadan names, obliterating all traces of their ancient faith and traditions, care to introduce the stories of Hindu princes and merchants into their *zenana* ? After they turned Muhammadans, not even their own kinsmen amongst Hindus would visit them within their houses, with the object of telling to them the Hindu folk-tales. The women generally tell these stories, but no Hindu woman would come in contact with a Muhammadan home, its kitchen savouring of beef and chicken roasted in onion-juice, at which she shuddered. Besides it is not true that these stories do not contain references to Hindu gods and goddesses. They sometimes do. I ought to tell you here that the Hindus and Buddhists often worshipped the same gods and goddesses. So that the mere mention of a god or goddess does not indicate to which of the two religious pantheons the deity belonged. In the story of Kānchanamālā by Mahammad Munshi we find the heroine Kānchanamālā suffering all that a woman could, from the maltreatment of her husband, who, out of prejudice and contempt, never looked at her face. She was a remarkable beauty ; but she could not show herself to her dear lord, who shut his eyes against her, following the wicked counsels of her sisters-in-law who had reported to him that her look was malignant. Despairing of gaining love from him, Kānchanamālā prayed to the

The reference to Hindu or Buddhist gods and goddesses in these stories.

goddess Sarasvatī for taking her away from this earth, for she could bear no more. She was a nymph and wanted to go back to her father's place at Alakā. The goddess came; and Kānchana must go back to her father's home with her. But her steps were slow; she glanced at her husband and found herself unable to move—a deep affection, inspite of all bad treatment, bound her to him and how could she give up the opportunity of seeing him, though he never looked at her? She now prayed for a little time to the goddess on some pretext or other. Here are the verses which are no doubt very old —

" Oh goddess, Oh mother, wait a while, I must wear my apparel before going to father's home."

And then again that little while passed, the apparel was worn, but she said again :—

" Oh mother, Oh goddess, wait a little more.
I must wear my eight ornaments before going to father's home.*"

This attachment to her lord is charming, for she secretly wept as she prayed for a little time to the goddess whom she had invoked to help

---

*"রহ মাগো দণ্ড চারি, গারের বসন আসি পরি,
আমি যাবগো মা বাপের বাড়ী।
রহ মাগো দণ্ড চারি, অষ্ট অলঙ্কার পরি,
আমি যাব নাগো বাপের বাড়ী ॥

her in going to her father's home. The merchant caught a glimpse of her for the first time in his life as she passed out of sight like a flash. He had never thought that his wife was so beautiful; he was dazzled by her remarkable beauty, but it was now too late. The remorseful husband passed through great adventures and perils with hair-breadth escapes, till he reached the fairy land. The condition of gaining his wife back was to recognise her and take her by the hand from the company of her sisters, all of whom assumed the same appearance; for they were nymphs and could take any shape. How could a mortal discover the subtle difference if any existed at all? She was dancing before the god Çiva with her sisters. Rūpachānd, the youthful merchant, sang a song understood by Kānchanamālā alone :—

> "Dance with one hand raised, my darling, so that I may know you.
>
> Dance, my darling, behind your sisters so that I may know you by your position.
>
> Shut one of your eyes, darling, and dance so that I may know you."

From a mere mention of Çiva and Sarasvatī we cannot say to which pantheon, the Hindu or the Buddhistic, the deities belonged as they are common to both. There are also invocations by Kānchana of Pārvatī and Gaṅgā in this story. We can cite many examples like the above, showing that in the Muhammadan versions of the tale, the gods and goddesses of the Hindu and Buddhist mythologies have found a place as in the Hindu versions themselves. This undoubtedly proves that the stories were current amongst the Muhammadans of Bengal, before they had renounced the older religion.

The only unfortunate thing about these stories is that we have had no opportunity to hear them from Muhammadan women. In that case it could have been understood they have been preserved by the Muhammadan country-folk in their original shape. As far as the printed versions go, they have not been preserved in this way. The Munshis have evidently introduced changes into the stories on the lines of Arabic and Persian tales; and, as I have already stated, the Hindu printed versions themselves are not free from Sanskritic influence. In the story of Mālatī-kusumamālā, the heroine Mālatī goes by her Hindu name, but her husband is called Alam which is a Muhammadan name. A clear influence of Persian is in evidence in the descriptions of the King's court; the language which is Bengali, has an admixture of Urdu and Arabic. But inspite of all these exotic traces, the original spirit of the story has, to a very considerable extent, been retained. The gander, the '*rājahansa*,' has been the traditional carrier of all news and a help in love matters, in the

A Hindu spirit permeates these stories.

Hindu tales ever since the time of Nala-Damayantî. And here also the bird appears discharging the same function. Alam, the merchant, appears before a '*muni*,' a Hindu or a Buddhist sage, and a *tāntric* who is engaged in *tapa* or religious austerities practised by the people of his order, with head bent downwards before a fire and legs raised above. These self-tormentings characterised the *tāntrikas* of the 8th and 9th centuries, when these stories were probably composed, though it cannot be said that there are not instances of similar self-torture amonst the *tāntrikas* even of this day. One curious point in regard to these tales compiled by Muhammadans is that we come across many examples of Buddhist phraseology in them, such for instance is the word '*niranjana*' which we find frequently in almost every one of these stories. The word is used for God. It often occurs in the Buddhist works like the Çunya purāṇa and Dharmamangala poems. The "*niranjaner usma*," or "the anger of Godhead," forms one of the most stirring incidents described in the Çunya purāṇa. Another word of Buddhist currency is 'Kāynur' for Kāmarupa, which is also to be met with in many of these stories. The Hindu and the Buddhist elements, as they were before the Pourānic Renaissance, form the characteristic features of these tales.

In the story of Jaminī Bhāna told by Munshi Muhammad Khater Marhun, the nymphs of Indra's heaven, that we find them in a similar tale told by Hindu writers, are changed into fairies. The deer in this story was a fairy; this will naturally remind one of the nymph who attracted the attention and love of the king Dandi in the guise of a deer. This legend of the king Dandi and his love with a nymph of Indra's heaven, who remained as a deer during daytime under a curse, is treated in detail in the Bengali Mahābhārata. The name of the hero--Jaminī Bhān seems to be an abbreviation of the word Jaminī Bhanu (lit. 'Sun of the night,' whatever it may mean) and reminds us of the hero of the poem of Harilīlā by Jaynarayan Sen, whose name is Chandra Bhān (moon-sun, an equally meaningless word). The other characters of these tales Jagatchandra, Mrigavatī and Rukminī bear Hindu names.

As already stated by me, these folk-tales, common to Hindus and Muhammadans alike, and a common heritage to them both, have got, in the Muhammadan versions, an exotic flavour, which is unmistakable. The story of Kānchanamālā, compiled by Munshi Muhammad, has a Hindu ground-work, and is essentially a Hindu tale in every sense; but even here the Muhammadan compiler has

The deterioration of the lofty Hindu ideal in Muhammadan versions of folk tales.

introduced some of the peculiar ideas current in his society. One of the brothers of Rupalāl goes by the Muhammadan name of Aftab. The name Taimus is also a Muhammadan one in the story. But these innovations are after all very superficial. Sometimes a deterioration in the standard of sexual morality in the Muhammadan versions of these stories is striking. This is what has shocked us in several places. The Hindu ideal of womanly virtues, of devotion to husband, of *brahmacharya* in widowhood, is the highest. Whether a woman should stick to her husband selected by her parents, or have a free choice in the selection of her mate, and change one who has ceased to interest her for the latest winner of her heart, is too complicated a question, raised by the modern rationalists, for me to enter upon in the present topic. In our social organism no doubt a change or rather revolution is coming on, and the time-honoured traditions and beliefs are now being scrutinised in the light of the reformer's new ideas, and the ground we tread upon, however firm in the past, has grown shaky in the present. But let us not fail to appreciate the type of the highest devotion and highest sacrifice in women, though we may break and rebuild our ideals. In the Muhammadan community here, a woman may take another mate if her husband dies. The fasts and vigils of widowhoood, its austerities and resignation,—the ideals set forth by the Hindu society, lost all its hold on the lay Muhammadan converts, and sexual depravity was not viewed by them in their lowest ranks, with the same feeling of horror. The Hindu folk-tales are free from all blemish in this respect. They were told by women to women and children, and every word that fell from the lips of their tellers was cautious and carefully weighed. The purity of these folk-tales strikes all the more, when we see that the poems and other literary works of the period, written by Hindus themselves, are not free from indecency and moral defects. The latter works were mostly written by men for men ; the fair sex had scarcely any thing to do with them. Female education, as we now understand by it, *viz.*, a knowledge amongst women of the art of reading and writing, had not spread so widely in those days as to enable the womenfolk to read the literature written in the vernacular. The writer therefore had not that sense of responsibility that he has at the present day. When men write something for themselves and not for the other sex, they may take some license and may not observe the too hard and fast rules of decency. But the folk-tales which used to be narrated to women, were generally composed with a far greater caution and sense of appropriateness than the ordinary written literature. In the

Muhammadan version we are shocked to find in the story of Kānchanamālā, descriptions of sexual vice that prevailed in the harem of the six brothers of Rupalal. This youth revelled in-unrestrained and gross incest with his sisters-in law. In the story of Çīta-Vasanta by Golam Kader, we are again shocked by the intriguing queen's throwing the two princes into the meshes of her abominable design. With what a sense of relief does the reader turn over the pages of a Hindu version of the stories. The situations are completely changed, and no suggestion of wicked indecency is to be found in them.

Çīta Vasanta as told by Golam Kader.

We are afraid that our critical review of this folk-literature may not appeal to you, as most of you are not acquainted with the stories. I propose here to compare several versions of the same tales obtained from differeut sources. First of all, let us take for example the story of Çīta Vasanta. There are altogether four versions of this story that we have come across. We shall first take up the Muhammadan one. It is compiled by Golam Kader and published by Afazuddin Ahmed from 155-1, Musjidbaree Street, Calcutta. A brief summary of this tale is given here.

In the city of Shahabad reigned a king named Ada Nasa. He got twin sons by his queen; they were called Çīta and Vasanta. One day the queen saw two birds near her compartment. Seated on the bough of a tree, they endearingly touched each other with their beaks and seemed bound in great love. They had several young ones. The queen was pleased to see the happy family. But a few days after, the female bird died, and for a day or two her mate screamed wildly in grief; but not long after, he brought with him another female bird, and they lived as husband and wife. The new comer killed the young ones, one by one, during the absence of the male bird. This incident moved the queen so deeply that she fell ill. She told the king of her fears, lest if she died and he took another mate, the condition of her dear sons might be like that of the young ones of the bird. The king of course swore that this could never be, that it was impossible that he would take another wife, if, God forbidding, such a calamity, as she spoke of, ever happened.

The queen's presentiments.

But the queen really died, and the Prime Minister gave a long course of religious advice to quiet the mind of the disconsolate king. His Majesty distributed charities amongst the poor, and did as he was advised for the good of the deceased queen's soul. In course of time, however, the king took

Her death and the king's taking a second wife.

another queen. Çīta and Vasanta had now grown up into manhood. The young queen was enamoured of the brothers and she did not make a secret of it, but plainly told them that she had conceived a passion for them. The brothers were shocked at this confession from their stepmother and fled from her presence in horror. But the infuriated queen maligned them before the king and gave out a false story complaining against their conduct. The king was very much enraged and gave an order next morning to execute the princes, and bring their blood before him. The executioner took compassion on the young princes, killed a goat and filled a cup with its blood to be shewn to the king, and set the two brothers at liberty in a deep jungle, advising them never to return to their motherland.

The brothers led to the execution-ground and their escape.

The brothers wandered in the forests for a long time, and heard two birds, endowed with the power of speech, talking to one another in the following strain: "If some one kills me and eats my heart, he will immediately become a king," said the one. "If any one eats me," said the other, "he will be in possession of a diamond every morning." The brothers were fine archers. They killed the birds. Çīta ate the heart of the

The eating of the hearts of the magic-birds.

first and Vasanta of the second bird. Now when the two brothers were straying apart from one another for a short while, the royal elephant of a neighbouring king's stall came near Çīta; the animal held a string of diamond of the value of nine lakhs by its trunk. The king of that country had died leaving no issue; the minister and the people relied upon Providence to give them a king, and the elephant was let loose on their decision that whomsoever it would bring to the palace on its back, he should be taken to be their king, elected by God. The elephant kneeled down before Çīta, put the string of diamond round his neck by its proboscis and carried him on its back to the palace. Çīta was thus installed as the king of that country. Vasanta wandered in the jungle in quest of his brother fruitlessly. He passed through great hardships and trials. Once he was taken for a thief of fruits and of horses, and arrested. After escaping from this danger, he came to a merchant who gave him shelter willingly, as to his great surprise he found that the handsome youth presented him with a diamond every day. The avaricious merchant made up his mind to extort from him information as to where his extraordinary treasure lay and insisted on his drinking wine so that in a drunken state he might make the disclosure. Now the condition

Çīta is elected a king.

of his receiving a diamond every day was that this power would fail if he drank wine. Being obliged to drink in the above way, he lost his power; and the merchant finding that he no more gave him any diamond, drove him away. He thus wandered about like a helpless man and was in great distress. The merchant had grown very rich by selling the diamonds and he now purchased a ship and planned to go on a sea-voyage for trade. But it so happened that, on the eve of starting, the ship would not float on the sea, and the captain said that unless a human sacrifice was offered, there was no chance of the ship moving on the waters. The merchant's men went to secure a person to be offered as sacrifice, and whom should they secure but the unfortunate youth Vasanta whom no kith or kin claimed as their own? The merchant's wife remonstrated, as he was a very handsome youth, but the relentless merchant would not listen to her words. He was dressed in red robes and garlanded. When led to the execution-ground, however, he begged of the merchant to spare his life, as he felt confident that if he simply touched the ship it would float by the grace of the Almighty. Vasanta was required to prove what he said. As

Vasanta loses his power of producing diamonds.

Led to the execution-ground.

he touched the ship it floated like a thing of cork. But Vasanta was not set at liberty, as the captain said that if the ship should again get stuck on the shore, his services might be required.

Is saved.

So Vasanta was on board the ship, and the merchant's daughter took a fancy for him and asked her mother to marry her to him. The merchant treated the request with contempt. Laden with merchandise, the ship came to the Chinese shore. The Chinese princess happened to see Vasanta from the window of her palace, and begged of her father to get her married to him. The king called the merchant to him and proposed the marriage. He would not listen to anything to the contrary. So the marriage took place with the usual pomp. And the princess with her large dowry started on another ship with her husband. The merchant paid a visit to them in their ship, and, one day, when they were passing through the vast ocean, pushed down Vasanta into the bottomless deep. He now asked the princess to marry him. The princess had thrown a *tumbā* for the support of her husband, and declared that she would be right glad to marry the merchant after the expiry of a year, the term of her vow. Vasanta, with the help of the

Marries a princess and is thrown into the sea.

tumbā floated on the sea and made a narrow escape from being seized and carried off by a great sea-bird. Once a crocodile had even swallowed him, but he came out with the help of the *tumbā*. He floated through the milk-sea, the butter-sea, the red-sea, the blue-sea, in fact all the seven seas, till some nymphs, taking pity on him, took him to Indra's heaven where the god granted him the boon that his evil destiny would soon be over. When he returned to earth, after passing through further vicissitudes of fortune, he came to the garden of a flower-woman, which was lying as a waste-land and desert for many years. But as Vasanta entered it, the withered plants all flowered and looked fresh and smiling. The flower-woman, coming to the spot at that time, felt as if some god had visited her deserted garden and worked wonders. She welcomed Vasanta, called him nephew, and treated him with great hospitality. This flower-woman had a means of access into the merchant's harem where the Chinese princess was kept. Getting a clue to this, Vasanta sent a message to her. And she now expressed a wish to celebrate the rites by which her vow was to be completed. The merchant was very glad that on the completion of her vow she would accept him as her husband. Invitation-letters were issued to all princes and Çīta who was now a king, and Adanās, the father of Çīta and Vasanta, as well as other princes of the country and its influential and rich merchants assembled to witness the function. The condition of the ceremony required that one who would be able to tell the whole story of the princes Çīta-Vasanta, would alone be privileged to hold the priestly office. Drummers were appointed to announce the condition laid down by the princess by beat of drums, and Vasanta came forward to accept the condition declaring that he fully knew the story. So before the assembled kings and merchants, he commenced to narrate the story of Çīta-Vasanta even from the time when their mother had seen the future of her sons in the fate of the young ones of a bird. As he related the story of his great miseries, one by one, the eyes of each one of that illustrious audience became tearful and many a time he himself had to stop to clear his voice, choked with emotion. A violent feeling was raised in that vast assembly, as brother recognised brother, and the king, his sons. The gladsome news of the lost being found again was announced by the music of *nahabat* orchestra. The king ordered his wicked wife and the merchant to be beheaded and the order was carried out then and there. The king elected Çīta to be his successor and Vasanta was made his prime minister. The Chinese princess

Vasanta holds the priestly office.

The merchant is beheaded and the happy end for others.

was brought to the palace. Vasanta, however, had to take a second wife, for the merchant's daughter had loved him with a whole heart, though her father had treated him cruelly.

We shall now briefly review another version of the story of Çīta-Vasanta by a Hindu writer. This compiler has tried his best to maintain his dignity as a writer of classical style, and the folk-tale he heard in his childhood he has thoroughly recast on a pouranic model, giving it an air of a full-fledged Sanskritic story, and eliminating all traces of its rural origin.

Harinath Mazumdar's version.

The story is not called Çīta-Vasanta. Somehow or other the author did not like the name of Çīta ; he has changed it into Vijaya. So that the story in this version goes by the name of Vijaya-Vasanta.

The author is well known in Bengal as a saint and a writer of spiritual songs. In the colophon of these, he subscribes himself as Fikir Chand Fakir. This is, however, his *nom de plume* ; his real name is Harinath Majumdar, but he is more familiarly known as Kāngal Harinath.

He wrote the story in 1859, when its first edition was published, and a fourteenth edition was called for in 1913, long after the death of the author. The book Vijaya-Vasanta was very popular at one time. The author's chief credit lies in his power of creating pathos in an extraordinary manner. No one can read the book without being literally swept away by emotion and by a feeling of compassion for the sufferings of the two forlorn children, especially Vasanta, the youngest child. But we are not concerned with the pathos of the story. A brief summary of this version is given below.

Parikshit, the king, one day went to the forests for hunting. He put a dead serpent round the neck of a saint, who, merged in contemplation, had not heard the king's request to give him some drinking water. The sage's young son Çṛngī came to the spot that moment, and, seeing his father insulted by the king, cursed him saying that he would be stung by a serpent within a week and die. Now the sage heard this curse uttered by his son and reprimanded him for this cruelty. He referred to a curse once uttered by two young ascetics, leading to disastrous consequences in respect of the Gandharva King Chitraratha, his wife and brother. The king sporting in a river with his wife had not paid heed to the young sages, and had thrown out water on the persons of their Holinesses in course of his sports. Chitraratha and his brothers were born into the world of mortals as Vijaya and Vasanta. Chitraratha's former wife became in the world a princess who was married to Vijaya in his youth. "What were

Çṛngī—the young sage hears from his father—the story of the Gandharva King Chitraratha.

the sufferings of these three?" asked Çṛngī and his father gave the following account.

"The king Jayasen of Jaypur got two sons, Vijaya and Vasanta. The good queen, their mother, died shortly after, and the king was disconsolate over her death for some time and his minister gave him a course of advice to alleviate his grief. Sometime after, the king, at the advice of his family-priest Dhauma, took another wife. The old maid-servant of the house Çāntā took charge of the young princes and was very devoted to them. Durlatā, a maid-servant of the new queen, advised her to take prompt steps to remove Vijaya and Vasanta from the palace for ever, by means fair or foul. For these children would, she said, stand in the way of her own sons, when born, succeeding to the throne. The queen took her advice and shut herself up in the "room of anger," and, when the king enquired about the cause of her sorrow, gave out a false story stating how she had been insulted by the children. The king, who was helpless in her hands, ordered the *kotwal* to arrest them and execute them in the morning. When they were bound with chains, Vasanta who was only four years old, said, "I will tell pappa how you treat me; see my hands are bleeding." Çāntā interposed and tried to take away the children from the *kotwal*

The step-mother's machinations.

who kicked her out. The boys were thrown into a dungeon and Vasanta said to Vijaya, "Brother, take away my chains. I cannot bear the pain." Vijaya heard him lament, and swooned away in grief. The next day they were brought before the king who gave the order to behead them at once. Vijaya said, "Punish me, sire, as you will like, but not Vasanta, innocent as innocence itself." Vasanta showed the blood on his hand and said, "Pappa, punish the *kotwal* and take me to your care. See I am in great fear and pain." But the king did not even look at the princes and was inexorable; his order must be carried out at once. The courtiers were greatly moved and they interceded in behalf of the princes. But the king said, "If some body else had insulted the queen, what would be his fate? I cannot show partiality towards my own children; that would not be just." So the just monarch's order was on the point of being executed, but the prime minister strongly condemned it, and the king had to yield a little. Order of execution was changed to one of banishment for life. The two boys were let loose in a jungle, far off from the capital. They came to the foot of a mountain where the valley was pleasant to see, with a spring of pure and transparent water. Vijaya left Vasanta for a little time and went in quest of food. The latter sat

Banished from the capital and sufferings in the forests.

there waiting, and tasted a fruit that had dropped from a near tree and became senseless,—the fruit was poisonous. When Vijaya saw his little brother in that condition on his return, he concluded that he must have been stung by a serpent. Seeing no help, he lamented, saying, "My darling, pappa did not show you any affection when you appealed to him; is it for this that, in wounded feelings, you are leaving this world? Wait, I am coming to you; alas, where now is Çāntā?" Saying this, he resolved to commit suicide. Just at that moment an ascetic appeared there and said, "Desist, my child, from the mad course. Self-murder is unrighteous." He gave some medicine to Vasanta by which he recovered, for he was not dead, but senseless. The sage gave the brothers shelter for the night. In the morning they again started in quest of some habitation of men. For miles and miles there spread a deep jungle from which they found no way out. In the night they climbed a tree, and hisses of cobra and the yell of wolves and a mingled uproar of other ferocious animals were heard around. Vijaya realised the situation and looked greatly embarrassed. Vasanta, who thought himself quite safe in the care of his brother, just as a baby in the arms of its mother, said, "Brother, if there is any danger, why not call Çāntā to our aid?" In the morning Vasanta felt so thirsty that he could not speak. Upon this Vijaya went in quest of a little drinking water, and when leaving Vasanta alone, he prayed, "Oh god, keep my little brother safe, do whatever you like with me." But as Vijaya had gone some way, an elephant gorgeously caparisoned ran towards him, and, gently taking him up by his trunk, placed him on the rich *hāwdā* on its back. It then walked rapidly towards the city. The people there on the death of the king, had set the elephant of the Royal stall to find out a king in that way, and when Vijaya entered the city, loud were the exclamations of joy in the public streets and he was immediately installed as king.

The elder brother is installed as a King.

The folk-tale ends here, and the remaining portion, tagged to it, is purely a creation of the writer's fancy on a classical model; though at the end, following the spirit of the folk-tale, he makes Vijaya, and Vasanta to be restored to the old king their father, who becomes repentant and receives them cordially. The wicked queen is punished as a matter of course.

The End.

The next version of this story we find in the Rev. Lalbehary De's folk-tales. It is called Çwet-Basanta; but the right word is 'Çita' which means 'cold' and not 'Çwet' which means 'white.' This ancient story is still told in the back-ward villages of Bengal and there we find the

Lalbehary De's version.

name as 'Çita.' Besides there is a sense in the names Çita and Vasanta as each signifies a season. The story told by Lalbehary De may be briefly summarised as follows.

Once a merchant married a remarkable girl, who was born of an egg of a bird called *tun-tuni*. She was very handsome and accomplished, and gave birth to two sons, Çīta and Vasanta. But unfortunately she died not long after the twin brothers had been born. The merchant married again, and after a few years lost all affection for the sons of his former wife. Çīta had by this time grown into manhood and married a beautiful girl.

About this time a fisherman brought a fish of wonderful properties. "If any one eats it," said he, "when he laughs, *maniks* will drop from his mouth, and when he weeps, pearls will drop from his eyes." The two brothers Çīta and Vasanta secured the fish and partook of it. Their step-mother was very jealous of them as they were sure to inherit the wealth of the merchant after his death. So she frequently quarrelled with them and one day she expressed her resolution at a moment of great anger, "Wait, wait, wait, when the head of the family comes home, I will make him shed the blood of you both before I give him water to drink." The brothers took fright at this utterance of their step-mother knowing what an influence she had

The brothers fly away from the capital.

over their father. So they fled from home in the night and Çīta's wife also accompanied them. They wandered about in the wilderness and as Çīta's wife was awfully thirsty, her husband left them in order to seek water somewhere near; but just as he had gone a few paces, an elephant gorgeously caparisoned, came to him, and taking him gently by its trunk, placed him on its back and then ran swiftly towards the city. The elephant was the 'king-maker' in that country. But for sometime past a tragic event occurred in the palace every morning. The elephant carried a man on its back every day and he was duly installed as king. He spent the night with the queen and it was found every morning that the king had died in the night. Çīta was also duly installed as king and was in the room of the queen that night. He, however, did not sleep but watched. In the depth of the night a thin thread-like substance came out of the left nostril of the queen; it increased in bulk till it assumed the shape of a terrible cobra and approached the new king. Before however, it could reach him, Çīta drew out his sword and cut it to pieces. The next morning the people of the city expected to see the corpse of the king, as usual, but they were glad beyond measure to see him living. He told them of what had happened to the former kings elected, and showed them the proof of his

Çīta is installed as a king.

valorous act by bringing the cup in which the serpent's body, cut to pieces, was preserved by him in the night previous.

Vasanta and his brother's wife, left alone, became tired of waiting for Çīta, and as the wife was very thirsty as well as anxious for news about her husband, Vasanta left her, to make enquiries about his brother and to fetch water, if available, from some neighbouring tank. He stood near a river, and not meeting his brother began to shed tears; these became pearls instantly. A merchant saw him in that condition, seized him with his pearls and carried him away in his ship. Çīta's wife was in extreme distress and all alone in that wilderness she gave birth to a son. She became senseless in consequence; and the *kotwal* of the neighbouring city seeing her in unconscious state, lying in the forest with an extraordinarily beautiful baby by her side, kidnapped the baby and fled away. The *kotwal* had no child and he adopted the baby as his son. Time passed on, and the boy grew to manhood. He overheard a conversation at this stage of affairs, between two calves in the cow-shed attached to his house, in which his whole family-history was revealed to him. He came to know that his mother had been saved from a tragic end by a compassionate Brahmin in whose house she still served as a maid servant. He also came

Çīta's wife gives birth to a son who is kidnapped.

to know how his uncle Vasanta was kept confined and was alternately flogged and tickled by the merchant, in order to yield pearls and rubies, for his tears produced the one and his laughs the other. The young man instantly applied to the king who was none else than Çīta himself. He listened to the strange story with attention and then sent men to the merchant's house to search his dungeon. As Vasanta was brought out from there, Çīta instantly recognised him though he looked greatly reduced and pale. From the Brahmin's house the king recovered his lost wife. How glad was he now to find again his own wife, brother and son so long known as the *kotwal's* son. The merchant, who had so cruelly treated Vasanta was buried alive in a pit which was filled up with earth and thorns.

The re-union.

Yet a fourth version of the story of Çīta-Vasanta we find in the collections of Babu Dakshina Ranjan Mitra Majumdar. It is in his first series of folk tales that appeared under the name of "Thakurmar jhuli," or "the grandmother's bag." The story runs thus:

Dakshina Ranjan's version.

A king had two wives, the more favoured one was the Suo Rāṇi, who had three sons; they were lean like jute stalks or bamboo-leaves. But the less lucky wife, the Duo Rāṇi had two sons, handsome as cherubs. They were called Çīta and Vasanta. Their step-mother was very jealous of them. So she first tried to remove their mother from the palace. One day as both the queens were bathing, the Suo Rāṇi on the pretext of doing the hair of her co-wife, tied a magic root with her hair; the Duo Rāṇi instantly turned into a bird called the *tun-tuni* and flew away. The Suo Rāṇi gave the report that her co-wife was drowned; and the king was now absolutely in her hands. She one day told a false story against the brothers Çīta and Vasanta, complaining that they had grossly insulted her. She demanded of the king an order for the immediate execution of the brothers and the king saw no way but to comply with her wishes. The executioner took them to a deep forest and said "Princes, I was present in the palace when you were born; I was at one time in charge of you; I cannot apply sword to your throat, whatever may befall me. Here take this bark-dress. No one will recognise you as princes in this dress. Go as fast as your legs can carry you to the farthest end of this jungle, and choose a safe place." Saying so, he unbound them, and set them at liberty. The executioner took a quantity of blood, killing a dog and a jackal on the spot, and made it over to the queen who was now satisfied that Duo Rāṇi's sons were now removed from this world for good.

The step-mother's witch-craft and the order of execution on the brothers.

The escape.

Now the two princes went on, but the end of the forest was not seen. Vasanta became very thirsty and wanted Çīta to get for him some water from the neighbourhood. He was not only thirsty, but so exhausted that he could not proceed any further. Çīta left him there and went in quest of water. He saw water-fowls coming from some place and understood by that sign that water was near. But on his way he saw a white elephant running towards him with a rich *howdā* on its back. The elephant took him by the trunk and, placing him on its back, quickly walked towards the near city. This white elephant was the 'king-maker' and as the king of that country had died without leaving an heir to succeed to his throne, it was let loose to find out a king for the people. The elephant wandered about, from place to place every day, and returned in the evening without carrying any one on its back, for he could not discover the mark of royalty in any person up to now. The sagacious animal after a long search found such signs in Çīta, so as soon as he was brought to the city, he was duly installed on the throne. All this time Vasanta was in great distress and was on the point of death by starvation and thirst, when an ascetic took care of him and kept him in his hermitage.

Çīta made a king.

Now the bird *tun-tuni*, to which the Duo Rāṇī was transformed by Suo Rānī's witchcraft, was caught by a princess named Rūpavatī. The king, her father, had proclaimed her *sayamvara*, or election of a bridegroom by herself from an assembly of invited princes. Many kings had come there and many a prince and nobleman stood suitors for the hand of Rūpavatī. But Rūpavatī, before she visited the court to elect her bridegroom, had asked the *tuntuni* bird "Whom shall I elect as my husband, bird?" The *tuntuni* gifted with the power of speech, said, "One that will bring you a rare pearl that grows on the head of an elephant on the sea-coast, will be your bridegroom, and none other." So before the assembled princes, Rūpavatī declared her condition, but she added, "He who will seek the pearl but fail, will be my slave." Many a prince went to the sea-shore and saw the elephant but could not secure the pearl. They became slaves of the princess Rūpavatī.

Rūpavatī's condition.

Now when Çīta, who was the paramount king in that country, heard all these, he was very angry and said, "Why should she make the sons of my feudal chiefs, the *Bhuia* kings, slaves?" He accordingly got Rūpavatī arrested and kept her in a compartment of the palace all alone. Now Vasanta one day overheard the conversation of two birds, Çuka and Çāri. In this conversation they disclosed the secret by which the pearl on the head of the elephant could be secured. There was a favoured spot in the milk-white sea, in which there grew a thousand lotuses in full bloom. The one in the middle was of the colour of gold. There the white elephant with the pearl on its head played with the lotus of golden hue. Vasanta learned the secret. He took from the ascetic, in whose hermitage he lived, his magic trident, and with it succeeded in reaching that spot in the milk-white sea. As soon as the sea was touched by the trident, it became dry. The elephant itself turned into a golden lotus, with the rare pearl inside it. Vasanta took it up and when marching over the sands of the sea he heard a cry, "We are your brothers transformed into fish; take us with you." Vasanta dug the sands and found three golden fish. He took them with him.

Vasanta gets the rare pearl.

Now after Çīta and Vasanta were driven from the palace of their father, he lost his kingdom and fled away in order to hide his shame. The Suo Rāṇi, reduced to abject poverty, begged from door to door with the three princes, her sons, for livelihood. She came in this way to the seashore. The sea roared in rage and coming over the banks swallowed them by its waves. These three princes had been reduced to the shapes of fish, whom the prince Vasanta now took with him.

The transformation of the step-brothers into fish.

Now the king Çīta one day had gone a-hunting into the depth of a forest; he came near a big tree which he at once recognised to be the very one under which he had left Vasanta, and had gone from there in quest of water, years ago. The recollection of his brother came back to him and he was overpowered by grief. His men, however, came to his help and took him to his capital, where he shut himself up in a compartment of the palace, and for seven days saw no one, nor ate anything,—for his grief was great.

At this time Vasanta came up to the palace and said to the royal guard, that he wanted to visit the king. He had come with the pearl which Rūpavatī wanted, besides he had brought the three golden fish with him. The guard requested him to wait for seven days. This he did and when the king broke his fast, the three golden fish were presented to him. They were made over to a maid servant of the palace. As soon as she tried to cut one of the fish and dress it she heard it saying, "I am the king's brother, do not kill me." The astonished maid servant brought this to the notice of the king, who wanted to see the man who had presented the fish. Vasanta came before Çīta, and there was great pathos as brother recognised brother. And as soon as they touched the fish, these assumed their own forms as their step-brothers.

"And where is our mother, Suo Rāṇi?" asked Çīta and Vasanta. And the reply of the princes was "Our mother died of grief." "Where is our father, the king?" He lost his kingdom and has gone away, nobody knows where."

The reunion.

Çīta and Vasanta shed tears of joy at meeting with each other, and of sorrow over the fate of their parents alternately. Vasanta now asked his brother to release Rūpavatī, which was forthwith done. Vasanta knocked at her doors and exclaimed, "See, bride, I have come with the rare pearl that you wanted, make me your husband." Rūpavatī turned to the *tuntuni* and asked if the youth had really got the pearl and was to be her bridegroom. "O yes" cried the bird. Whereon Rūpavatī welcomed him and put the garland of flowers, that she had wreathed, round his neck as a sign of choosing him to be her husband. Rūpavatī was so glad that out of gratitude to the bird who had helped her to get such an excellent husband, she bathed it in milk and scented it with perfumes with her own hands; and in doing so she found something tied with the feather on its head. She took it out and lo! as soon as she had done so, the Duo Rāṇi once again gained her own form. She said that she was the mother of Çīta and Vasanta and the news spread with the

The Duo Rāṇi is restored to her human form.

speed of lightning, throughout the whole city. And Çīta and Vasanta and their step brothers were in a moment down upon their knees before her, weeping in joy to meet their mother whom they had taken to be dead. The old king who had been wandering like an ascetic came back to meet his lost family. Çīta and Vasanta and the three young princes, their step-brothers, helped him to gain his lost kingdom back and they lived long years in happiness and prosperity.

It will appear from the four tales summarised above, that there is little room for doubting that all of these are different versions of one and the same story. An alien influence is distinctly marked in the Muhammadan version. The way in which the step-mother shamelessly offered her love to the two princes has not been mentioned in my summary for the sake of decency. The wickedness of the woman, her unrestrained passion, coquetry and vulgarism are of a shocking character. Such a tale could not be told in a Hindu household. The way in which the merchant's daughter and the Chinese princess declared their love for Vasanta in the Muhammadan version also discloses a lack of that self-control which characterises the heroines of the Hindu folk-tales. We need not

The language of the Muhammadan version.

comment on the language of the Muhammadan version. It is no doubt Bengali but bears in a large measure an admixture of Arabic and Persian words. As a specimen we may quote a few lines:—

উজির নাজির ওমরা সকলে হাজির।
রাজারে বুঝায় সবে না কর ফিকির॥
এই হাল দেখ জাই সকল সংসারে।
ছনিয়াতে খালি মায়া গেরেপ্তার করে॥
আপে ছুই ফরজেন্দেরে করিবে মেহের।
কাহেক আন্দেশ গম কর বেরবের॥
পেরাসনি না হইবে শুন আলম্পনা।
ছনিয়া জাহানে আল্লা করিবেক ফানা॥
এতেক শুনিয়া সাহা হায় হায় করে।
দেলে দর্দ্দ মুখে আহা চোখে পানি ঝরে

Nor is the next version—that by Harinath Mazumdar—less interesting from the point of view of the changes and innovations introduced into a simple folk-tale. The author is resolved upon improving the rural story by his pedantry and scholarly knowledge of Sanskrit. A tale, to possess an air of authority, and classical dignity, in his opinion, must be derived from Paurānic sources. So he altogether conceals the fact that he had heard the story originally from the old women of the country-side. He puts the whole story in the mouth of that unweary sage Vaisampayana, who has from age to age added to and replenished the store of tales in the Mahāvārata. Vaisampayna tells

The version of Harinath Majumdar.

and Janmẹjaya hears. From hoary antiquity down to the year 1859, when Vijaya-Vasanta was written by Harinath Mazumdar, the teller and the listener had sat facing each other ; and we are not sure which to admire the most—the power of narration without a limit, or that of attentive hearing which knows no fatigue or weariness. The Gandharva king is introduced ; and following the characteristic traditions of the Paurānic Renaissance that all evils of the world are brought on by the curses of Brahmins, Harinath traces the career of Çīta and Vasanta before they were born on the earth, and makes them victims to Brahminic ire. But the changes are not merely these. All descriptions of men and women and of nature are indebted to Sanskritic sources for their elegance and classical style. The characters cite Paurānic stories by way of reference in their daily conversations. They are all up-to-date and show a liking for modern topics as well. Dissertations on patriotism are given on p. 80, on female education on pp. 107-110, on widow remarriage on p. 85. Other burning questions of the day are also treated by the author whenever an opportunity presents itself. The king Vijayachandra and his wife Bimalā visit the prison-houses of their capital and give sermons to improve the morals

The Paurānic elements introduced into this version.

The up-to-date questions.

of the prisoners. His Majesty makes a laudable and vigorous effort to spread a knowledge of science and general geography amongst his people. In one place (p. 84) we find a character crying hoarse against the rite of Satī on the lines of Rājā Ram Mohan Roy. The names of the characters are elegant Sanskritic words; Vijayachandra, Ramanīmohan and Vimalā may be cited as examples. The king's priest is Dhouma of the Paurānic tradition. Harinath is not only a pupil of Sanskrit poems and the Purānas, but shows his knowledge of Kalidāsa's poetry by referring to *udyanlatā* and *āçramalatā*, the creeper of the king's garden and that of a hermitage, in a passage of his work (p.99). He belonged to the society of educated Bengal in the early part of the 19th century and the age spoke through him. So how could he help giving all that was fashionable in the cultured society of his times in a work which, though based on an ancient rural story, was recast and re-written with a view to entertain the young men of his generation. The style has the stamp of that of Vidyā-sāgara, refined, rigidly accurate and heavy with pompous classical words. We need only quote the first sentence which is typical of the style of the entire work.

Specimen of language.

"একদা পরীক্ষিৎ রাজেন্দ্র সসৈন্যে মৃগয়ায় গমন করিয়া অরণ্য অবরোধ করিলে বিপিন বিহারীগণ ভয়াকুল হইয়া ইতস্ততঃ নিবিড়ারণ্যে প্রবেশ করিতে লাগিল।"

This reminds us at once of the characteristic style of Vidyā-sāgara's Sakuntalā and Sītār Vanavāsa. The rural element in which, however, lay the unassuming poetry and simplicity of the people was out of favour in the early part of the 18th century, and Harinath as an exponent of the taste of his times changed the manner and style of narration of the folk-tale by giving in it a preponderance of Sanskritic words. But as stated by me in the foregoing portion of this lecture, the work of Harinath possesses remarkable pathos in the earlier chapters, such as only Vidyāsāgara alone could show in some of his finest works.

Lalbehari De's Story.

Next if we take up the version of the story given by the Rev. Lalbehari De, we find that his account is not always an accurate one. True, he reproduced it as he heard it, but being a Christian, he could not always get the materials of the folk-tales at first-hand. In his version we find a portion of the story of Malati Kusuma dove-tailed into that of Çīta-Vasanta. The account of a baby who was kidnapped by a nobleman from the arms of its mother, lying senseless after delivery, and the subsequent union of the mother with her son grown up to manhood, forms a part of many old folk-tales in Bengal. This account we also find in the story of Çankhamālā in Dakshinaranjan's second collection called the

Thākurdādār Jhuli or the grand-father's bag. We think that this episode was originally a part of the story of Cankhamālā from which it was taken and joined to other stories. But whatever it be, the Rev. Mr. De has described in this story how the kidnapped child, when he grew up to proper age, conceived a passion for his own mother without knowing her to be so. This seems very repelling. And as we have condemned a similar thing in the Muhammadan version of this story we do it also here, though it must be said to the credit of the Rev. Mr. De that he has dealt with this part of the story very cautiously so that its impropriety has not become too prominent. Mr. De tells us that his old friend Sambhu's mother from whom he had heard many folk tales had died before he collected the stories for his work, "The Folk-tales of Bengal," and that therefore he had to depend for them upon a christian woman who evidently had lost some of her old memories. At least she could not have given him a strictly faithful version of the Hindu folk-tales. The episode of one of the brother's eating the flesh of a bird or fish by which he got the power of producing rubies and pearls by smiles and tears is analogous to the European story of the Salad in the Grimm Brothers' Collections.

Last of all is the version of Daksinaranjan Mitra Majumdar. It is not affected by any pedantry or scholarship in classic literature or any modern propagandism; for Mitra Majumdar is too humble a scholar to aim at higher things. He is in love with the tales as they are related by the rural people of the lower Gangetic valley, and gives a faithful version of what he has heard. Nor do his stories bear any exotic influence—Persian, Arabic, or even Sanskritic. The language is that in which our grandmothers used to tell tales,—simple, even archaic, full of naïve rural charms, and always to the point. There is nowhere a display of vain learning or straying out of the main subject in order to hold disquisitions on the burning questions of the day. But as we shall have to deal with his folk-tales more elaborately in course of our lectures, we cut short our comments here.

The superiority of Dakshinaranjan's version.

There are many folk-tales which we have got in common from the Hindu and Muhammadan sources, and this we have already noticed. Another very interesting story repeated by many writers is that of Sakhi-sonā. The compiler of the Muhammadan version is one Muhammad Korban Ali—an inhabitant of Butuni in the sub-division of Manikgani, Pergannah Sindurijan in the district of Dacca. The story of Sakhi-sonā that he gives, is briefly summarised as follows.

The story of Sakhi Sonā.

Muhammad Korban Ali's version.

In a place called Taef, there lived a poor man named Syed. He had a wife, and none else in the family. As they were in extremely indigent circumstanes, Syed had frequently to bear insulting treatment from his wife who was a shrew. One day when Syed could by no means secure food, his tart-tempered wife rebuked and insulted him grossly, taking him to task for indulging in the luxury of a wife before he could provide for her comforts. Syed bore the insult quietly but resolved to put an end to his wife's life and thus be saved from the state of things that occurred every day. He accordingly secured a poisonous cobra and put it inside an earthen pot and carried it home. He planned to open the cover of the pot at the dead of the night, and to place it near his sleeping wife. But when at midnight he actually opened the cover, instead of the venomous animal that was inside the pot, he found it filled with gold coins. He was of course very glad at the discovery, and his wife's anger against him was all gone when he produced the pot before her, and said that he had earned the wealth by great labour. By Syed's order, his wife took the pot to the palace of the Badsha of that country and sold the gold coins to his Begum for a thousand rupees.

Syed carried home a cobra to kill his wife.

The cobra turns into gold coins.

The Begum thought that she had made a bargain, and kept the wealth in her iron safe, and when in the morning she brought it out to show to the Badsha, he, instead of finding the gold coins that she had seen there the day before, found in it a smiling baby—a girl of exquisite beauty. The King who was childless was right glad to have this baby,—far more glad than if the pot had actually contained gold as had been reported to him by his wife. The news was announced throughout the capital that a girl was born to the Begum and there were great rejoicings in the palace over this event. The girl was named Sakhi-sonā. Just at the moment when the king's palace resounded with the music of the *nahabat* orchestra announcing the glad news, the mansion of the Uzir of the king's court witnessed similar festivities, though on a much smaller scale, on the occasion of a son being born to him. This son was called Mānik. The Badsha's astrologers prophesied that Sakhi-sonā, who was born under the influence of the Scorpion, would elope with a youth when she had reached womanhood.

The strange baby in the earthen pot.

The Uzir's son Mānik and the princess Sakhi-sonā read in the same Mokhtab. When they grew up to youth, they fell in love with each other; but one could not speak of "the passion that burnt within" to the other for shame.

One day, however, an opportunity presented itself. Sakhi-sonā's paper in the school dropped from her hands below, and she asked Mānik to get it from the ground and hand it to her. Mānik eyed her with a look in which a longing desire was hardly suppressed, and said that if she promised to pledge something to him, he would do so. Sakhi-sonā agreed knowing full well the significance of his suggestive words, and from thence they met in a compartment of the palace every day. A maid-servant of the princess one day dicovered their intrigue and advised them to go away from the palace as they were sure to be detected some day or other.

Mānik and Sakhi-sonā in love with one another.

Sakhi-sonā dressed herself as a young valorous youth with a sword hanging by her side and Mānik was also similarly dressed. Both mounted swift horses and left the palace at the dead of the night. From a deep jungle they came out after a day's fatiguing ride and coming near a cottage stopped there. The old lady of the house seemed very hospitable, but she was the mother of seven dacoits who just at that moment were not in the house. She gave her guests wet fuel and rice mixed with grains of stones, so that it took them considerable time to kindle a fire and cook the rice. But a woman of that house had whispered

They leave the city.

in their ears that the house belonged to dacoits who would soon return and rob them of every thing they had. Mānik and Sakhi-sonā instantly mounted their horses and fled away; but the old woman had, before their departure, tied a small bundle of mustard-seed to the tail of each of the horses. So, as they proceeded, the seeds fell on the ground marking their path, without their knowledge of the device of the cunning old woman. The dacoits, seven brothers, returned home, and their mother regretted their lateness in coming back, saying that the guests who had escaped, were enormously rich, their crowns, and necklaces sparkled with pearls and diamonds. The seven brothers lost no time but mounting the swiftest horses in their stalls marched with the speed of lightening and overtook the princess and Mānik. A fierce skirmish ensued, and Mānik who was a superior swordsman killed six of the robbers: but the seventh who was a lame man, implored for mercy and Mānik granted him life. Sakhi-sonā was not for showing him any mercy, but Mānik was kind to him and appointed him to be in charge of the horses to give them food and drink. But the dacoit felt a flame of passion for Sakhi-sonā, and secretly planned to kill Mānik and seize her. So when one day Mānik had fallen asleep and Sakhi-sonā was busy

In the hands of the dacoits.

Mānik kills six and is killed by the seventh.

in the kitchen, the dacoit took a sword and cut off the head of Mānik. Sakhi-sonā lamented the loss of her husband and killed the lame dacoit and then prayed to god to restore her husband's life. A *pir* (saint) came there at this stage of affairs and taking pity on Sakhi-sonā, restored Mānik to life. The couple were now happy beyond measure on being restored to each other, and they rode their horses again till they came to the cottage of a flower-woman named Champā. She at once conceived a passion for Mānik, and by witchcraft turned him into a monkey; Sakhi-sonā, who was not just at that moment with her lord, knew nothing about his strange transformation, and seeking him everywhere in vain bitterly lamented for him. The monkey in the night assumed the form of man, by the spell of Champā, and she spent the night with him. If he attempted to escape he was again turned into a monkey.

Mānik restored to life and is transformed inte a monkey.

Sakhi-sonā now led the two horses, the one that of herself and the other that of Mānik, by their reins and walked from place to place enquiring about her husband. She was dressed as a man and was arrested by the officers of the king of that country on a charge of theft of the two horses from the royal stall. She was thrown into prison. At this time a very large serpent appeared in the city of the king; it ate goats, cows and men; even tigers and bears were devoured by this dreadful reptile. The king's officers with guns shot with fruitless aim at it; the shots failed to pierce through its tough skin. The king proclaimed a large reward to one who would kill the animal and save his subjects from destruction. Sakhi-sonā dreamt in the prison that a *pir* (saint) appeared to her and told her the secret of killing the serpent. In the morning she sent word to the king, that if she were released, she could kill the serpent. She was of course all along taken for a young man and the king forthwith ordered her release. She approached the serpent from behind and struck her sword in the manner in which she was advised to do so by the *pir* in her dream. She had therefore no difficulty in killing the animal. When she succeeded in this enterprise, the king gave her his promised reward. And when she told her story of the sufferings caused to her by the king's Police officers on mere suspicion, declaring her own innocence in respect of the charge of theft of the horses, the king was very much ashamed; for, he could not disbelieve anything that she said. The king, as a token of his appreciation of her heroism, and also to make up for the injustice done to her, resolved to give his only daughter in marriage to her, taking her to be a valorous and an

Sakhi-sonā kills a serpent and marries the princess.

accomplished youth. She readily consented to the proposal and married the princess. But the latter, after a short time, felt that there was something strange and mysterious in the conduct of her husband; for, Sakhi-sonā kept aloof from her for fear of detection. Meantime the monkey who assumed his human form every night, wrote a letter to Sakhi-sonā describing his condition. As soon as she read it, she asked the king to get for her the particular monkey belonging to the flower-woman. Inspite of the latter's protestations, the monkey was brought to the palace, and when in the night he got back his own form he related the story of his sad transformation into the shape of a monkey by the witch-craft of the flower-woman. The woman was obliged to undo her spell on him. So he was himself once more. The flower-woman after this was beheaded by the order of the king for her wickedness. The king, knowing now that Shakhi-sonā was a woman, married his daughter to Mānik with the consent of Sakhi-sonā. And he lived long in prosperity and happiness with both his wives.

Mānik restored to his own form.

Mānik marries another princess and is happy with two wives.

The story of Sakhi-sonā was rendered into Bengali verse by the illustrious poet Fakir Rama Kavibhuṣana, who was a native of the Burdwan district and flourished in the middle of the 16th

Fakir Rama's version.

century. The story as told by this writer who was a poet of the Hindu Renaissance is briefly summed up as follows.

The princess Sakhi-sonā and Kumāra, the son of the *kotwal*, or the prefect of the Police, used to read in the same school. The seat of the princess was an elevated platform over the gallery in which the classes were held. Sakhi-sonā's pen one day dropped below, let us say, by a mere accident, from her seat. And she asked Kumāra to pick it up for her. Not once, but thrice did the pen drop that day, and on the third time Kumāra extorted a promise before he would pick up the pen for her, to the effect that he would do so on condition that she would comply with his wishes whatever they might be. Heedlessly did Sakhi-sonā run into the agreement, but what were her wonder and indignation, when Kumāra demanded to marry her and run away with her from her father's palace? For after such an inequal marriage, the king would not brook the pair to live with him, though she was the only legal heir to the throne.

Kumāra and Sakhi-sonā in School.

Sakhi-sonā said in rage, "You villain, dare you say so? Do you know that your body will not bear the burden of your head if this be brought to the notice of the king? For a trifle of help that you did me, you venture to insult me in this way."

Kumāra said, "If you say so, no more. I do not press my request. But the moral binding

The inviolable promise.

nevertheless remains the same in either case. You can kill me, princess, but if you break your promise you cannot avoid the eyes of God who sees everything.

"Rāma, for a simple word that he had given to his father, left his kingdom and turned an ascetic. Dasaratha, his father, died of grief, but yet did not break his promise. Rāma, the pure-hearted killed Vālī in a questionable manner, simply for a promise that he had given to Sugrīva. If you break promise, well and good, you will be lowered in my estimation and that of your Maker, what more?"

Sakhi-sonā felt humbled, before this appeal to God. For she had given a promise and there was no doubt about it. After many conflicting emotions which caused her sleepless nights, she decided to leave the palace and join Kumāra. She excused herself of a little delay that had occurred, in the following manner:—"my maids are constantly with me; how for shame can I come out? The queens will not leave my side for a moment. Some cover me with the hem of their garments; some fan me, and some wave the soft *chāmara*. One offers me betel, and another kisses me with great love, and a third calls my attention by such words as 'Hear me, my dearest child, I will tell you a story.' And yet another weaves floral wreath for me and wants to know if I like it."

Before leaving the palace, she had taken a parting view of the sleeping queens and soliloquised in this way: "Henceforth we shall meet no more. Like a boat trusting itself to the current, I trust my youth to fate. Do not weep, dear queens, when you miss me—your hapless child. Burn my throne and royal couch, for they will torment your eyes. Offer all my books lying in heaps in my chamber as a present to the Brāhmins. Forbear to enter into my apartment, it will grieve you ever so much. My golden plates and cups and vessels adorned with precious stones, distribute among the poor. My jewels and ornaments send to the royal treasury, and adieu queens, adieu for life."

The Princess's lament.

She had met her preceptor in the way who advised her not to take the rash step, but to return to the palace. But she said that as she had given the pledge, it was sacred and inviolable.

In the way the princess did not say any word to signify her love for Kumāra. She was far too much moved by her grief in cutting off her home-ties for ever. Like Gareth following Lynette, Kumāra followed his love—wooing her at every step. But she heeded not, now looking at the cow that had

They leave the palace.

lost its young one, and then sighing over some other thing she saw in her way that reminded her of the home that she had deserted. But when the spring came and the trees that had looked like skeletons in winter became covered with luxurious foliage, "the Princess and Kumāra delighted in each other's company and the former forgot her old sorrows for a time."

The advent of spring.

"Nature had given her a form of surpassing beauty; now the dawn of youth made her a marvel. She never had passed the threshold of a kitchen; and if her hair was untied, never did she adjust it with her own hands,—but her maids for her. Never had she learnt to blow the fire with her breath; and as she did it now, the smoke of the wet fuel made her face pale and sad. The smoke stifled her breath and the fire of the hearth wel-nigh burnt her skin. Alas, once even the heat of a lamp-light was too much for her; but with the smoke and fire of the hearth she continued her struggle to cook a humble meal."

The cyclone.

Both of them were journeying on horseback when a great cyclone overtook them. "The trees of Cuttack were carried down to Hinglat. Goats and cows were forced to fly on the high air like winged things. Seldom from the palace had the princess walked abroad on foot, and when she passed from one room to the other, the maids spread a rich carpet on the court-yard ; and when walking in the sun a guard used to hold a golden umbrella over her head. But now the hailstones beat incessantly against her head, and it seemed at each stroke her very skull would break. "O my love" she asked, "what will become of us? From the storm, the rain and the hailstones no escape I see. What path should we follow. The thick hailstones will ere long kill us both. The lightning's flash frightens my steed, and the striking of his hoofs on the hard ground produces fire. The storm suffocates me and I feel as if the breath of life itself would cease."

Suffering in this way from the furious weather and her own mental anguish, she with her husband came to a cottage which belonged to seven robbers. Kumāra killed six of them, but the seventh implored pardon which out of magnanimity he granted. But when Kumāra fell asleep, the miscreant killed him. Sakhi-sonā prayed goddess Chandi for mercy, and she restored Kumāra to life. Kumāra was next turned into a goat by the witchcraft of a flower-woman named Hīrā and the king of that country Naradhaja carried Sakhi-sonā by force into his compartment for females. Sakhi-sonā said that, before she would agree to marry the king for which he

In the cottage of the robbers.

Kumāra killed and restored to life.

pressed, she must perform some religious rite, which was to be completed after a year, with due solemnity. The king agreed to wait till that time. And at the end of the year, when her period of religious observances was over, she asked the king to provide her with a particular goat that was in the possession of Hīrā, the flower-woman. For Chandi had appeared to the princess in a dream, and told her that her husband had been transformed into a goat by Hīrā. Hīrā was obliged to produce the goat by the king's order, and the princess by the power of the spell that Chandi had taught her, forthwith restored her husband to his own form. Naradhaja saw in the transformation of the goat into a man the mercy of the goddess Chandi, and ungrudgingly shared in the joy of the couple who had met after a long year of bitter separation. Meantime the old king Vikramajit, the father of Sakhi-sonā, had heard all about his daughter and Kumāra, who had been so long missing, and now pardoned their marriage, and took them to his own city and made them heirs to his throne at death.

Kumāra transformed into a goat.

The reunion.

The most authentic version of this story, however, is the one compiled by Babu D. R. Mitra Mazumder. The story is called Puṣpamālā and not Sakhi-sonā. Mitra Majumder has

Dakhina Ranjan's version.

given the oldest form of the story, which is also the most accurate form. Whether the name Sakhi-sonā or Puṣpamālā is the older name of the heroine is open to question, but that is an immaterial point. In briefly summarising this version of the tale, I beg leave to state that the peculiar excellences of the original form of some of our folk-tales will be the subject of a somewhat elaborate analytical review in one of my future lectures. Here for the purpose of comparison, I subjoin a very brief summary of the story under review.

The Raja's pledge.

A Rājā happened to enter into a contract with his *kotawal* that if a daughter be born to him and a son to the *kotawal*, they would be united in marriage. But if instead, a daughter were born to the *kotawal* and a son to the king, the *kotawal* would be beheaded. These were the whimsical ways of the autocrats of those days. So no question was raised as to the propriety of the oath insisted on by the sovereign, and the *kotawal* had only to submit. It so happened that just at the same moment the queen and the *kotawal's* wife ran into a similar agreement, while they were bathing in a tank called the *Putra-sarovara*. The world knew nothing about these pledges. The king with the point of his arrow wrote his pledge on a fig-leaf and handed it to the *kotawal*.

A daughter was born to the king and a son to the *kotawal*; the princess was called Puṣpamālā and the *kotawal's* son Chandana. They used to read in the same school and each day from the high seat on which the princess sat, she dropped her pen below, and Chandana used to pick it up for her at her request. One day when he picked up the pen, and she bent herself a little to receive it from his hands, their eyes met, and Chandana the next day said, "Princess, if you exchange garlands with me, then shall I pick up the pen from the ground for you; else I will not." An angry look came from the princess as she said, "Don't you remember, lad, that you dwell in my father's kingdom? Have you no fear of life that you dare say so?"

Chandana and Sakhisonā at school.

Chandana said, "Why should I fear, princess? I know that my ancestors have for several generations shed their blood to build up this kingdom for your father."

The princess said nothing more that day. The next day her pen did not drop. But as Chandana was cleaning his own pen, it escaped his hand and fell on the the princess' apparel spotting it with ink. Chandana was abashed at this, and the princess also felt a shame which she could hardly conceal, but she pushed the pen with her finger so that it dropped below. Chandana took it up and said, "Many a day did I pick up your pen from the ground, to-day your gentle hand has pushed mine down to reach me. This earth is sacred because the flower blooms here. I charge you by the sacred earth and by the sun and the moon that illuminate her, that there has been an exchange of some sort." Saying so Chandana went away silently with the pen touched by the princess leaving his books and other things in the school. The princess was lost in her thoughts, and it was at a very late hour that she returned home that afternoon. The maid-servants had been long waiting with soaps and perfumes for her toilet.

But Chandana one day brought her a leaf on which the king had written the pledge, and on another occasion she came to know of the promise made by the queen to Chandana's mother. The king had absolutely ignored his promise and the queen would not even bear to be reminded of hers. If the *kotawal* or his wife ever alluded to it, they were threatened with death.

The princess, however, felt that the pledge was solemn in the eyes of God, however lightly her parents might now regard it in the pride of their power. She said to herself, "Alas, now I feel why my pen dropped from my hands every day. A destiny binds me to the young

Chandana, my parents' pledge must be fulfilled. I must be his wife."

She wept and could not sleep, the floral fan dropped from her hand on her breast; and the next morning a change in her was observed by all. On other days when she came to school, the jingle of her ornaments sounded like the merry hum of bees, but that day she stole into the room like a guilty soul quietly and silently.

They leave the palace.

The teacher marked it and said, "Princess, on other days the sweetness of your voice, while reciting lessons, pleases every one; how is it that your voice to-day seems so dull?" Chandana looked at Puṣpa and Puṣpa looked at Chandana; their eyes met again and she blushed drawing the veil over her face. Then the princess with hands that trembled produced the fig-leaf containing the king's pledge. Both of them said to their *guru*, "Should we, or should we not, keep our parents' pledge?" The teacher felt alarmed when he saw the leaf and read its contents, but collecting himself after a while said in a clear, firm voice, "If you keep the pledge, your seat will be in heaven, if not, your place will be in hell." Then the princess made Chandana sit on the high throne reserved for her in the school, and she sat below where Chandana used to sit. They bowed to their teacher, and the princess laid her ornaments, her bracelets and necklaces, studded with precious stones, at his feet and asked him to accept them as her humble present at the close of her school career. And both of them said, "To help the king to keep his words is to maintain the honour of his kingdom. We leave the city to-day."

Before she had left her father's palace, the princess cooked a good meal herself. It was a great strain on her nerves to leave her father's house for good, and frequently did she wipe away her tears with her *saḍi.* She offered the food to her parents, relations and servants and even to the domestic animals. It was the last time that she was permitted to serve them. Just at the time Chandana signalled to her; as she heard it she did not wait to take her own meal. She ran to Chandana and bowing low at his feet, fainted away. For the whole night Chandana fanned her with the cloth that he tore off from his turban and said to himself, "How can I preserve this jewel stolen from the serpent's hood?"

But she was all right the next morning, and both of them rode on and on, till they reached a cottage standing in the middle of a clearing. It belonged to an old woman, the mother of seven robbers, who had just a moment before gone abroad on their wicked trade. She showed great hospitality to the couple and

In the cottage of the robbers.

marked with delight the precious ornaments on the person of the princess. She gave them rice mixed with gravels, pulse which was old and dry, and a wet hearth and damp fuel. All these caused delay in cooking. The princess and Chandana went to bathe, but the landing steps were made slippery for them by water; and when they tried to come up to the bank by some other way, the old woman cried, "Not that way, dear, it is unclean." And when they tried a different way, the old woman came again and said, "Not thither, my children, there are thorns." By such petty devices she caused delay, expecting her sons to come in the meantime and plunder the guests.

The pair came to the kitchen and the torn turban now stood them in good stead. Fire was kindled by means of it. And they, rightly suspecting danger, came out by the back-door, and got on their horses and fled. The fire on the hearth gave a wrong impression, for, the old woman thought that her guests were busy cooking their meal. But what was her surprise when peeping into their room she found them gone. And from the stall their horses were gone too. She was, however, a very clever woman; for as soon as the couple had entered her house leaving their horses in the stall, she had collected some white seeds. These she had put in small pieces of cloth and tied to the horses' fetlocks. The small bundles had been pierced through with a needle, so that when their riders fled, the seeds fell on the ground by twos and threes all over the track, and as they fell they turned into white flowers. The robbers on return easily overtook the guests by these beautiful signs. There ensued a fight and the six brothers fell as Chandana was a superior swordsman. The seventh implored mercy. The princess said, "No, dear, it is not safe to keep a part of debt, however small; all should be cleared; do the same with an enemy, howsoever lightly you may think of him." But Chandana said, "Foolish, what can he do? he will be our attendant." So the life of the robber was spared and he became their servant. He burnt, however, with vengeance, and when one day Chandana had fallen asleep, killed him with his sword. The princess did not weep but smiled, and said, "What am I to do now?" The robber was very glad at this and said, "All right, now come to my house, dear." The princess assented. So both of them rode back and Puṣpa said, "It is surely a happy day for us both, will you not accept this betel from me?" He, in eagerness, stretched himself forward to receive the betel from the princess, as a sign of her love, and she in the twinkling

Overtaken by the robbers, Chandana kills six and is killed by the seventh.

of an eye cut off his head with a stroke of her sword.

Now she alighted from her horse and threw herself on the ground where her husband's head lay severed from the body; she had so long controlled herself by superhuman efforts but now her tears were unceasing. She held the head close to her breast and cried, "How long, dear, will you remain silent and not talk with me?" "From morn to noon" she wept and "from noon to dewy eve." It was a dark night. The god Çiva and his consort Pārvatī were passing by the sky at this time. The goddess said, "Stop, husband, who is it that is weeping below?" Çiva replied, "No matter, who, let us pass on." Pārvatī said, "That can never be. A woman's lament I hear. O who art thou, unfortunate woman, grieving over a dead child or a dead husband? I must see thee." Then as she looked down below, her eyes met a sad spectacle. A woman was bathing a head, severed from the body, in her tears and crying, "O my husband, O my darling." The goddess was moved by the sight and restored Chandana to life.

Restoration to life.

After thanksgivings and great elation, the couple again rode on, till they reached the house of a flower-woman. She was a witch. As soon as she met them, she eyed them malignantly, and Chandana turned into a goat, but her charm did not affect Puṣpa as she was true and chaste. Puṣpa was dressed like a young soldier. She approached the king of that country and said, "Here am I seeking service in your majesty's personal staff." "What can you do for me; lad, and what should be your pay?" asked the king. "My pay is one shield full of gold coins per day, and I can do what others cannot." The king assented to her demand and employed her. Just then a huge reptile appeared in the city of the king, and swallowed

Puṣpa kills the cobra.

men and beasts every night, for in the night only it made its appearance and none could kill it. It was generally seen by the side of a large tank near the palace and passed by a deep forest abounding with Sāl trees. The young soldier was ordered to kill it. She was busy in the afternoon cutting the tall sāl trees with the fine end of the sword with such wonderful dexterity that the trees stood as before and none could know that they had been cut in the middle. At night a deep uproar mixed with a hissing sound was heard as the serpent moved about in the jungle, and no sooner had it come to the bank of the tank, than the trees touched by it, fell in hundreds upon its body, and the monster lay crushed under their weight. The young soldier next engaged herself in cutting the body to pieces. But when the animal gave up its ghost, there sprang from its body a middle aged woman. She told Puṣpa that she was her mother transformed into that shape because she had failed to fulfil her pledge to the wife of the *kotwal* and Puṣpa recognised in her the queen—her own mother, who also stated that the old king, her father, had become a sweeper in that palace for the sin of his breaking his pledge. And as she said this she died at the spot and where she died a flower plant grew as a memorial.

Not long after Chandana was restored to human form by the grace of Pārvatī who was pleased with Puṣpa's devotion. Puṣpa told Chandana, "What is the good of my life when

The happy end.

my father is a sweeper and my mother died as a serpent because of me?" She was resolved on committing suicide, but Pārvatī's grace again helped them, and the queen got her life back and the king was restored to his kingdom which he had lost by divine curse for breaking the pledge. Chandana and Puṣpa were united in wedlock by the sanction of the king and the queen. The *kotwal* was raised to the status of a feudal chief so that the king was no longer ashamed of calling him a friend and relation. The *kotwal's* wife, now a lady of high rank, became a fast friend of the queen. They now lived in happiness and prosperity for long years.

In the version of Fakir Ram Kavibhuṣaṇa the father of the princess Sakhisona, is King Vikramjit. There is a village called Mogalmāri two miles to the north of Datan which some of our scholars have identified with the ancient historic town of Dantapur in Orissa. At Mogalmāri there are ruins of a palace which people of the locality ascribe to Rājā Vikramjit and they say Sakhisonā of the folk story was the only daughter of that king. A mound of earth is still pointed out there as relics of the schoolroom of the princess where she pledged her hand to the *kotwal's* son. Many places of our country are associated in this way with our legendary heroes and Paurānic characters. But unless we have clear evidence we cannot accept such accounts as historically true. What happens is this. A man gives out a story in respect of some ruins in his locality consulting his fancy, and his statement is taken as a historical fact by the simple village-folk and it passes current throughout the neighbouring locality and goes unassailed from generation to generation. I do not believe that these attempts to connect places with the heroes of legends and popular romances should be treated as having any historical value.

All these stories, I beg to repeat, have been greatly abridged by me, and if the reader wants to compare them and have fuller knowlege of their details he must go back to the originals themselves. If we take up the Muhammadan version for a critical review, we see, as we have already observed, that with the loss of the Hindu ideal of womanly virtue amongst the rank and file of converts to Islam, immodesty in sexual matters was no longer thought of as a matter of serious social condemnation. The lower class of Muhammadans revel in unrestrained language while dealing with the topics of the passion of the flesh. The self-immolation of a Satī, though its propriety is justly called in question on humane grounds, the self-denial and austerities of widowhood enjoined by the Hindu scriptures, the loyalty that does not break after husband's death but continues to inspire a woman's soul through the rest of her life—these ideals of women were withdrawn from the community of converts, and the result was that the folk-lore amongst them degenerated from the standpoint of the high Hindu conception of devotion and purity. The story of Sakhisonā shows this decadence of the lofty Hindu spirit in a striking manner. Sakhisonā with her hair all loose and dishevelled stands on the roof of her palace enjoying the warmth of the sun on a wintry day; her charms are exposed to the gaze of Kumāra who feels the "dart of Cupid

The deterioration of the Hindu ideal of chastity in the Mahomedan version.

pierce his breast outright," and then when they meet in the school he seduces her in the language of a low class debauch. She listens to him with her heart throbbing with passion ; and they meet shamelessly in a room of the palace every night. What a contrast does such a scene of lust, introduced by a Muhammadan writer, offer to that quiet self-control which we find in the original Hindu story ! Pre-nuptial love is unknown in our community but sometimes it finds a place in our folk-tales, as it does in the present case. It is, however, couched in guarded language showing a high sense of sexual purity even amongst our rustic folk. In the Hindu version of this tale, stress is justly laid upon the word of honour and upon the pledge of parents, justifying the abandonment of home in the company of a lover, which divested from any such moral obligation, is in itself a horrible thing to our men and women. Peruse the Hindu tale and nothing will jar against your ears in respect of the elopement of a princess with a youth of humbler rank. The woman stands elevated in your eyes inspite of what she did. And yet what she did was deliberate and well-planned, not conceived at the spur of the moment. A grossly sensuous element, on the other hand, permeates the Muhammadan version. The immodesty of the princess meeting a lover before she is married to' him will strike every

Hindu reader and in our Zenana the women will not bear to hear a story like that. The robber, whose life is spared, feels a passion for the princess, and says or thinks nothing of his murdered brothers. The flower-woman also conceives a passion for Kumāra, whom she transforms into a goat but restores to human shape every night. The writer says "they spend the night in jolly spirits." We need not comment on the conduct of the flower-woman. She may be equal to this action or things even more hineous, but the hero of the tale becomes contemptuous by his tacit submission to the will of the debauched witch. The king seizes the princess when she is forlorn and there is again a love-proposal. The whole story in the Muhammadan version has thus been worked up to pander to a vulgar taste which repels us. We would not have cared to notice the story, were it not for showing how the original Hindu tale has been vitiated in its Muhammadan version ; but let us very clearly state here that we do not believe that the Muhammadan women tell this story in their homes in the shape in which it has come down to us in its printed form. The version current in Muhammadan homes may be truer to the original, and let us believe that it gives a decent and becoming account of Sakhisonā's love and trials. What seems to have happened is this. The

Muhammadan writer, whose readers are no doubt a few rustic men who have just learnt to read the Bengali alphabets, in his zeal for showing himself a dilettante and well skilled in the art of expressing the softer emotions of the human heart, has introduced these incongruous elements into the original Hindu story which is so rigidly pure.

Fakir Rama introduces classical elements in the story.

So far with the Muhammadan version. Let us next say a few words about this story as related by Fakir Rama Kavibhushana in the middle of the 16th century. That Fakir Rama was a true poet admits of no doubt. His taste is rigid and he gives very fine touches showing a real mastery over the poetic art in many of his elegant passages. For instance, he begins his tale with a dialogue between the princess and Chandana. The latter proposes elopement. The princess should leave the palace and both of them go to a different country and live as husband and wife. The indignant princess expresses her vehement rage at this unbecoming proposal and threatens to bring the matter to the notice of the king. This would lead to his immediate execution. But Chandana cites Pauranic examples; how Rāma left the palace and became a beggar for a simple pledge; how Daçaratha died of grief yet dared not break his pledge; how Rāma himself did an act which was blamed as one of questionable integrity, simply because he had pledged his word. These references to Pauranic examples of faithfulness completely conquered her spirit. For being a scholar herself, she dared not violate the ordinances laid down in the holy books. The Puranas guided the social lives of the Hindus of the 16th century. Even the literary characters were bound down by the commandment of these scriptures. The preceptor of Sakhisonā dissuaded her from flying away with Kumāra, but she cited an example from the Rāmāyaṇa referring to the case of the washer-woman who was afraid of scandal in the Uttarākānda; and this completely outwitted the preceptor. The descriptions of Nature given by Fakir Rama are all on classical lines. The animated account of a hurricane is interesting, and so is also that of Sakhisonā's full grown charms on the attainment of womanhood. Her feet are like lotus buds, her eyes soft as those of a gazelle and her face lovely as the moon. These are of course stereotyped objects of comparison which abound in Pauranic literature. But inspite of his classical taste, which is a marked feature of the story related by Fakir Rama, we admire his keen appreciation of the rural element in the original folk-tale which he retains in his version in a considerable measure. His writings show a combination of the classical elements with the rural, and his style is light occasionally verging on the humorous and far from the monotonous and heavy sweep which often repels us in most of the vernacular poems of the Hindu Renaissance.

But when we come to the version of Dakshinaranjan what a sense of relief do we feel! This scholar has taken down the story as told by old women of the country-side. He has added nothing himself. He has even tried, as far as possible, to retain the very language in which these tales were delivered. This takes us back to a state of things which existed in the country before the Muhammadan invasion. Those that are acquainted with Hindu life in the Zenana, especially in the remote Mofussil villages of Bengal, will bear testimony to the fact that time has changed but little of the ideas and thoughts of our womenfolk and even of the dialect they have been speaking for all these long centuries. We find in these country-tales some of the simple charms of old life, before the Brahmin priests had made it a complicated and artificial one. These beauties grow up everywhere in the tale and are abundant as field-flowers. The princess and Chandana take the vow of adherence to a life of devoted love, but they do not swear by gods and goddesses nor by the holy writs nor by the words of the Brahmins. Chandana says "We shall be true

The excellence and genuineness of Dakshinaranjan's version.

as the earth is true where flowers blossom." The flower is the emblem of innocence and truth; and the earth is sacred because the flowers blossom here! When the queen breaks her promise, Chandana's mother—the poor wife of the *kotwal*—comes to the bank of the Putra-sarobara and before the lotuses which were the witnesses of the queen's pledge, sings her lament, the quiet pathos of which appeals to the heart, offering a contrast to the Pauranic allusions made in Fakir Rama's version to prove that breach of promise is not good. Here the *kotwal's* wife says in rhymed verse:—"Oh lotus, why do you blossom still and do not blush and fade for shame? For did she not make a pledge here and has not she broken it here and in your presence? The bank of this lovely tank is no longer sacred. How strange that in spite of the breach of faith that took place here the sun still throws its reflection on this tank by day and the moon and stars by night!"

The princess has a dim knowledge of the pledge given by her royal parents. She comes near the tank and sees the birds Çuka and Sāri perched on the bough of a near tree. The shade of the evening spreads around her and she says: "O birds, Çuka and Sāri, O waters of the tank, can you not tell me what this pledge is? For its fulfilment I am ready to take out a rib of my heart and offer it, if necessary." The ideal of loyalty and devotion is here even more strikingly shown than in Pauranic tales; but they are simple virtues of the innocent human heart, and for following these no Pauranic rules needs be quoted. The plant with its floral wealth, the tank with its transparent water and the lotus in its full-blown beauty appeal to the rural people more than the Brahmins and all their holy writ would perhaps do. The thought of the pledge weighs upon Puṣpamālā, the princess, and makes her sad. The next day, the preceptor marks it. On other days the jingle of the gold cymbals on her feet pleased the ear of everyone that heard it, to-day she steals into the room quietly, and the preceptor says, "How is it that your voice on other days sounded so sweet when you recited your lessons, and to-day it is dull like that of a dry piece of wood?" When the preceptor learns the whole thing about the pledge from Puṣpa and Chandana, and when both of them seek his opinion as to what they should do, he does not play the part of the vociferous Brahmin of the Renaissance giving a catalogue of the Pauranic allusions to bear upon the question, but briefly says, "If one keeps the pledge he goes to heaven, he that violates it, goes to hell." But before this Daniel delivered his judgment, he had sat quiet for a minute with brows that were darkened and pursed up, for he realised the fact well, that his judgment would make the princess, the heiress to the throne of that country, leave the palace and seek a life of poverty and distress. But in his regard for truthfulness, he did not yield to the Brahmanic enthusiast of the Pauranic revival, though he was not at all prolific in his speech like the latter. The princess after hearing this judgment from his Guru, made Chandana sit on the throne, while she sat below; this simple act showed that she elected him as her bridegroom. Without the sound of conch-shells and the recitations of Vedic hymns, and a hundred rites which are held indispensable, they became bound in wedlock in response to the call of a higher duty which gave a solid grounding to love and sentiments. Before they departed they said, "To keep the honour of the pledge of a king is to keep unimpeached the honour of the country; so do we follow this course." The princess took her diamond necklace and bracelets off and offered them as fees to the preceptor. We all feel that he richly deserved them; for even at the risk of everything enviable in this earth, he could not advise the pair to swerve from truth. He knew that if this were known to the king, he would punish him with death.

One thing that strikes us as very remarkable in these stories is the control exercised on feelings and speech of the great characters. This affords a contrast to the literature of the

Pauranic renaissance where descriptions of simple things often weary us by their monotony and unnecessary repetitions. Here the women-

Brevity and want of repetition.

folk are generally the listeners of these tales and they are also the story tellers. This accounts for the excellent brevity—the characteristic of the stories—which as a great poet has said "is the soul of wit." For though we read in modern romances long speeches on love delivered by women, these people of the tender sex are, as a matter of course, averse to such speeches, when their feelings are deep. This is true especially of the Hindu women. One of our great poets has put this in the mouth of his heroine "We are called Abolās (speechless), for though we have mouth, we cannot speak out our sentiments." In fact, deep love is not consistent with long professions. It is silent and full of sacrifices. Words are generally frothy and they often disclose shallowness of the heart. Did ever a mother deliver a long speech to her child to prove how dearly she loved him? Even so it is with nuptial love; when it is deep it scarcely speaks. In the modern Bengali romances, the heroines are given to long speeches and long love-confessions. But here we find the highest and deepest love shewn in action and in sacrifice at every step, but the characters seldom make speeches.

The look of the flower-woman's malignant eyes turned Chandana into a goat. She wove a garland of flowers without the help of thread and blew into the air by her breath. These had no effect upon Puṣpa. For, says the folk-tale, she was chaste and pure. It is interesting to notice that in spite of the many superhuman actions, charms and spells, with which these stories abound, the rural people realised the power of simple truth and faith in a wonderful manner. A woman who was loyal and true and who sacrificed everything for love, and suffered without complaint, was a proof against all kinds of spell. Truth and devotion were the armour against which no witchcraft or charm could stand. Human virtues are appreciated in these simple accounts of rural life in a remarkably convincing manner. Gods and even devils bow to a true heart. This gives the stories a great ethical status. We shall, however, show a striking example of these great human virtues in the typical story of Mālanchamālā of which a full translation will be appended to our concluding lectures.

The country life, with its charms and simplicity and with its deep poetry, finds a most unassumingly fascinating expression in these stories. Not a word more, not a word less than what is required; the words are all to the point, and the descriptions are not made ingenious or heavy by scholarly effusions; the little songs interspersed in the stories are full of poetry, wit or pathos. In this very story of Puṣpamālā, there are many small songs which shine like gems; they were not composed to illustrate classical canons of rhetoric, but coming direct from hearts that were charged with emotions and true pathos, they appeal irresistibly and remind us that there is nothing so beautiful as simplicity. Puṣpa had disguised herself as a warrior but the king's guard while trying to take off the soldier's coat from her body, makes a strange discovery. The folk-tale here introduces a song :—

" How does her rich braided hair become open to the gaze! The green outer skin of the mango had hid its wealth of ripeness but the beak of a crow strikes it, and lo! the golden colour is out. The water weeds had covered the lotus, its soft stalk lay hid under thorns, the bee touches it and lo! a hundred petals spread out and show the full bloom."

This passage reminds us of a few charming lines in Goldsmith's "Hermit." The beauty of words like "বরণ চোরা আম" is untranslatable, and belongs to the rural dialect of this province. Their rich suggestiveness can hardly be conveyed to foreigners.

The descriptions sometimes consist merely of a number of onomatopoetic words. They are, however, more expressive than those which are verbose and written in a grandiloquent classical style. The great reptile, the Çankhinī, that swallowed men and beasts, approaches through the forest lands.

Onomatopoetic words and their pointedness.

"কন্যা শুনেন, গাছ মড় মড়, হাত রুড়্ রুড়্ নিমিষে লেজের দাপটে বন জঙ্গল কাঁপাইয়া শঙ্খিনী সরোবরে নামিল, তিন শোষে সরোবরে কর্দ্দম শোষ করিয়া ডাক ফুকারিয়া চলিয়া গেল।"

These few words call up the hideous imagery of the Çankhinī, which many of our modern writers would fail to produce by writing a number of pages.

CHAPTER V

Four kinds of Folk-Tales

There were four kinds of folk-tales prevalent in Bengal. First of all, to begin with, the *rūpakathās*,—they are simple tales in which the superhuman element predominates. The Rākṣasas, the beasts and celestial nymphs often play the most important parts in these stories. The tales of heroism related in them are sometimes fantastical. The sages of these kinds of tales in Gaul could tell you the age of the moon; they could call the fish from the depths of the seas and cause them to come near the shore; they could even change the shapes of the hills and head-lands; they

The rūpakathās.

could utter incantations over a body cut to pieces, saying, "Sinew to sinew and nerve to nerve be joined" and the body became whole again; the Druid priest could hurl tempests over the seas; the heroes with one stroke of their favourite swords beheaded hills for sport; when they sat down to their food, they devoured whole oxen and drank their mead from vats. In the legend of Mainamati, we find the Haḍi Shiddha displaying similar feats; with golden shoes on his feet he could walk over big rivers; he kindled fire with the water of the Ganges instead of oil; the river was bridged at the mere words of his mouth; at his command the tree laden with fruits drooped low to the earth to yield its treasures to him; the gods came down to offer their services to him; he was so powerful that with his rod he even chastised Yama, the god of death. The attribution of superhuman powers to mortals, held in higher rank than even the immortals, was a special feature of the *rūpakathās* and legends from the 8th to the 10th centuries all over the world. In a tale called the "Field of Bones" in the collection of Bengal folk-tales by Lal Behary Dey, we find a sage, like the Gaelic physician Miach, son of Diancecht, joining the different parts of a dead body by incantations; and the legend of the beautiful nymph Caer, who became a swan every summer and smote Angus with her charms, will ever remind us of many stories current in Bengal like those of Dandi, Jamini Bhan and Chandrāvali, to which reference has already been made. This episode, differing in some of its details in various versions, recurs in many Bengali stories as well as in those of the other parts of the world. The genuine *rūpakathās* and legends all over the world have many strikingly common points in them. Those that are indigenous to Bengali life have the special feature of having some great ethical aim while imparting instruction with amusement to the young. It is now admitted by European scholars that many episodes of the Arabian Night's Tales owe their origin to Indian stories, such as are to be found in the Kathāsaritsāgara. The story of Saharia and Sahajeman is an Arabic adaptation of the story of the two Brahmin youths and their religious sacrifice described in that Indian work. The story of Sindabad the sailor, that of the King, the prince, and seven ministers, of Geliad, his son and minister Senmash, in the Arabian Night's Tales, are derived from Sanskritic sources. We have already mentioned how the Panchatantra which professed to teach the princes of Pataliputra rules of conduct and politics, presented in the garb of animal stories, got a world-wide circulation. This represents one of the forms of *rūpakathās*. But the true *rūpakathās* are those where fair ones are won by the heroic feats of dauntless princes and young merchants after a conquest over the Rakṣasas or achievements of other feats equally hazardous and glorious. These at one time carried the young children breathless through every stage of narration; the spirits of the air, the beasts of the forest and the monsters of the deep took part in human affairs in these stories creating a romance which produced and excited interest around the hearth of each family.

Often in particular classes of *rūpakathās*, the human powers were exaggerated, till imagination feasted itself to a satiety, and in Eastern tales the romance of these was not bound by time and space, but transcended limits of all sorts. In the Edda the giant Skrymmer notices the dreadful blows of Thor's hammer as the falling of a leaf. In the English story of Jack the giant-killer, Jack under similar circumstances, says that a rat had given him three or four slaps with its tail. But these feats are nothing as compared to those described in the Bengali tale called "The wrestler 22-men-strong, and the wrestler 23-men-strong." The tale is a typical one showing the wild excesses of Eastern imagination. The wrestler 22-men-strong heard that there lived in another part of the world a wrestler 23-men-strong. His

The wrestler 22-men-strong and the wrestler 23-men-strong.

pride was wounded, so in great rage he started for the country of his rival who claimed the strength of one man more than himself, in order to challenge him to a fight. In his hurry he forgot to take his meal. But on his way he found that his bag contained 24 maunds of flour. Where was the plate to be found from which he could eat so much food? Finding a tank on his way he threw the flour into it and then quaffed off the whole mixture. This appeased his hunger for a time. He now took a mid-day nap, but a wild elephant that had come to drink water from that tank was enraged to see it emptied of its liquid, and trampled the wrestler under its feet; the sleeping man was disturbed, and half-opening his eyes from which sleep had not yet vanished, gave a slap which killed the animal as though it were a gnat, and then he turned on his back and slept again.

Arising from his sleep the wrestler came to the house of his rival 23-men-strong, and knocked at his gate. But as no one responded to his call, he kicked at the earth as a sign of his rage, and this caused a great sound. A girl nine years old came out and wonderingly said, "You, a man? I thought the cat of the house was scratching the earth as it does every day?" The wrestler felt himself humbled by this remark, for his feats were belittled by a girl and declared to be worthy of a cat. Then reclining upon a tall palm tree he asked the girl where the wrestler 23-men-strong was. "You mean my father, wait a bit, he will come presently. He has gone to the river side," said the girl and added "Dont push the palm tree in that way, it may fall down." "Why, what if it does?" The girl repiled "My father will make a tooth-brush with it, when it grows stronger." The wrestler did not relish this remark also and wondered what the man would be like, who thought of making a tooth-brush with such a tall palm-tree. He did not wait, but ran to the river side to meet his rival. They met and forthwith began to fight.

An old woman with a herd of goats was passing that side, and seeing the two wrestlers fighting, said "Children, forbear your play for a moment, and let me pass." The wrestlers stopped fighting and wondered that such giants as they were could be addressed as children and their fight described as play! But the woman did not wait long; she took the fighting heroes upon her shoulders and forgot all about them, and tying her cows and buffaloes to her apron, passed by. The king of birds Gaḍura was passing by the sky above them at this moment and he saw the prospect of a good feast, and carried in his beak the woman with all that she carried.

There lived a king in a certain country who had a daughter. She was taking rest on a couch on the roof of her palace, and one of her attendant maids was narrating a *rūpakathā* to her. The breeze was pleasant and the princess enjoyed it no less than the tale, when suddenly she rose up from her bed and said, "Maid, see what has fallen into my right eye, it may be a dust-grain." The maid took a straw in her hand and put a bit of cotton around it, and then with its help drew out the dust-grain. The princess felt a little pain in the eye from which fell a drop of tear. The dust-grain when brought out proved to be nothing less than the woman with two fighting men on her shoulders and with a whole herd of beasts tied to her apron! The gentle breeze that the princess enjoyed was a cyclone which had caused the king of birds to throw the woman from his beak! The dwellers of Brobdingnag who are "as tall as an ordinary spire-steeple" sink into insignificance before this mighty host of the Bengali tale.

These *rūpakathās* introducing nymphs and fairies, where the hero and the heroine suffer for their love and pass through risks and sacrifices in an adventurous spirit, have interest for the young as well as the old, rousing the imagination of the former and old memories of the latter. And what people of the world have not heard these in their infancy, and not admired them with all the warmth and eagerness of their souls ? Sometimes the grim and terrible element in these tales fills the young minds with awe, and sometimes the picturesque natural sceneries drawn in a few lines—the flowers of the valley, the evening stars and moon light—diffuse a charm which make a lasting impression on the young. And many a time and oft the story carries them through the dangers passed by the hero,—in the land of Rakṣasas or of giants or in cities depopulated by tigers or cobras. And the young listeners sigh and pray for the end of the hero's troubles and when he is restored to his love's arms, feel extreme gratification and sense of relief. Sometimes as in the story of the Field of Bones, the stillness of a dark night, in the depth of an impenetrable forest, mixed with awful incantations and the grimness of Tantrik worship, recalling the dead to life, awaken the soul to mystic emotions and thoughts that transcend the limits of time and space. In stories like that of "The Origin of Opium," through the various stages of ambition presented in the form of a legend, the ethical lesson that contentment and not self-aggrandisement should be the true object to be aimed at, prepares the temperament of the young aspirant to high moral life.

Humorous tales.

The next species of folk-tale in Bengal consists of those in which there is an attempt at humour. These may not be often too pointed and subtle, but they show the power of appreciating humorous situation by the rural-folk in their own simple way. They call up associations of merry laughter of children and smiles on the bashful lips of youthful women. One of them begins in this way :

Habuchandra and Gabuchandra.

" There was once a king whose name was Habuchandra. His minister was called Gabuchandra.

" The king was the very jar of wisdom and the minister a palm-tree of sagacity.

" Both kept company day and night, and did not leave each other for a moment.

" How could injustice prevail in a kingdom ruled by such a pair of prodigies ? They were determined to protect the country from harm in every way.

" The king used to laugh loudly, ho—ho—ho at every thing, and the rejoinder was sure to come from the minister who in his deep-mouthed voice coughed kho—kho—kho.

" Each admired the other's wisdom and was full of praises of the other.

" The king had a wall raised round his Audience Hall, his minister kept his nostrils and ears shut by putting a quantity of cotton in them. This was a precaution lest the royal and ministerial wisdom should disappear from the court.

"It happened one day that a boar passed near the palace making a sound with its nose, *ghonth, ghonth, ghonth.* The king saw the animal and said, 'What is it, minister?' The minister looked at it with scrutinizing eyes, and said, 'Your Majesty's servants in charge of the stall are thieves. This is an elephant famished and reduced to this size; the servants have not evidently provided it with food.'

"At once an order was passed to imprison the servants belonging to the royal stall!

"Another day the same boar passed by the palace again. The king looked at it and said, 'How is it, minister, that the elephant has not improved in size though the servants have been punished.'

"The minister said, 'Your Majesty, this is a mouse, for were it an elephant, its trunk would have come out by this time. The kingdom is in a great peril. The mice have become fat, feeding on the royal store.'

"'Does the matter even stand so?' cried the indignant king. Orders were at once passed to behead the sentinels of the royal store.

"The royal store was now saved by the sagacity of the king and his minister; they drew a breath of relief and sat in a chamber after this great labour and the servants fanned them in order to remove the weariness caused by the toil of administration."*

The story goes on to narrate a number of episodes illustrative of the sagacity of the king and his minister, and the humour throughout, though not pointed as a needle, is neither blunt as a wooden sword. They best show the joys and merriments of simple village-folks, and are purely indigenous in character. The sequel is worthy of the beginning, comic and tragic at the same time. The king, counselled by the minister, orders the execution of a man, as innocent as you or I, on a charge of heft. A stake is raised for the impalement of this criminal. And the king and the minister are present to see to the carrying out of their command. Now the *Guru* of this unfortunate man came to the spot at that moment and cried out, "Do not put him to the stake for god's sake ; let not a criminal be rewarded in the way deserved by saints." "What is the matter ?" "What is the matter ?" asked the king and his minister with gaping mouths. Now the *Guru* who was dressed as a hermit said, "I have found it in the holy writs that the man who is impaled at this most auspicious moment will go to heaven straight, no matter what heinous crime he may have

* Dakhina Ranjan's Thakurmar Jhuli.

committed in this earth ; so keep his punishment in abeyance for a while, and put me on the stake instead, so that I may at once pass from earth to the heaven." The minister said, "This cannot be, if this death is so glorious, why should an outsider be rewarded with it? Put me there." But His Majesty whose imagination was inflamed by the description of the nymphs of heaven that he had heard, cried aloud, "The king must go to heaven first." So by his royal order he was impaled by the executioner and by his wish loud music was kept up all the while drowning his screams, and when the crowd at last saw him, they found him stone-dead, with a horrible grimace on his face.

The fox in charge of the tortoise's young ones.

There are many stories that we heard in our childhood containing rural sketches full of humour and jovial spirits, and not in an inconsiderable portion of them are the animals, the chief actors. The fox is often the hero of these stories. In one of the tales we find him in the capacity of a village pedagogue. The tortoise has seven young ones; he is anxious for their education and leads them to the school of the veteran teacher. The wily fox is well pleased to see the young ones and casts on them hungry looks, but says he, "You need not at all care for them now. Their interest is my look-out from this day." The tortoise now goes back fully convinced of the sound education its young ones will get at the hands of such a well known scholar as the fox. On the third day, his fatherly care made him feel some anxiety about them and he paid a visit to the school-master. One of the seven had meantime served for the light refreshment of the latter, but the cunning fellow brought the little things one by one and showed them to their father, the sixth one was brought twice so that he could not perceive any diminution in their number. In this way when all but one remained, the cunning fox brought it out and then took him back to his school chamber and in this way produced it seven times, on which the tortoise felt that all the seven were alive and doing well. But when the wily animal had finished that one also, the tortoise on his visit again was told that his seven young ones had completed their school-education and gone to college for higher academic distinction. How long could such a pretext hold water? The tortoise now realised the truth that his young ones had gone up indeed to a higher world but through the jaws of the wicked Reynard. And he took a solemn vow of retaliation. One day the old fox was crossing a canal and the tortoise caught one of his legs tightly within his jaws. "Ha'-Bah!" cried the prince of cunning, whose presence of mind never failed him. "What a narrow escape!

The foolish tortoise has but caught a log by his teeth, my legs are quite free." Whereupon the latter let it go, thinking that it was a mistake on his part. Another day the fox was thinking to how to cross the small canal. He had urgent business on the other side, but dared not cross the canal lest the tortoise who was on the alert, might catch him again. The tortoise was weary of waiting, and at last showed himself on the surface of the water. He abused the fox to his heart's content and said that there was no escape from him, sooner or later. The fox also gave replies which enraged the tortoise. In his indignation he floated in mid-water in a careless manner; and lo! clever Reynard sprang up in all haste and resting his feet for a moment on the back of his enemy went to the other side of the canal by a heroic leap. "Ha'-Bah!" cried Reynard safely landing on the other bank, and the tortoise felt greatly disappointed. The tortoise thought "The wily fox outwits me in this way each time but I will prove too clever for him this time." He came up to the bank of the canal and landing ashore closed his eyes and lay like one dead. "The old fool Reynard must take me for a corpse and come to partake of my flesh. Let me wait." The fox came up there as usual for an evening walk and noticed the father of the deceased young ones lying there inert and motionless. In a moment he understood the device of the tortoise and said: "The tortoise, poor fellow, is dead. But stop, I am not sure if he is completely dead; for he does not shake his ears as tortoises do when they die." The tortoise thought that it must be a sign of death of the species to which he belonged, to shake the ears after death. So he gently shook his ears as a convincing proof of death. But the fox said: "The tortoises open their eyes after death and shut them again." Whereupon the foolish animal did as he was told, shutting his eyes after opening them once. Reynard approached him and gave him a kick and fled in all haste into the depths of the forest. This part of the story has a parallel in the story of a hare and a fox current among the Negroes.

The *brata kathās*.

The third class of these stories comprises the *brata kathās* or tales interspersed with hymns and attended with religious observances. Some of these seem to have come down to us from hoary antiquity. The deities addressed are those for the most part to whom the Aryan pantheon has not opened its doors. Their names are unknown and non-Sanskritic, and the mode of their worship is strange. The deities called the Thuā, five in number, are to be made with clay. Their conically shaped figures are like miniature pyramids and the hymns addressed to them are couched in the oldest form of the Bengali dialect akin to Prākṛita. The meaning of this mystic hymn is not very clear.

The language of the hymns.

"থুথু থুয়ন্তি
আঘন মাসের জুয়ান্তি
অকালে ভাতন্তি
সকালে পুতন্তি
বনে বনে আয়তি
ধনে জনে স্বয়তি
থুয়া পুজে মোরা জন্মায়তি॥"

The origin of the worship of the Bengali woman's god Lāul is also lost in obscurity. Like Thuā he is represented by a conically shaped piece of clay. This is covered with floral decorations, and two sticks of flowers representing two arms are attached to the figure; but this seems to be a later innovation. The religious observances in regard to Thuā and Lāul seem to be a sort of pyramid-worship; and it is difficult at this stage to say if these forms of worship belonged to the indigenous non-Aryan population, or were introduced by the Dravidians or some other people. One point to be noticed in regard to such worship is that the elderly women of the Aryan homes seem to have been originally opposed to them. It is the young wife that introduces them at the teeth of great opposition. This we find in the sacred tales by which every such worship is consecrated. The Aryans did not at first tolerate these practices; but the brides were initiated into the rites probably by the non-Aryan people with whom they came in contact and amongst whom the Aryan homes were built. In the stories attached to the worship of these local deities, we find the mothers-in-law resenting the practices, nay sometimes setting their feet on the sacred things with which the wives worshipped these deities privately. We all know that the worship of Chaṇḍī and Manasā Devī was not at first favoured in the Aryan homes. The young wives introduced it at great sacrifice on their part and bore all manner of oppression for doing so.

The indeginous form of worship among the non-Aryans.

To some of the deities of this nature, such as Chāṇḍī and Manasā Devī, the Brahmin priest opened his temple-door latterly. They were connected in some form or other with the legends of Hindu mythology. But Thuā and Lāul are worshipped by womenfolk alone, without being recognised by the Brahmins, and are now in their last struggle for existence in Bengal. The archaic forms of words in the hymns addressed to these deities carry us to the 8th or 9th century A.D. and even earlier times; and there

Admitted to the the Aryan pantheon.

is no lack of other internal evidences to prove that some of these forms of worship originated when the Bengalis were at the height of maritime activities. The chart of worship of the goddess Bhāduli is full of symbolical things denoting sea-voyage. There are seven seas, thirteen rivers, the sandy sea beach, rafts, sea fowls, palm tree, etc., in the chart. The prayers all refer to the safe landing on the home-shore of those dear ones and relations gone by sea to distant countries :—

Evidence of maritime activity in the tales.

"Oh river, Oh river, whither do you run?
Before you pass by, say something of my father and his son.
Where do you go so fast, Oh river, Oh river,
Tell me how my husband and father-in-law fare.
Oh sea, Oh sea, peace be with thee, grant what I pray,
My brother has gone for trade, may he return to-day.
Oh sea, Oh sea, peace be with thee, hear what I say.
My father has gone for trade, may he return to-day.
Oh raft, Oh raft, dweller of the high seas thou art.
Keep my father and brother safe from all harm and hurt.
Oh sea-heach, Oh sea-beach, smile when they pass by thee.
Watch them, keep them safe, this boon grant me.
Oh sea-fowls, Oh sea-fowls, tell me I beseech thee.
Where did you see the ship, that carries them in the sea?"

The little girls worship the image of the sea, of the rivers, sea-fowls, and rafts, preparing the figures by a solution of powdered rice, and address these short prayers and hymns, wishing the safe return of those dear and near to them, engaged in sea-voyage. Who the goddess Bhāduli is, no one can tell. In one of the hymns, she is called the mother-in-law of Indra, as Lāul is called in another passage the elder brother of Civa. These are no doubt mere attempts to connect them in some way or other with the deities of the Hindu pantheon. Bhāduli is worshipped in the month of August, when the rivers are full and the monsoons are high, and the anxiety of tender hearts becomes greatest in respect of their husbands, fathers and brothers whose ships not so secure by scientific methods and appliances, as now, were often a plaything of the deep. The little girls observed fasts and prayed to the raft, the seabeach, the ship and the sea-fowls to keep their kith and kin in safety. There is a simplicity and tender pathos in these unassumingly beautiful prayers of the child's heart which cannot but appeal. The images of men and women are drawn in *alipana* paintings and this is an essential rite and part of the ceremony of worship. These figures are often like crosses; a line is drawn in addition, to each cross towards the end; for otherwise the figure would have but one leg. These are also made of clay and sold in the country-side. A distinguished European scholar once expressed great surprise at seeing one such clay figure, and told me that it was the exact likeness of some of those clay-figures which Mr. Evans discovered along with other things in Crete, all belonging to about 3000 B.C.

The agricultural element.

The agricultural element, an indispensable factor of country life in Bengal, is in evidence in most of these songs and tales. We find that in the Çunyapurāṇa, written in the 10th century, Çiva appears to us as an agricultural god engaged in reaping the harvest and doing other field work, with the help of his chief assistant Bhīma. The peasantry of the country-side attributed their own calling to the deity, in order to bring him nearer to their comprehension. There is a humour which almost reaches a pathetic interest in the description of Çiva applying lime water to the roots of rice-plants in order to destroy insects. Well is it said, that if a bull were to make an image of its god, the horns would be considered indispensable for such a divinity. Some of these *bratakathās* attribute an agricultural life to Indra as the Çunyapurāṇa does to Çiva. One of these runs thus:—

"Where is the god Indra?
Indra is husking rice."

One of the most popular of these Bratas, or religious rites performed by our girls, is the *Sejuti*. In the prayers and songs relating to this *brata*, we have a vivid sketch of the Hindu girls of the old school with their ideas and feelings. The typical girl of our society expresses in simple language all that she feels to the deity she worships. Her ambition, her sweetness of temper and even bitterness of feeling and jealousy are all expressed in her prayers. There is much crudeness but the simplicity is most attractive. There are prayers for a pretty son being born to the mother; "Let me be borne in a stately palanquin from my father's house to my father-in-law's" is suggestive of a desire of being married to a rich husband; "May the refuse in the plate of my brother be the meal for others." "May my brother be lovely as the moon-beams." "May he be a favourite in the king's court"; "May I eat off a plate of gold and may I wear golden bracelets"; "Oh god Çiva, Oh god sun, may I not be married to an illiterate man"; "May my husband be a prince;—elephants at his door and steeds in his stall, heaps of grain husked in his courtyard and cows breeding evermore in the cow-shed, and may we have a son of a swarthy colour." The liking for a child of a swarthy colour is inherent in the Hindu mother with

The hopes, aspirations and wishes of Bengali girls.

her love for the child Kṛṣṇa of the religious legend of her country. "May I have a son in my lap, and one in my arms, and may I have a *sāḍī* of Benares-silk to wear in the night"; "May I be a sister of seven brothers."

With a solution of powdered rice she makes a bracelet and with joined hands she prays, "I worship thee, Oh bracelet of powdered rice, may I have a pair of golden bracelets, grant me this boon." Then she makes a kitchen, a cow-shed and a dwelling house with the same material and prays to them each, in the aforesaid manner that she may have these made of bricks. She prays also for diamonds and jewels to wear in her person. Her concluding prayer is, however, the purest gem amongst her sincere expressions of the heart: "I take a vow of *sejuti* worship so that I may be as virtuous as Savitrī."

But if the above show her crude simplicity and anxiety to lead a virtuous life, she is not free from that fear which was once a Hindu girl's nightmare. In those days Hindu girls were plagued by a number of co-wives; and the favours and likings of the husband fluctuated whimsically, but invariably with the approach of age in his consort the favourite of to-day became the cast away of to-morrow. The fear in respect of a co-wife was, as I have said, the very nightmare of her existence, and this will be illustrated from the following :—

"Oh mirror, Oh mirror, may I not have a co-wife.
"Oh squirrel, Oh squirrel, keep my husband in peace but eat my co-wife's head.
"Oh broom, Oh broom, may my co-wife never have a child.
"Oh bird, Oh bird, may my co-wife die below and I behold her death from above.
"May her sleeping-room be the hut for husking rice and there may she die.
"Oh knife, Oh knife, here do I dress vegetables with thy help for a feast to be given on my co-wife's death.
"What is the red dye that adorns my feet? you ask, it is the blood of my co-wife whom I have killed."

We have some very old specimens of the songs of the sun-god, which at one time were recited by girls and young women. The sun was probably called Viṣṇu in the earlier Riks. In fact, in Vedic literature there are enough hints suggesting that the word Viṣṇu implied the sun-god amongst the Hindus in ancient times. Even in the days of Rāmāyaṇa the Viṣṇu of the line "বিষ্ণুনা সদৃশোবীর্য্যে সোমবৎ প্রিয়দর্শনঃ seems to signify the solar god. The sun according to the Ptolemaic theory, as also that of the early Hindus, made his round through the solar system. The theory of Copernicus gives this motion to the earth. According to the Hindus the sun met

The legend of the sun-god.

the constellations রাধা, অনুরাধা, বিশাখা and passed through কালিয় হ্রদ মণ্ডল, কংসমণ্ডল and other signs of the Zodiac of the Vedic times in its course. The worshippers of the sun-god, created legends out of this astronomical theory, describing the marriage of the sun-god, and his play with his planetary companions. In a song of the sun-god we find him in a boat with 1,600 Gopis or milk-maids. It is quite probable that these 1,600 maids were meant to symbolize the innumerable planets of the solar system. Whatever it be, there are good grounds for believing that Viṣnu or the sun-god of the Vedic hymns became in later times identified with Kṛṣṇa and as the worship of the sun-god lost popular favour in preference to the worship of Kṛṣṇa, the legends that had gathered round the bright luminary of the day in a previous epoch of history all passed to Kṛṣṇa, who ousted the former from the temples of this country—the popular Vaiṣnava religion of to-day thus seems to have evolved out of the worship of the sun-god.

The song, to which reference has been made seem to have been composed in the 10th century or so, judging not only from its crude language, but also from the fact that the forms of worship and the legends which they treat of, were those of that early epoch of our religious history.

Like a thing carried by the waves from the Atlantic or the Pacific ocean to the shores of Bengal, these literary and historical relics, the subjects of the songs, have come floating to us from the Vedic or Upanishadaic times.

The young sun-god, in this song has attained a fit age ; yet his parents do not think of marrying him. "The beautiful saḍis of two Brahmin girls have been spread to the sun,—the young sun-god casts a longing look at them,—O mother of the sun-god, he is now grown up, why not get him married ? A girl on the other side of the river is sitting with her hair spread before the sun,—look there, how the young sun-god roves about in order to see that hair.

Oh mother of the sun-god, why not yet get him married, he is quite grown up.

Another Brahmin girl walks with the cymbals jingling on her feet. The young sun-god goes so far as to propose to marry her. Why not get him married ; he is quite grown up."

My audience should excuse any indecent suggestion in this rustic song. This was the way how the old village people felt that the time was ripe when they should look for brides, for their young lads.

But the real pathos of the song is centred in the touches with which young Gaurī's marriage and separation from parents are described. She is below twelve, she must sever all connection with her parents at this tender age. The relatives bless her saying,—

"Go O Gaurī, weeping to-day, but come to-morrow smiling and rejoicing."

As the boat carrying her passes through the stream that flows fast by the village, Gaurī says to the boat-man, "Brother boat-man, ply your oars slowly, my mother is crying, let me hear her voice a little more; Oh my brother boat-man, ply the boat slowly, my sisters are crying, let me catch their sound; Oh brother boat-man do not ply your boat so fast, yet my brothers are crying, let me hear their voice a little more." At the time she left home the relations were weeping, for she was a little girl and never stayed even a day away from her home. Her father hid his face in his scarf and wept. With a basket, full of toys, with which they used to play together, Gouri's brothers and sisters wept, but her mother threw herself on the bare earth and cried beating her head against a stone. The little girls after their marriage, went to their husbands' home and were subjected to the maltreatment of their sisters-in-law and mothers-in-law. This accounts for the tender pathos of such situations.

But the Hindu wife, in that tender age had need of parents and brothers and sisters. She could not think of her husband alone as satisfying all the needs of her tender mind. The home meant to her, the home of parents and it would take years for her to grow up and accept her mate as her all absorbing care. How touching is the following conversation between the grown-up husband and his girl-wife ! So long her parents were ministering to her wants and now she feels helpless not knowing exactly on whom to depend.

"I shall go to your country, my husband, but ill will it fare with me when I am in need of apparel."

"In my fair cities a colony of weavers will I found for you."

"I shall go with you, my husband, ill will it fare with me when I want shell-bracelets for my hands."

"In my fair cities will I make the bracelet-makers dwell, who will cut shells to adorn your hands."

"I shall go to your country, my husband, but where shall I get vermilion for my brow."

"From the adjacent countries will I import Bānias to my fair cities to sell vermilion to you."

"I shall go to your country, my husband, but where will a supply of rice come from ?"

"In my fair cities the ploughmen will be busy reaping harvests for you, my love."

"I shall go to your country, my husband, but who will be my mother there."

"I have my mother and she will be a mother to you."

"I shall go with you, my husband, but who will be my father there?"

"My father will be your father as well."

"I shall go with you, my husband, but who will be my brothers and sisters there?"

"My brothers and sisters will, my darling, be brothers and sisters unto you."

In our country, the gods are not unapproachable divinities—the dwellers of high heaven, they are merely those whom we see around us in our home. The rustic songs draw the gods after the models of the rural people. Hence so much tenderness attaches itself to the tales of the gods.

In this song, there is frequently a reference to money received by a girl's parents from the bridegroom at the time of marriage. In one place, I find Gaurī's mother began to weep and cry (when Gaurī left her parents for her husband's home), but she tied Rs. 1,000 in the edge of her sāḍi. The consideration received by the girl's mother was nearly tantamount to her price with all its legal bindings. In one place, Gaurī, the young girl was unwilling to go and wept, "Oh my papa, Oh my mama, won't you keep me near you?"

"But we have taken money before the whole village people, how can we keep you?"

Alas, these old good days are gone. In those days a daughter used to be called কন্যা-রত্ন which suggests a purchase value. How the social aspect is changed, not daughter, but the son is a valuable thing in the Bengali matrimonial market.

The rural songs have a simple charm of their own,—even now, when refined ideas and Sanskritized Bengali have driven the charming things of the village into a corner. These songs sometimes under a religious garb and at others without any such garb at all,—indicate the soft feelings, the sorrows and joys that are nourished every day under the shade of green mangoe trees in a Bengali village. I remember to have heard a Bengali shepherd, a lad of barely 16,—filling the whole air with the pangs of a widow's heart, conveyed in a song which he sang one evening, while returning from the field. The widow of the song is young and just stricken by her great calamity. I remember a line "Oh my darling, why have you left me—making me helpless, driving me mad with sorrow! In some past life did I purchase fish from a fisherman and forgot to pay the price, for that fault am I a young widow to-day." Alas! the Bengali widows are not allowed to take fish or meat of any sort, the passage has therefore a special appeal for us.

The Gīta Kathās.

It is the fourth class of these folk-tales that are by far the most important of all. They are the *Gīta Kathās*, lit., tales interspersed with songs. In Eastern Bengal, old widows of the humbler classes, assisted by a chorus, used to recite them before ladies of high rank during the days of their confinement. On the sixth night particularly, when the Fortune god—the Vidhātā Puruṣa—is said to come down in order to write on the forehead of the baby its future fortunes, the mother and her attendants remain awake ; and how can they do so better than by listening to the stories narrated by these story-tellers ? These *gīta kathās* are not merely nursery tales. For the education of women, according to the ideals of the East, there cannot be anything more sublime or edifying. They smell of fresh grass and field-flowers that grow plentifully by the country-side and in them are embodied lessons of the highest renunciation and sacrifice. Some of them are distinctly and peculiarly Indian ; so that none of the foreign nations that have imitated or adapted many of the Indian tales could reproduce them in their own language or assimilate them in their stories.

Babu Dakṣiṇā Rañjan Mitra Majumdār has done yeoman's service to the cause of Bengali literature by collecting some of these. The first edition of his Thākurdādār Jhulī reproduces the stories almost as he heard them from old women of the rural villages of Eastern Bengal. Their very language is preserved in this edition, as it was in some cases recorded by means of phonograph. The story of Mālañchamālā which is typical of these tales, and has unique excellence, was obtained from an old woman of the Yugī caste. This woman was aged over 100. People said she was 150 years old at the time. She was an inhabitant of a village near Pinger in the sub-division of Tangail in the district of Mymensingh. The stories of Thākurdādār Jhulī were collected during the years 1896-1902. As the language of the first edition of this book proved too archaic and antiquated, the compiler at the request of his publishers had to change it in some places in the later editions. But though the language in the new editions is now closer to current Bengali, the intrinsic worth of the tales has to some extent suffered by the change. It must, however, be said in favour of these changes that the book could not have commanded the popularity that it now enjoys, if the archaic forms had not been changed in many places. But the alterations are not always happy. When an army marched in a hurry, what a dash and sweep of the movement of a large mass of human beings is implied by the line "জলা জাঙ্গাল নদ নদী

উজাইয়া বুজাইয়া" (p. 18, first edition), which means that the low marshy swamps were raised to the level of plain land and the rivers were run up the stream and crossed, but this translation scarcely conveys the precipitous hurry and the dash implied in the original line. This line is omitted in later editions. The words "দণ্ডধরের পুতি" (lit., the son of the wielder of the sceptre, p. 22), "বায় বাতাস নিগুম" (p. 20) "থির থাপাল কর্যা" (p. 25), "নিরবাতি আঁধারপুরী" (p. 40), "বায় বাতাস" (p. 49), "দেখলে বাঁয় থামারে" (p. 49), "নিগুম নিশুতি রাতে" (p. 55), "গহিন পাতার নীচে" (p. 127), "দুয়ারে পাথালে মানুষ" (p. 131), and many such expressions have been changed or paraphrased in a simpler language in the succeeding editions. What words can convey the awful stillness of the night so powerfully as "নিগুম নিশুতি রাতি"? The very word "নিগুম" which means "without sound" and "নিশুতি" which means "merged in profound slumber" recall to us by association the terrible calm of a midnight in a child's dream. Put any Sanskritic expressions in the place of these two Prakritic words, however pompous and grand they may be, they will fail to make a similar impression. But we, in whose ears still ring some of the powerful expressions of country-Prakrit by associations of childhood, do understand and appreciate their rural charm and significance. Our younger generations accustomed

The Thakurdādār Jhuli, its first edition as contrasted with later editions.

to Sanskritic words have not learnt their meanings partly because they have lost touch with the old country-life, and partly because the present vocabularies scrupulously avoid illuminating scholars about Prakrit expressions, confining themselves to Sanskritic words. It was therefore prudent from the publisher's point of view to change এহি into এই (p. 53), একহি into এক (p. 58), বিহা into বিয়া (p. 60). But the old fascination still lingers in the archaic forms and the same literary beauty, I am afraid, is not preserved in the tales.

How unfortunate is it to substitute গহিন পাতা by কচি পাতা (p. 127). গহিন means impenetrably dense. In our childhood we understood by this density as if it could not be pierced by the point of a needle. কচি means tender.

But the versions of the tales given by Dakṣiṇā Rañjan, in spite of the occasional changes in the style, which he was obliged to make in view of making them suitable for popular use, possess a unique merit. Sir Rabindranath Tagore has written in his introduction to one of these compilations that no other man in Bengal has succeeded in reproducing the tales in the popular dialogue so well as Dakṣiṇā Babu has done. The compiler put aside his own learning, his own notions, and his own language and did almost the part of an automatic machine. Thus the old world is here with its antiquated forms, with its mannerisms and with its ideals, unvarnished and unmolested by modern influences. The old Bengali life of the 10th century is vividly before us in the story of Mālaṇchamālā. The professional women who used to recite these tales in the palaces of the kings as well as in the huts of the poor had a formed style with fossilised ideas. The stops, the sighs, and even the caughings passed from one generations of reciters to the others, preserving the original stories in a really wonderful manner, not indeed like the Egyptian mummy which is lifeless, but like a flower-woman's wreath, fresh with life and fragrance. If the stories were not preserved in this manner, how could an illiterate woman, who did not even know how to sign her name, reproduce such an excellent thing as the tale of Mālañchamālā ? Dakṣiṇā Rañjan got it from one of these women, as an automatic record. In reading these tales, we need not attach any importance to the name, that appears on the cover, of one who compiled them except for the purpose of grateful acknowledgment of his unselfish labour. He had simply acted as a medium in bringing down to us a treasure that lay hidden in the rustic villages of Bengal. He did not, like Harināth Majumdār, build a new tale out of the materials of the past, nor did he, like Lāl Bihāri Dē, give a

Dakṣiṇā Rañjan compared with other compilers of Bengali folk-tales.

gist of the stories in another tongue, nor like the Mahomedan writers did he introduce into the stories foreign elements divesting them of their original elegance ; neither did he like Fakir Rām Kavibhuṣaṇa try to invest the old stories with a classical dignity and adorn them with borrowed metaphors from Sanskrit. Dakṣiṇā Rañjan is an elegant writer of Bengali prose and we can well conceive what a control he had to exercise on himself in order to shut himself up altogether while compiling these stories. But a deep love for the rural life inspired him ; and merged in his cause he forgot himself altogether like all great workers.

We shall attempt here to reproduce the story of Mālaṇchamālā, as we find it, in Dakṣiṇā Babu's compilation. As some of the great merits of Bengali tales will not be understood or recognised until the readers find an opportunity to be acquainted with this story, I may be excused for introducing a full narrative here at this fag-end of my lectures. There are many stories which may be more or less elegant and attractive than this, but it presents the old ideal of womanhood in the most striking manner, and is typical of the great virtues of the fair sex as conceived by the Hindu nation.

Malanchamala

The King is childless.

His Majesty called all the astrologers, all the Brāhmaṇs and all the hermits of his country, and had sacrifices performed by them with a view to having a son. At the end of the ceremonies, the Sacred Oracle said :

The story of Mālañchamāla.

"Observe fast, O king, for three days and three nights. On the fourth day pay a visit to your orchard. In it you will find a pair of mangoes of golden hue. Break your fast with them."

The Oracle further had it that the fruit on the right side should be taken by the king and that on the left by the queen.

The king gets a son.

By the king's order all music in the palace was stopped, the royal court remained closed for three days. His Majesty shut himself up in his room bolting its doors. For three days and nights the king observed fast and vigil. On the fourth day the favourite horse of his stall, the Pakṣīrāj, stood near his door-way. The king took his bath and performed the usual religious rites. He bowed to the sacred dust of the temples and then rode the Pakṣīrāj. Instantly he was in the orchard. There was a mango-tree in this orchard that had not borne any fruit for three generations ;

this tree presented two beautiful mangoes of the colour of gold. The king rubbed his eyes with his two hands and when he was sure of what he saw, promised offerings of sweets to the gods.

The gold-coloured fruits lay half-hid under green leaves, hanging from one stalk. The king shot arrows, but the fruits did not fall. He pulled them by means of a hook, but still the fruits could not be brought down.

His Majesty said, "How strange! I am not able! The smaller stalks joining the fruits should be kept as they are, let some of you pluck the gold-coloured fruits, if he can."

The ministers, the architects, the courtiers all tried one by one, but failed. The arrows were shot, but they flew into an opposite direction. They applied hooks, which broke half-way; they tried to climb the tree, but the trunk became slippery, and they could not succeed; one broke his arm and another his leg in the attempt. With broken limbs they all returned and sat crouching in the meadow.

The king tore off his pearled necklace and threw down his crown. He himself tried to climb the tree. The *kotwal** was there. He came forward and said, "Victory be to the king. One who is a master of good qualities himself can

* The *kotwal* seems to be a police man of the status of an Inspector.

recognise the same in others. If Your Majesty permits me, I may try."

" The elephants and horses are drowned, the grasshopper says, " Let me fathom the waters."

All cried, " Shame" and hissed.

The king said, " All right, if you succeed, there will be a *shawl* for your reward ; if you fail, you will go to the scaffold."

The *kotwal* bowed low till his head touched the very ground and observed, " If I am to kill any living thing, let me try the elephant ; if I am to plunder, let it be the royal treasury, nothing short." Saying this, he took up a clod of earth and muttering some mysterious words, threw it at the furits. The fruits fell down at the first stroke and rested at the hands of the king. All hang down their heads in shame.

The great music instantly sounded in the king's palace. The horses neighed in the stall ; the queen awoke from her sleep. The king threw his own *shawl* over the *kotwal's* shoulders, and riding the Pakṣirāj returned to his palace.

But the stalks broke in the way and which of the fruits was on the right, and which on the left, could not be known. The queen ate the one that was on the right, and the king the other.

Some months passed ; the queen became *enciente.* The king was glad beyond measure.

He distributed the pearls and jewels of his necklace amongst his courtiers, and the royal treasury was opened for charity.

Ten months passed. By the king's order drummers were brought from the city of drummers ; tabor-players were brought from the city of tabor-players. The great sound of kāḍā, nākāḍā, sānāi, chakaḍā, mṛdaṅga and other musical instruments was heard for ten days, and all this time no bird dared to come down on the earth for fear. On the night of the tenth day, a baby was born in the palace ; the full moon of the sky was no match for it. In the natal room the baby prince lay surrounded by a halo of light.

The kingdom flourished. The king made offerings to God and distributed food amongst men and animals.* He had tanks and ponds dug in many places, established markets and opened roads ; and everywhere his praises were sung.

The writings on the forehead of the baby.

The sixth night came. The king covered his courtyard with canopies, fringed with golden pendants. Three series of lamps burnt, fed by butter. There were 101 musical bands, they played incessantly. On four sides there were made four fire-places. The soldiers, sepoys,

* This is a Buddhist or Jain custom.

sentinels and armed men kept watch in the palace whole night. Paths strewn with flowers were opened up to the natal room. Over the posts, raised for the occasion, hang garlands of flower; and sandal and vermilion were sprinkled over the path. By this path, Dhārā, Tārā and Bidhātā would go to write the luck of the baby-prince on the forehead.

The sentinels kept watch, and at intervals the bands played. The maid-servants and nurses lay cross-wise at the threshold and narrated to the queen tales of princes and their lady-loves. The queen fell asleep as she heard the nursery tales. The flower-woman who was reciting the story, last of all, dozed till she also fell fast asleep. The mid-night clock rang and the sentinels were feeling sleepy. Dhārā, Tārā and Bidhātā chose this hour to visit the natal room by the path strewn with flowers, scented with sandal and reddened with vermilion. They carried with them bundles of pens. When about to enter, they saw a person lying cross-wise at the threshold. The gods had raised their feet but they withheld; all of them whistled together; but the person did not awake. Time passed, what could they do? They called the three stars of the sky to witness, and stepped over the sleeping person. They now entered the natal chamber.

It was Dhārā who first held the pen. He indicated the learning, intelligence, wealth, number of followers and other fortunes of the child by signs. On his palm the signs of banner and lotus were marked, and the god took notes from them, and wrote details in full three hours; all the pens he had brought with him were thus exhausted.

As he finished, next came Tārā. He held the pen and touched the child's forehead with it, but threw away his pen forthwith, and rose up. Dhārā asked, "What do you find?" Tārā turned his face and said, "What more? Let us go, the baby-prince's life extends to 12 days only.".

The baby is to die on the 12th day.

"Only 12 days? Let me see." Dhārā began to count for his satisfaction; each time he calculated, the same result—12. Dhārā put a zero after 12, but the zero mysteriously vanished.

Then Dhārā threw away the pen with disgust. If the gods wept, the whole world would cry and be wretched; so they hid their tears with the edge of their clothes and came out. But at the threshold was the flower-woman lying cross-wise. They called the three stars to witness and stepped over. Dhārā succeeded, but Tārā's feet touched the flower-woman; she awoke and caught hold of the feet of the god. "Who art thou?—a god—a man—a spirit—or a robber? The king's darling sleeps inside the room and I, the flower-woman, keep watch at the threshold. Even Death has no power to come here." Tārā said: "Flower-woman, I am the god of luck, leave my feet." "God of luck! Tell me what hast thou written on the forehead of the prince?" The god felt troubled, and said: "You need not hear that, flower-woman, leave my feet." The flower-woman tied, instead, the feet of the god tightly with her apron. Then the god let fall the drop of tear, that he had hid so long, over her and said: "What more shall I say, woman, the prince's life will extend to 12 days only."

"Only 12 days!" the woman burst into loud bewailings. The drums suddenly burst; the music stopped; the sentinel's spear pierced his own breast. The queen arose with a start and asked "What is the matter?" The king himself came out asking "What is the matter?" The ministers, the courtiers, in fact the whole city came out enquiring "what is the matter? what is the matter?"

The flower-woman beat her head against a stone and cried "How many sacrifices did you perform, oh King, and as a result got this child bright as the full moon. Not even a fortnight, oh King, this moon will vanish after 12 days. Oh God, is it just and fair?"

The king, his ministers, his courtiers fainted in grief. The queen lay as one dead.

The elephants broke their chains and fled from the stall. The horses died in the stable, the

Pakṣirāj, the favourite horse of the king, did not touch any food. The kinsmen of the king and the Brāhmiṇs of the city assembled near the mango tree and observed fast, resigning themselves to the will of God. Dhārā, Tārā and Bidhātā visited the other gods and said, "What justice is this that a son born after so many sacrifices and offerings to gods will live for 12 days only ? The king's country stands on the verge of ruin, and the earth is flooded with tears."

The gods said : " Yea, have things come to such a pass ?" Their chief assumed the guise of an old Brāhmiṇ and came near the mango tree. The Brāhmiṇ was surrounded by a halo of light. The citizens approached him and said : " Who are you, oh Brāhmiṇ ? A light emanates from your body ; whoever you be, the prince is going to die shortly. This is his fate. Pray, Save him if you can." The Brāhmiṇ said : "Even the sun and the moon fall into the jaws of the Demon of Eclipse. Who can alter the divine decree ? Yet despair not, I shall be able to say more if I see the child once." The king and the ministers took him to the natal room. The Brāhmiṇ examined the palm, the forehead and the face of the child and said : " The life of this baby, seven days old, may be prolonged if you can get it married to a girl who has completed her 12th year to-day. Adieu" The king placed the richest stones and other valuables of his treasury at the feet of the Brāhmiṇ. What will a god do with them? He, however, chose a bright diamond and carried it with him. On his way he threw it towards the cottage of the *kotwal* and then departed.

The night passed. The flowers bloomed in the garden and the birds began their songs. Messengers were sent all over the country, seeking a princess, just 12 years old, to be the bride of the baby prince. The messengers returned from far and near and reported that not one was found who had completed her 12th year that day. They all went to the selfsame mango tree and waited observing fast.

The baby to be married to a girl of 12.

On the other side of the tank facing the tree stood Mālañchamālā (*lit.* the garland of the garden), the daughter of the *kotwal* who had completed her 12th year that day. She was washing the diamond, thrown by the god. She had picked it up from her cottage-compound, where it had lain, covered with mud and dirt, as it had rained only shortly before. She carried a pitcher with her and the cymbals of her feet made a merry sound on the landing steps of the tank.

"Who is it whose cymbals sound so sweetly—a goddess or a maid?" wonderingly asked all. The musician playing on stringed lyre stopped and said "Is it the hum of bees flying near a hive in the flower-garden ?" Another who played on a musical organ, cried " Is it the cackle of the merry geese swimming in the tank ?"

"Not so, then what ?"

The ministers and courtiers came near the tank and saw that it was a girl of 12, whose cymbals had sounded.

" A girl of 12! whose daughter is she ?"

She is the *kotwal's* daughter. The king fell into a mental confusion. The sound of the cymbals of her feet is like the humming of bees ; flowers bloom in the path which she treads ; her arms are like swan's neck ; her hair is of wavy curl ; the face is like the moon and she looks like an image made of gold. But after all, she is the *kotwal's* daughter. The king was perplexed. The report was carried to the queen who said " If the girl is so handsome, no matter, though she is the *kotwal's* daughter marry her to the prince and raise the *kotwal* to the status of a feudatory chief."

" What am I to do ?" asked the king to himself ; he pondered over the matter. Sometimes he sat in a pensive mood and then rose up and after a good deal of thinking he commanded,—

" Well, be it so. Send words to the *kotwal*." The report went there forthwith. The *kotwal* put on the shawl presented by the king. He took a spear in his hand and visited his neighbours. He told them "I plucked the fruits. The results is that my daughter is going to be married to a prince. The king will be my brother-in-law now. You must pay me *nazar*."✓

The . *kotwal* made a spacious road in his courtyard. The main door of his house, he changed into a gate ; he did not know what he should do to meet the occasion. The *kotwal's* wife said "Here we humble people live in huts and the sneeze of the king is even heard here.* We are required to give our daughter in marriage to a baby who will die after 12 days. Tell the king I am not going to comply."

Mālañchamālā, the daughter said "Pappa and Mamma, allow me to go, as it is the king's command. But Pappa, go to him and first ask if he will agree to my conditions."

"What conditions ?" "Whether the bridegroom will be permitted to visit his father-in-law's house ?" The *kotwal* said "Certainly." Mālañcha said "Another condition, whether my father-in-law, the king, and mother-in-law, the queen, will agree to partake of the food prepared by me ?" The *kotwal* said "Yes, daughter." "The third" she said "is whether they will be prepared to give mė dowries and presents as usual

* The king would oppress us though we are so humble.

on the marriage night." The *kotwal* came to the palace to meet the king. Meantime Mālañchamālā said " Mamma, help me to dress myself." What would the *kotwal's* wife do ? She opened the toilet box and with tears in her eyes helped her daughter to dress herself.

The *kotwal* addressed the king thus, "Oh thou, King of kings though thou art, yet I shall have the privilege of calling thee a brother, be it to-day, be it to-morrow. Thou wilt accept my daughter but shalt not thou allow the prince to go to the house of his father-in-law ?" The king glanced at him crookedly and brushing his hair with fingers

Mālancha's conditions.

said " let the girl first come to the palace on the marriage night, the question will be settled then."

The *kotwal* next asked, " Will Your Majesty and the queen eat the meal prepared by my daughter ?" The king said " Take care, *kotwal*, these matters will be settled on the marriage night." But, "Oh king, will not my daughter receive the dowries and presents that are usual in marriages?" " Look here, *kotwal*, but stop I say, I will tell everything, when the girl comes to the palace."

The *kotwal* returned and told all these to his daughter. Robed in her best of attires she touched the feet of her parents and said " Mamma, grant me leave, Pappa, lead me now to the palace ; but Pappa, tell the king, if my husband dies on the first night of marriage, may I be permitted to take away his dead body ?" The *kotwal* went to the king and said as instructed.

Now the king was wrath " Such big words from this mean fellow ! This rustic girl has the audacity to extort pledges from me in all matters and dares worry me again and again ; she crosses me beforehand and speaks evil things. Who is there ? Put the *kotwal* to prison and bring his daughter here through the air path and get her married to the baby-prince."

It was the king's command. His people forthwith went. They tied a palanquin high up to the tops of some tall bamboos, and carried Mālañcha by the air path.

It was a mockery of marriage ; there was no present of scents, oil, no fasting and other rites usual before marriages. Only one musical pipe sounded, and the marriage came to a close. The Brahmins recited the *mantras*; the new born baby cried, the queen came to suckle it and the drummers tried to stop its crying by beating their drums. No flowers, no garlands ; the bride went seven times round the baby-prince, and then carrying him in her arms entered the nuptial room. As soon as she came to her apartments, there came down an outpour of rain ; the towers of the palace broke and the palace itself caught fire ; the

The baby dies and Mālancha's punishment.

baby-prince vomitted milk and died in the arms of his wife. There was a great bewailing in the palace; the king ran mad and the queen fainted. The citizens in bewildered grief came to the palace, and waited near the room where Mālañcha lay with the dead prince. The king said "There is no doubt of it, she is a witch, catch her by the hair and drive her out of the room. Pick out her eyes and burn them." There was a great agitation among the crowd. They forced open the room. Mālañcha said to the nurses and maid-servants "Ask my father-in-law and mother-in-law what will they do regarding the words they pledged." "What words?" "They gave assurance that the bridegroom will be permitted to go to my father's house; will they agree to it now?"

"Who is there?" cried the king, "send the *kotwal* to the regions where the prince has gone." A sound indicated that the *kotwal's* head was struck off. Mālañcha said "I have seen enough, O nurses, ask the king and queen about the other words that they selemnly gave me." "What are those?" "Will they not eat the meal prepared with my hands?" "Nurses, cut off the hands of the *kotwal's* daughter." The nurses cut off her hands, with the knife that was among the dowries; blood gushed out and flowed past the drain. Mālañcha said, "I see it clearly, what about the other promises that he had made." "What promises?" "Tell the monarch to give me as dowry a milch cow, five lights fed with butter, sandal-wood, a stove of gold, a spoon of pearls, cups of silver and gold, pillows of white mustard seeds, hand-made beddings of fine needle-work, silver pencil to put the black paint in the eyes. Let him not make any enquiries about his son and the bride."

"See how audacious is this daughter of the *kotwal*! Who is there, break open the doors of her room." Then the dowry was offered in the following manner; an ass for the cow, gravels for sandal-wood, a basket of cane for the golden stove, a broken earthen pitcher in place of the spoon and cups. And the shells of cocoanut fruits were strung together and put around her neck. A basket was filled with cow-dung and tied behind her back. She was made to put on rags and refuse-clothes picked up from the cremation ground, and with a looking glass in her hand she was made to ride the ass, and in this condition was carried round the city. Her head was shaven and order was passed to banish her, as she was a witch. Mālañcha said "Ask my father in-law and my mother-in-law what about their other pledges?" "What are they?" "My husband died in the nuptial room. They had promised to make a gift of him to me." "A gift?" "All right, who is there, kindle the funeral fire." The fire was prepared, the flames rose up and there was great noise. The dead prince was given to Mālañcha. Her nose and ears were cut off and she with the baby was thrown into the fire.

On the funeral fire.

Then came down a great outpour of rain, *jham*! *jham*! *jham*! The fire was nearly extinguished. The gobblins and spirits of the air came there with hungry looks. The Pakṣirāj horse went mad; it neighed and came there. The king, the ministers and his people left the funeral ground and saved themselves by shutting the city gate. In the midst of the funeral fire, Mālañcha sat with the baby-prince in her lap.

The trial.

Mālañcha asked, "Is my husband dead or asleep?"

"Dead."

Malañcha again asked, "Is my husband dead or asleep?"

"Dead."

Again the same query "Is my husband dead or asleep?"

"Asleep."

She smiled and took up the child in her arms and pressed it to her breast. Blood gushed forth from her nose and ears that were cut; The gobblins licked them.

"Mālañcha, is it you that are sitting there?"

"Yes."

"What will you do with such a husband? Offer us the dead body."

"No."

The wood of the funeral pyre gradually became stirred with life; hands and legs grew in them, they walked *hop*, *hop*, *hop*.

"Is it you, Mālañcha, that are sitting there?"

"Look here Mālañcha, so many of us are lying in wait for the dead body, give it to us."

"No."

Sometime passed; the smoke issuing from the funeral pyre took the shape of a series of grim teeth. Loud laughter came all on a sudden. "Mālañcha, are you still sitting there?" "Yes, what of that?" "Give us the dead child, the fire will be extinguished." "No, I will not give." "Will you not give?" "No."

From one side rose an old woman with a strange and coarse voice "Màlañcha, you are going to be killed, make over the dead body to me." From the other side, an old man sprang up with a grimace, "You will be killed ere long, give me the child and save yourself." The crocodiles and sea-fishes came up to the river-bank and called out, "Mālañcha, make over the child to us, we will appease our hunger with it." In the sky the very rains and lightnings and the spirits that rove in the air gaped open their mouths, sneezed and yawned, exclaiming "Mālaṇcha, give us the tender bones, how glad shall we be to eat them up."

Mālaṇcha did not heed all these. She clasped the baby close to her breast and sat quietly. Days and months passed on ; on the sandy shore of the river a great forest grew up. The brother of the Messenger of Death was Kāladuta, his brother was Çāladuta who approached Mālaṇcha and said, "It is the command of the Lord of Death, give up the dead body." Mālaṇcha replied, "Who are you ? Take, if you have the power to do so." Kāladuta and Çāladuta melted away in the air. There was moon-light all around. Next came an exceedingly pretty girl with a bright complexion and lovely intelligent face. Her hands and feet were tender. She said, "Is it you Mālaṇcha ? We were great friends when we were children. You seem to have forgotten all. Oh, what is it ? Oh God, what a condition ! With a dead rotten baby in your lap ! Throw it away, throw it away." Mālaṇcha said, "Who are you that profess friendship to me ? Have you no feeling of a wife for her husband ?" The girl said, "Alas Mālaṇcha, is this corpse your husband ? Make it over to me for a moment and go and fetch a little water from the river." "There is no water in the river." "Oh yes, if there were water in the river, things would not come to this pass." "Bring some medicinal herb." "There is none." "Oh Mālaṇcha, look up there, the sky is overcast with clouds, the floods come pouring, arise, dear, here is my hand, place the baby in my lap, arise, haste, I say." Mālaṇcha clasped the baby closer to her breast and said, "Be witness, oh gods, here is my baby-husband in my lap, if I am chaste and devoted, oh you tempter, do but touch me, and you will be reduced to ashes; I am Mālaṇcha and none other; you are an evil spirit, go hence. Oh thou night, if thou dost not pass away, with my baby-husband in my lap, here do I solemnly say, I will transform the stars to fire and flowers to stars." The night was frightened and passed away trembling; the dawn peeped into the forest-lands. The girl, her friend, said, "Mālaṇcha, look at the baby." Mālaṇcha felt that the apparitions were all gone. The baby in her lap was gently moving its hands and feet, and she seemed to be in the midst of a vast expanse of sands. Mālaṇcha, intensely willing to see the baby, gradually got her sight; she went in quest of a pitcher for milk. Ready for service she felt that her hands grew. She recovered her ears;

The dead baby gets life and Malancha recovers her eyes and limbs.

her nose became what it formally had been; the hair of her head fell in luxuriant curls behind her back. Mālaṇcha addressed her girl-companion and said, "May your husband be long-lived. Who are you? I abused you, look at my condition and pardon me." Mālaṇcha found there a stove of gold, sandal-woods, pillows of white mustard seed and spoons made of pearls. She made a fire with sandal-wood, warmed the milk and put it in a silver cup; then with the spoon made of pearls, she fed the baby; she wiped away the neck and the face of the baby with her silken apron; then on a bed delicately wrought with needle, she made the baby sleep, resting his head on the pillow. She sat with her back towards the sun, and with a silver pencil applied the black paint to the baby's eyes.

Thus did she live in the sandy shore with her little husband. She fasted all the while. She got milk and every thing, and fed the baby. She applied the black paint to its eyes, and warmed it with her apron. There she sat all the time, gazing at the child. The little husband laughed, and she smiled; he cried, and she wept. When he began to utter inarticulate words, she gave replies; the little thing moved hands and feet, she played with him; she bathed him with tears, wiped away his dust with her hair, warmed him with her breast, covered him with the edge of her cloth and sat clasping him close to her breast.

The nursing.

Days and months passed, and even a year rolled away in this way. Mālaṇcha had a pitcher of milk which was never to be empty. The gods, with mouths, pointed like needles, drank off this milk. Mālaṇcha found there was no more milk in the pitcher. Carrying the baby-husband in her arms, Mālaṇcha set out in quest of human habitation for cow's milk.

In that limitless expanse of that alluvial land, she walked on and on. If the sun smote the baby's face, she covered him with her cloth; if rain fell, she protected him in her bosom; if dust blew, she kept it away by spreading her hair; she fanned him with her flowing hair. She went one step and then stopped, thus did she proceed in her journey. At last she reached a dense forest. Alas! where is human habitation? Where is milk? She saw, instead, a large tiger; it approached her with a hungry growl. "I am grown old, dear maid, I have no strength to go seeking for prey, I am almost starved. I must eat this baby," it said. "Look here tiger, he is my husband, he is so small that if you eat him, your hunger will not be appeased, so eat me instead." "Is he your husband, child? With such a one you are in a dense forest! I will eat none of you; live here, child, I will be your guard."

In quest of milk.

Mālaṇcha said, "Uncle, that's good, but how can I feed my baby husband? Where is milk to be had?" "Milk? Yes, you are human beings the baby must drink milk. All right let me see, if I can secure a cow for you." The tiger went away. Mālaṇcha wept and said, "Where are ye, oh gods? The baby is crying for hunger; if by sacrificing my life, one drop of milk I can get, I am ready to do so." The tigress appeared at this moment with her cubs. She said, "Who art thou, child, weeping for milk in this forest? If my milk will do, you can have it from me." "Yes, it will do." The tiger meantime returned and said that he could not procure a cow and looking at the tigress exclaimed, "You are here, now see, I forgot all about it." Chandramānik (the baby prince) was suckled by the tigress and grew up. The tigress and her mate were their guards. Mālaṇcha thus lived in that forest; she watched her little husband at every step; she walked keeping pace with him; she gathered flowers and fruits for him; she sang lullabies to make him sleep and played with him when he awoke, and thus spent five years.

In quest of a tutor.

With tearful eyes, Mālaṇcha one day said, "Uncle and aunt, I have to leave this place now." "What word is that? Do not say so again. Tell us what has happened, whose neck shall we break? Name the offender; we will instantly eat him up." "No uncle and aunt, nothing of the sort. You do not know it, my husband is a prince; he has just stepped into his fifth-year. How can I avoid placing him under a tutor." "Is that all? Then make arrangement for it at once. There are so many scholars who rove here in mornings and evenings, crying out '*hukkā huā*'[1]; you have simply to ask for it and we shall secure some of those from the forest for education of the prince." "No uncle, they will not do for us, I am going away; enquire about us now and then, I shall live close to some city." Mālañcha took leave with tears. The tigress and her mate accompanied her till she got out of the forest. For four days after her departure, the grisly couple of the forest ate nothing. The cubs wandered about uncared for.

Mālañcha proceeded in her journey with Chandramānik in her arms. After some days she came near a garden, belonging to a flower-woman. The tank there was without water and no flower had bloomed in it for twelve years; the garden had become a regular forest of thorny plants and an abode of snakes. It was a hot day and Mālañcha rested there a while, greatly fatigued.

---

[1] "*Hukkā huā*" is the familiar word in Bengali to denote the yell of the fox.

As she sat there, the bees began to hum and birds with coloured wings flew near about her in numbers. Each tree became covered with green leaves, and each of them had on it a creeper laden with flowers. Their fragrance drew the attention of the flower-woman, who came out.

In the flower-woman's cottage.

"For twelve years there has been no flower in my garden, no water in the tank, but to-day the garden smiles with flowers, and a beautiful lotus has bloomed in that tank. It seems there has come a change over my luck. What is it that has made the garden so to-day?" As she looked out, she saw that under the shade of a Vakul tree on which sat a cuckoo making the place resonant with its cooings, there sat a goddess with a baby in her lap, bright as the moon. The flower-woman approaching her said, "What heaven is that of which you are a dweller, child? Your presence makes a desert bloom, tell me who you are?" Mālañcha said, "I am a humble being of the earth, I have sat here to rest a while." "Come inside my cot. Your face and hands and complexion resemble those of my niece who died twelve years ago. All this time, I have wept over her untimely death; is it she that has come back to me in the lovely form I see before me?" "I do not know that aunt, I have just now come to your garden." "Never mind, come to my house." The flower-woman was pleased that she would be able to sell flowers to the palace every day, and Mālañcha felt she would be able to get information regarding the city from her. Both entered the cottage. The flower-woman said, "You look pale, child, take some food." Mālañcha said, "Give me some milk if you have it." Mālañcha fed the child and dusted the room fixed for her and brought some flowers from the garden, which she placed around the bed of her little husband. And then she told the flower-woman, "Aunt, I do not take meal prepared by others, help me to get things, I shall cook for myself." The flower-woman was pleased and did as she was asked. Mālañcha did not disclose to her that the child was her husband. The cottage of the flower-woman was a wretched one. Mālañcha said, "It is not a good house, aunt, appoint men to build a good one." A new house was built, formerly there had been only a single hut in the house and now it contained three huts. In one she lived with the prince, in another the flower-woman and the third had no occupant. Mālañcha asked the flower-woman one day, "Where do the students read in the city?" "Why, there is a teacher in the palace who has a number of scholars in his charge. There is quite a legion of them! There are hunchbacks and frog-voiced scholars, there are those who have elephantiasis and others who are huck-shouldered. Besides there are sons of the king also. Day and night, they hum like bees and croak like ravens. It is a sight worth seeing—a veritable mart of crows and cranes."[1] "Then aunt, the prince must go there. Get for him inkstand and pens and take him to the school."

Chandramānik goes to school and returns with marks of ink all over his face. The room that was unoccupied serves now as his reading room. Mālañcha engages the flower-woman to help him to bathe, to wash his face marked with ink. Mālañcha cooks the meal and keeps it ready and then goes away. The flower-woman brings him to the dining place and sits by him when he eats. But Mālañcha no more appears before Chandramānik, fearing lest the child takes her for his mother. Mālañcha remains in her room and from there gazes at her little husband with eyes full of love; but she retires when Chandramānik comes to a place from which he may see her. Thus passed another seven years.

The name of the king of that country was Dudhabaraṇ or 'milk-coloured.' His seven sons and the young princess read in that school. But the latter makes no progress in her studies.

---

[1] "কেন রাজার বাড়ীর পণ্ডিত কত পড়ুয়া পড়ায়। কুঁজো, সুজো, গেঁগো, গোঁদা কত পড়ুয়া! আবার, রাজার রাজপুত্তুর ও আছে। দিন রাত হিলিমিলি কিলিমিলি, কাক বকের হাট।"

The brothers ask, "How is it, Kānchī, that you make no progress in your studies, though you evidently take pains?" "Look at him, brothers, how glorious does he look like the moon-beams; his face, and his forehead have the air of a god. They say that he is the son of a gardener. I have acquired all the learning that is in the four Vedas and eight Puranas by gazing at his face. Was ever a human being so handsome?" The princes were startled at these words. They all said, "We must see that the gardener's son never comes to the school again."

The discovery by the princes.

They called him to their presence and said, "Your face and hands are spotted with ink; we shall not allow it. If you come to the school with dirty clothes to-morrow, we shall hand you over to the public executioner." The princes thought, "How can the son of a gardener be expected to have clean clothes, he will not attend school from to-morrow."

They conspire to plan some impossible conditions for Chandramānik.

Chandramānik left his books and returned home weeping. Mālañcha said, "See aunt, why is he weeping?" The flower-woman—"He tells me there are only a few nours of the day and the intervening night, in the morning he would be made over to the public executioner." "Why?" The flower-woman gave out the history. Mālañcha said—"Aunt, here is the money, go and get such fine dresses as may even be coveted by a prince." Mālañcha was in possession of immense wealth as she had got the diamond. The next day the princes were surprised to see Chandramānik robed like a king's son. "Where could the fellow get such a splendid dress that even we have not got ?" Kānchī said to her seven brothers, "What do you say now ? Does a gardener's son look like that ?" The princes then addressed Chandramānik and said, "You little gardener, you have come with a gorgeous dress ! But shame ! with such a dress you came walking. If you do not come to-morrow in a stately palanquin, we will make you over to the executioner." They thought "He may have got a gift of the dress, but it will not be possible for him to get a stately palanquin, so he will not be able to attend school to-morrow." Chandramānik returned home that day also weeping. He left aside his dress and threw himself on the dusty ground. Mālañcha asked the flower-woman the reason. "There are a few hours of this day and the intervening night, after that he will be handed over to the executioner." "To-day also to be handed over to the executioner, why ?" "He dresses himself well but goes walking." "Very well take money, bring all the best palanquins available in the city." The flower-woman went, but no palanquin-bearer would consent even for wages to carry a gardener's son. Mālañcha said, "Pay each man ten gold coins,"

So a basketful of gold coins was distributed, and the best of the palanquins were brought. There was among them one used by princes and noblemen only, with a gold umbrella overhead and in this sat Chandramānik, and other palanquins went surrounding it. Men assembled to see the procession in the street. The scholars sprang to their feet. "Come princes," said Kānchī, "See how glorious the school looks to-day! Like a jewel shining in the middle of a gold-string he looks. I am your only sister and you are seven brothers; if you do not marry me to Chandramānik, I will commit suicide." The seven brothers found themselves really in a puzzling situation. They said, "You gardener's son, you have done all, now you must have a horse. The horses of us, seven brothers, will be at several points within the range of seven and a half miles. Your horse will occupy the last point. We will apply whip to our horses, if you can win the race, well and good, if not, you will be handed to the public executioner." The princes thought "The gardener's son will never be able to ride a horse, as soon as he will try to do so, he will fall down and die." Chandramānik was sorrowful again and returned home with tears in his eyes. Mālañcha said, "Aunt, see what has happened again." The flower-woman gave the account. "All right aunt, here is the money. Spend it as need arises. I shall go in quest of a horse. I will stay out not more than three days at any event, but return with the horse within the time."

Mālañcha went on and on. She passed through 13 territories that belonged to 12 Rājās, and then came to a city where she saw the palace-gate closed and doors of houses all bolted from within. The courts did not sit, their doors lay closed also. The good luck of the king had left him and the city looked like a desert. The Pakṣirāj, the favourite horse of the king, had run mad; it ran wildly and killed every man that walked in the city. Mālañcha, when she heard all these, cried out "Where art thou, Oh Pakṣirāj? Dost thou remember Chandramānik?" The voice reached the horse, and it ran up to her with ears erect. It said, "How could you know the name of Chandramānik, child, shall I ever get him back?" Mālañcha said, "Pakṣirāj, come with me then." Mālañcha set out for her place, followed by the horse. The citizens were astonished. "Chandramānik died years ago. She names him; she catches the mad horse; what charmer is she?" They all felt a surprise. The queen said, "Who is she? Go and find her out." Mālañcha sang as she went "O king, it is the self-same horse which you rode when you went in quest of the two fruits. You got a son whom you married to *kotwal's* daughter, carrying her through the air-path. It is she that has come back to take away the horse. Only a few days still remain to complete twelve years. After that you will have the full account, not now." And Mālañcha went away. The king said, "What? Is it Mālañcha? Mālañcha has saved the city from the horse. Mālañcha has caught it. I had her hands and ears cut off and punished her in the most cruel manner. Alas! has she come back? Open your doors, citizens." Her mother recognised her, her brothers recognised her. To-day her ears and nose are fine as flower-buds, the fingers look like *champaka* flowers; her eyes have a keen sight, bright as the sun or the moon. They all cried out, "Mālañcha, Mālañcha," and ran after her. But they could not find her for she had left the city with the Pakṣirāj by that time. The king sent messengers in all directions. He invited the *kotwal's* wife to the palace and entertained her with a rich banquet, and the queen herself dined with her. Days and nights passed, they anxiously waited for news about Mālañcha.

Now in the city of Dudhabaraṇ, the king, the morning conch-shells sounded. The scholars rose up and attended their lessons. The words of a true woman never fail. She had returned with the horse. The flower-woman saw fire coming out of the eyes of the animal; its ears were erect, and the sharp hoofs cut the earth that trembled under their strokes. The flower-woman said, "What am I to do now, child?" Mālañcha said, "Take the horse, it is ready." "What else you would say, I am ready to do, but I venture not to come near that animal." "Don't fear, it will not hurt you, aunt." "No child, for my life I will not be able to do it." Mālañcha hang her head down for a moment; she wiped away the sweat from her brow, and then spread a beautiful seat on the back of the horse; with eyes downcast and head drooping low, she helped her husband to ride the horse. She then tied several knots in the edge of her *saḍi*, and addressing the animal said, "You know what you should do; my husband is a boy, I place him in your charge. I will open the knots in the course of the day. By the time all be opened you must bring him back to me." At this moment she held up the reins so that her husband might catch them, and took the opportunity of seeing his face for a moment. On the plea of dusting his shoes, she bowed down to his feet. Chandramānik said, "Who are you? You are always near about me, but do not speak to me. You cook my meal but do not serve me. I have seen your hands and feet to-day, you have to-day looked at my face and touched my feet. Who are you *to me*?" "Who? You ask me, I am the daughter of the *kotwal*." She hid her face with her hair on the pretext of arranging them, stopped a little and then in haste drew out a thread from her cloth and put it round the neck of the horse and let it go. The Pakṣirāj ran as if flying in the air. Mālañcha threw herself down on the bare ground near the tank in grief.

In the school the princes were surprised to see the horse. "It is of the Pakṣirāj-species, we have not got such a horse in our stable; where could the gardener's son get it ?" Like the young one of a bird feeling its wings just grown, the horse brooked no delay. Chandramānik held the reins tightly. The horse's body moved like a wave, its four feet struck the earth in impatience. The princes were at their wit's end. They spoke between themselves, "As we have given word, we must be ready for the race. Even if he wins, the kingdom is ours, who will prevent us from sending him to the scaffold ?" They cried out, "Ho, gardener's son, if you go ahead of us, we will put you to death. You must be seven and a half miles behind." This really was the arrangement. Each rider was ahead of the next by a mile and the last of all was Chandramānik. He called out, "Have you commenced the race, or have you not ?" No reply. They had set out long before. Now Chandramānik started. The Pakṣirāj flew through the air, and went ahead of the others in no time. The princes exclaimed, "No. The race is not yet won, it is only the east, now come to the north." Chadramānik only smiled and beat them in the north. In the west also he beat them and he won also in the south. The princes said, "We are satisfied. Your horse is a very fine one; now the people of the palace will like to see it. So let us return." "Yes, be it so," said Chandramānik and applied his whip to the Pakṣiraj. The stroke tore off the thread Mālañcha had tied round the neck of the horse. The thread was wrought by all the virtues she had acquired in her past lives, it was charmed by her tears. It fell in the earth's dust—uncared for. Pakṣirāj drew a heavy breath, and then set off. It stopped near the gate of the palace, and all voices cried, "Who is it that has won the garland of victory?" On the golden tower of the palace where lay the golden cup, sat Kānchī, the princess, who herself looked like a statue of gold. From that height she observed Chandramānik coming, and flung down the garland she had woven; the garland touched the head-dress of Chandramānik and then hang on his neck.[1] The multitude cried, "What is it? What is it?" But the princess had given her garland to Chandramānik and this implied marriage and there was no help. All became silent. The seven princes came, and with outward cordiality escorted Chandramānik to the court of the king. The king called his councillors and said, "Does our law permit that

Winner of the race.

[1] The present of a flower-garland to a man implied his election by a woman as her bridegroom.

the king's daughter should marry a gardener's son?" They said, "It may be so, if the gardener's son remains in prison for 12 years." There was no alternative left. The marriage took place. For three days and three nights there were great amusements in the palace. On the fourth day, the seven princes put a chain round Chandramānik's neck and led him to the prison and there left him.

Marries and is imprisoned.

Now the Pakṣirāj came back where Mālañcha lay on the bank of the tank. She was on the dusty ground and saying to herself, "Alas! why did I not let him know who I am! Why did I not tell him when he asked it?" Then she saw before her the Pakṣirāj. She asked, "What is it Pakṣirāj, where is my husband?" Mālañcha's eyes became fiery. She rose from her dusty bed, "Alas, what do I see? what have I done?" She threw herself on the ground in grief.[1] The Pakṣirāj said, "What should I say to you, child? On the tower of the palace there sat the princess with a garland in her hand, that garland has drawn your sweet husband to the palace." As she heard this she rose up, but did not weep.[2]

[1] She felt misgivings as regards Chandramānik's life, not seeing him on the horse-back; she regretted having sent him for the race.

[2] Mark the change of emotions in her. There had been a presentiment of something wrong having befallen her husband, but now she was assured that he was safe and happy. Her own happiness was lost for ever, but she did not care for her personal sorrows.

She said, "Pakṣirāj, it is all right now! My mission in bringing up my husband for these 12 years is fulfilled to-day. To-day the 12th year is complete. Pakṣirāj, I have given you trouble, pardon all, and remember me the fortunate[1] one. I will give you a letter. Please give it to my father-in-law, the king. Then Mālañcha, wrote thus: "Oh king, my father-in-law, the life of the prince was to close on the 12th day. Twelve years are now complete. If you come to the palace of the king Dudhabaraṇ, you will find there the prince, your son. The princess there is an expert weaver of garlands. He has married her and all his trouble is over. When this letter will reach you, Oh great king, my father-in-law, dip your toes for a moment in the water of the tank where you first saw me, recollecting me—the *kotwal's* daughter." She gave the letter to the horse. She gave it some grass and water and then bade adieu. With her clothes soiled with dust, with dusty feet, she returned not by the roundabout garden-path by which she had been used to go, but by the road facing the cottage, which she had

[1] The word 'fortunate' has a significance. The mission of her whole existence was to see him happy. That mission was now fulfilled. She was not swayed by any personal consideration. She called herself fortunate, because her husband was now happy in every respect; for a parallel passage one may quote Chandi Dās's familiar lines, "আমি নিজ সুখ দুঃখ কিছু না জানি। তোমার কুশলে কুশল মানি।"

not trodden before.[1] She arranged all her things and made them over to the flower-woman, saying, "Aunt, I did not disclose to you all this time, but I do so to-day. He whom I brought up all these years is my husband. All that I have, I give to you. Do not remember my faults, dear aunt, I shall bear the burden of my debt of gratitude to you for the rest of my life. Aunt, I have come to bid adieu to you." The flower-woman saw everything dark before her eyes and almost fainted. And Mālañcha went away from her presence and set out for her own city, in order to drown herself in the tank of her father's house. "In the tank near which I got the diamond, in the city where I lost my father, will all my griefs come to an end. How happy is the princess Kānchī in the arms of her husband! How happy shall I be to-day drowning myself in the beautiful water of the tank!" Mālañcha thought, "What fault can I find in my husband? He wanted to know who I am, I never told him that he was my husband!"

She resolves to drown herself.

Mālañcha followed her course. The flower-woman's garden was left behind—the big and small tanks were left behind. In that path

[1] She did not appear before Chandramānik when he was grown-up lest he called her mother; this was the reason for her avoiding the main road to the cottage.

neither any human being nor any animal was to be seen. Proceeding still further, she met the tiger and the tigress. Mālañcha said, addressing them, "Aunt, eat me up, uncle, eat me up;" she turned to the cubs now grown to full vigour, and said, "Ye are my brothers, eat me up." "Oh child, here are you again, tell us where had you been all this time." "In the garden of a flower-woman." "Where is he whom you carried in your arms and whom we nourished with our milk, where is that darling child of ours—Chandramānik?" "The princess of that country has given him her garland. Aunt and uncle, what day can be more happy to me than now? Eat me up to-day." The tiger and the tigress heard the whole story from Mālañcha and sat crouching near her, "Child, then it is not the marriage-garland, it is the prisoner's chain." "Prisoner's chain, why?" "If a gardener's son marries the daughter of a king he shall be subjected to a penalty of 12 years' imprisonment. This is the custom of the land." Mālañcha bit her lips and firmly stood up.[1] The tiger said, "Take this glue from our head and put it on yours. Now let us all go to the city." Mālañcha said nothing, as soon as she applied the glue to her hair, she became

[1] She had thought that there was nothing more in the world, for which she would care to live! But there was a complete change in her attitude. She was resolved to rescue her husband from danger.

invisible to others. The tiger and the tigress with their whole flock started for the city of Dudhabaraṇ.

Meantime the Pakṣirāj returned to its own city. It carried the letter to the king When it came up to the palace-gate, the whole city was frightened. The king and the queen trembled, fearing that the horse must have killed Mālañcha and come back. The Pakṣirāj said, "No cause of fear, Your Majesty may read this letter." "If it is a letter, let it be carried to me by means of a hook from a safe distance." The king read the contents and became greatly elated with joy. He said, "I have got my Chandramāṇik again." "Where is he?" cried all. "In the kingdom of Dudhabaraṇ." The king called back all the messengers that he had sent in quest of Mālañcha; he called all his army and sent them out in four divisions, *viz.*, to the east, west, north and south, in quest of the capital of Dudhabaraṇ. The king after much search arrived at a place where a mad flower-woman was found to tear off flowers by her fingers, break small twigs and branches, pelt clods of earth into a tank and cry "Oh my niece, Oh my darling boy."

Song.

"My darling Chandramānik is in chains. The chaste wife, my niece, has gone away to the forest losing her husband. Here in this tank, my niece, used to bathe every morn and eve; here by this path she used to come to the cot with her pitcher filled with water. Chandramānik, my darling, used to sit and read here; and there on that couch he used to sleep."

The king said, "It is all right. Stop and pitch our tents here." The king sent a letter to Dudhabaraṇ to the following effect. "King Chandra of Chandrapur sends this letter to Your Majesty. Is my son in your palace? Hear, Oh Dudhabaraṇ, give me the right information, where have you kept my son and how is he doing in the palace. Chandramānik is the name of my son; he used to read in the school attached to your palace. Is it true that your daughter has given her garland to my son? If you wish everything well, give back my son to me and take away his chains, and also send to my camp my daughter-in-law who belongs to our family now."

Dudhabaraṇ said in reply, "If he is your son, come and fight. If you be the victor, take him by force." The king gave order to attack Dudhabaraṇ's capital, and himself led the expedition. Dudhabaraṇ's army was stronger, so he could not succeed in his attempts and became a prisoner himself.

The king of Chandrapur is imprisoned.

The day passed and the night approached. Made invisible to others by the charm given by the tiger, Mālañcha went inside the prison-room where her husband lay. He was reduced to half his normal weight. There under the heavy chain he lay in the dust. Mālañcha wiped away her tears and went near him. She had nothing with her. She took up the iron chain and applied all her might to break it by her teeth. Was it possible to do so? In full three hours she broke one of the four folds of the chain the attempt costing her eight teeth; thus losing all her teeth towards the end of the night, she broke the four-fold chain. The chain broke and fell down with a sound. Blood streamed forth from her gums; she smiled in her triumph but fainted.

She breaks all her teeth and the chain.

Chandramānik now awoke from his sleep; he did not notice Mālañcha lying there in an unconscious state. He, however, found that the chain was broken. A tigress had suckled him; so his strength was great, he rose up and broke open the door and came out. Chandramānik was surrounded by a halo of light, and it took the tiger and the tigress no time to recognise him. They said to their companions, "Now we have got our Mānik; let us go and eat up the inmates of Dudhabaraṇ's palace." The tigers in great number came and attacked the palace. They killed the horses and elephants, the domestic animals

The havoc made by the tigers.

and men, and made a feast with them. They ate up Dudhabaraṇ and his seven sons, they all growled setting up a terrible roar and went in quest of Dudhabaraṇ's daughter—the princess Kāñchi. Now Mālañcha had come back to her senses, she ran like a mad girl towards the tigers. "What are you doing, Oh uncle, you have indeed done a great evil; you have left no one to light the evening-lamp in this great palace. Don't eat my husband's father-in-law, his mother-in-law and their sons. Don't eat the princess Kāñchi, the treasure of my husband's heart." The tiger said, "Alas, what have we done? We have eaten the king, the queen and their sons and followers! we have been greedily pursuing the princess. You forbid us to do so." Mālañcha beat her head against a stone and said, "Don't do so, if you are still hungry, eat me." Mālañcha approached them and the tigers left the princess and said, "We have had a sumptuous feast, we are now very thirsty." Mālañcha brought some pitchers and went to the tank to fetch water.

Dudhabaraṇ's city was thus depopulated by the tigers. The captive king now came out, and Chandramānik was in the midst of his own men. The king ordered drums to be sounded, and with his son and the new bride marched towards his own capital. On his way he descended the landing steps of a tank to wash his face and hands. Mālañcha was filling her pitcher with water at the time. She placed two pitchers filled with water on the left of the king, put two blades of green grass over them and then bowed to him. The king said, "Who are you?" Mālañcha's reply:

Song.

"What a good fortune to-day! Miserable as I am all my life, I have seen the feet of my father-in-law after 12 years. You are now going to your palace. A woman's highest heaven is her father-in-law's home. I have been denied the good fortune of getting a place there. Oh my father-in-law! what consolation have you to offer me?"

The king exclaimed, "Here is that *kotwal's* daughter again! I shall have nothing to do with her. No more, my men. Do not tarry here, but proceed; I have got a princess for my daughter-in-law. The case of the *kotwal's* daughter is out of the question now." His counsellors said, "She saved us by putting the *pakṣirāj* in check." "What of that?" "Your Majesty knows it is she that had set the tigers against Dudhabaraṇ's city."

The case of *kotwal's* daughter is out of the question.

"What of that?"

"Your Majesty, it is she to whom the prince owes his life."

"Now listen to me, my men. If you speak a good deal, you will die; this will be my sentence. Whatever she may have done, she is a *kotwal's* daughter. Whoever has heard that a beggar became a queen? If she wants audience, tell her to approach me in true dignity worthy of a king's daughter-in-law in stately conveyances."

Mālañcha gave water to the thirsty tigers and borrowed money to secure state-palanquins. She now set out in a right royal palanquin attended by the tigers. The old tiger stood in the king's presence and said, "She has now come here in a way worthy of the palace, accept her and take her with you." The king's reply was a shower of sharp arrows. The tigers said, "How can we, Oh Mālañcha, bear this? Permit us by a mere word, and we will eat up this army; we will eat up the princess—the new bride and give you your own Chandramānik."

"Say not so, uncle; before you eat up my father-in-law's army, eat me, I pray.

Song.

"I will dust the path for my father-in-law with my hair. I will go by the thorny path, but still accompany him. Uncle tiger, aunt tigress, do not take offence, but leave me."

The unflinching devotion.

They, however, did not leave her. The king went with his army by the royal road and she followed him close by the thorny path.[1] And the tiger with his flock accompanied her. The king entered the palace with the prince and the new bride, to the sound of the drums and other music. But she remained at the gate in grief, and the tigers also remained there, because they would not go away leaving her in her destitution. For seven days she was there. She wept and sang.

Song.

"This is my father-in-law's place—my heaven. To me the place is sacred, for here did I get my husband, here was I married; this house of my father-in-law appears to me more precious than a house of gold."

"I must stay here, uncle tiger, leave me here." But the grisly uncle said, "Say even now, we will eat up the king and the new bride and restore you to your Chandramānik." "How could you say such cruel words? Why not eat me up? Even if I be here as a servant of the cowshed in charge of the cow dung, I shall prefer such a life and dwell here for ages. Uncle and aunt, I bow down to your feet, leave me now and go." They said, "Now what to do, she will not in any case take our advice. Let us depart for a time." When they went away, the king felt greatly relieved. "She sheds tears at my gate, what an inauspicious thing! Drive her

[1] As the king would not allow her to go by the main road by which he passed, she had to choose the thorny path lying in the jungles.

away." By the king's command, they not only drove away Mālañcha, but also her mother from the palace.

The mother and the daughter wandered about weeping. The mother said, "What is the good of leading such a life? No more, let us drown ourselves." And she drowned herself in a tank. Before she had done so, Mālañcha wept and sang:

"Oh mother, do not die, leaving me helpless. I venture not to drown myself as my hopes are unfulfilled. I am not allowed to see my father-in-law's face, nor of Chandramānik once before my death! Wretched woman, as I am, how can I die now?"

But forlorn by all, she could not bear her lot, and went to drown herself. But whatever tank she chose for the purpose, she found filled with thorny plants or with earth, or watched over on four sides by guards, appointed by the king. Mālañcha knew not if she should be sorry or happy at this. "My father-in-law will not permit me even to unload the burden of my sorrow! Let him however do as he likes. Whom else have I in this world even to give me pain?"

At the interval of every three hours in the night, the drums sounded in the palace.

In the nuptial room.

Mālañcha went to the palace at that opportunity so that the sound of her footsteps was not heard. She advanced slowly, step by step, and reached the room where the prince and the new bride lay. Slowly did she open the doors; the beauty of the full moon burst to her sight! Eight lamps burnt fed by butter,—the room was fully lit up and bright; on a golden couch with beddings fringed with gold over it, slept the prince and the bride—like two flowers of a moon-lit night soundly did they sleep. Mālañcha stood at the door awhile and saw the sight;—she came in and saw,—she brightened the lamp and saw,—she came near them, stood near their pillows, near their feet, and beheld them for the rest of the night, yet her eyes did not feel a satiety. "Oh God, did you give to such a prince the wretched *kotwal's* daughter!" As Mālañcha saw the pair, her unbraided hair fell profusely behind her back, the flower-buds on the bed bloomed at her breath, her tears of gladness fell there like pearls. The crowing of the crows indicated the morning. Mālañcha rose up and from the sacred plate took a few blades of grass and some grains of rice, and she tore off two hairs from her head—with these she blessed the new bride and then put them at the feet of her husband and sang:—

Song.

"Be happy, Oh prince, be happy, Oh princess,
"Be it so, if the prayers of a devoted woman, are ever fulfilled.

"May the candles that are lit up here brighten this house for generations to come and the royal umbrella of this house may remain unfurled for all future time!

"Oh forests, Oh trees, Oh land, Oh water, keep guard over this house.

"May the tower of this palace ever remain high and unconquerable.

"May the sun and the moon with their golden rays brighten the ever glorious pinnacle of this royal home for long ages.

"May the house of my father-in-law and the throne of my husband be ever preserved as the seat of power and victory in this land.

"May the princess be happy and prosperous with her husband through long years; I seek this boon.

I have brought him up with great pains; a sight like this immensely pleases me. What-ever may befall my lot—whether I am reduced to dust or water or transformed into a bird or a lower animal no matter, a sight like this will ever delight mine eyes!"

Every night Mālañcha stole into the room in this manner. Three nights passed, and on the fourth, Mālañcha was singing her song in a humming tone, but suddenly the prince awoke; he rose up and said, "What is this? Who are you that sing in this way in our nuptial room?" Mālañcha said in a low voice, "One who has a right to enter here. I have disturbed your sleep, prince, pardon me—do not take offence, I am a servant of this palace. You have no reason to fear, sleep prince as you were doing, I depart." "A servant? Tell me the truth, or else look here at this sword of mine.

Song.

"A servant? But that can never be. It is the same face that I saw in the garden-path of the flower-woman's house. If a servant, why is it that through my body passes a thrill of delight and there is an ebb and flow in my blood? I recollect as if I was brought up by those tender hands of yours. You a servant? Tell so to one who does not know you. I know you, but tell me to-day who are you *to me*."

"Prince, through yonder window see the first streak of dawn's light. I cannot say anything to-day, I cannot stay." As Mālañcha turned her steps Chandramānik held her fast by the edge of her *sāḍi*. "No, I will not allow you to go if you do not say that." Mālañcha bent her head down and said, "Prince you do me wrong."

"What?"

The guards came up there, the sentinels hurried, the king himself came. "Who is it that has entered the nuptial room of the prince? Whose footprints do we see in the path?" On other days Mālañcha took care to wipe away her footprints when she returned. To-day they are detected. All came close to the nuptial room. They saw a strange light, they could not bear to look at it. The king hid his eyes from the dazzling light with his hands and said, "Who are you?" The prince replied, "Father, it is the *kotwal's* daughter." "*Kotwal's* daughter?" The prince said, "If she is to be treated so, because she is *kotwal's* daughter, who will deserve a better treatment?" "Son, tell her not to tread this compound any more, let her go away by the path by which she came." Mālañcha could not say what she had to say. She went away by the path by which she had entered.

She is turned out.

Thus did Mālañcha depart from the palace. From that time evil befell the city. The high towers fell, the triumphal arch broke and many disasters overtook the palace. Twelve years passed in this way. Seven children were born to the prince and all of them died. The king said, "It is all the work of that witch." Seven or eight days passed after he had said so. One day as the king was passing by the main road, he saw the soft flowers blooming on each side; at every halting station the sound of the musical pipe *sānāi* was heard. He looked at the tower of his palace, it seemed to be restored to its former condition. His seven grandchildren came back from the regions of death and stood around him. The king wonderingly asked, "What is this ?" The prince said, "It is all the work of the *kotwal's* daughter. She can break and rebuild." "False," exclaimed the king, "if she could restore the dead to life, she would make her dead parents alive again, first of all." The king entered the court. The *kotwal* came up to him to his astonishment and said, "Hail Your Majesty, the king of kings." The queen was in her appartments, the *kotwal's* wife came up and accosted her thus, "We lived together for many years, I have come to see you, sister." The king said, "It is all very puzzling, I do not understand what all these mean; I must clear up my brain in free air, and go a-hunting in the forest." The king lost his way, and his attendants were devoured by tigers. He wandered about losing his way, and suffered greatly from thirst. There, by the side of a tank, the water of which was dried up, he saw a beautiful damsel with a pitcher in her arms. The king said, "If there is water in your pitcher, child, will you save my life by giving me a little?" The beautiful damsel said, "There is milk in my pitcher, no water." "Milk? But milk does not satisfy thirst, can't you give me a little water?" The damsel smiled and gave the king sufficient water from her pitcher. The king was very pleased and said, "Whoever you may be, child, may you adorn your

For the first time she hears sweet words from her father-in-law.

father-in-law's home, and as you have made me happy by giving me drinking water, may you be happy all your life." Her pitcher she placed on the ground and reverentially bowed to the king's feet and sang.

Song

"I am made happy, oh my father-in-law, oh my king, happy beyond what I can express. Fortunate am I to-day, for the first time I have heard sweet words from your lips. If I die to-day I shall die in happiness, oh father, allow me to touch the dust of your feet."

"Who child? *You* the daughter of the *kotwal!* Are you Mālañcha?" Thrice did the king touch the ground with his hands and touch his head again. He said, "Come now child, come to the palace." Mālañcha sang.

Song

"This forest plain is my home now, for you have sweetly addressed me here. This place is heaven to me. I have got what I had wanted, and I care not for life in the palace now. Here on this earth, made sacred by your shoe-dust, shall I build a cottage and live for ever."

The king's eyes became filled with tears. "Child, I have given you much pain without knowing your virtues; pardon me and come to my palace." Mālañcha replied:—

Song

"I have heard you address me sweetly in this forest, how can I leave this dear forest, father! But I shall go, not now, but a few days hence."

The king said, "Why should you stay here? The kingdom is yours, pardon me and come to my palace." "What do you say, father, about pardoning? It is not right for me to hear such words from you, revered sir." She bowed at the feet of the king and said, "Father, I shall go to the palace after a few days, meantime I shall enquire about my uncle and aunt, and about the flower-woman whom also I call aunt." The king said, "Allow me then to go back. I shall meanwhile prepare roads, dig tanks and make other preparations for receiving your uncle and aunt with their train."

Preparation for reception.

The king returned to his city. He distributed his treasure amongst his people, opened roads, dug tanks and set up camps everywhere. On both sides of the roads he placed heaps of cowries for distribution amongst the poor, while the roads themselves were reddened by vermilion.

The musical bands played, and he himself with his seven grandsons and the citizens waited at the gate to receive Mālañcha.

**

Meantime Mālañcha went to the forest, and saw the tiger and the tigress wild with grief for her. She took them with her. She went to the cottage of the flower-woman. She found her beating her head against a stone for grief. Mālañcha wiped away her tears with her own hand. She went to the palace of the king Dudhabaraṇ. It was desolate, there was none there to kindle the evening-lamp—no heir to the vast kingdom. She wept as she saw all these. On the night of the full moon, she tore off a few shreds from her own clothes and kindled eight lamps with them. She kept them burning with butter. She took her seat in the great hall in the middle of the palace and sat in the attitude of *yoga*. Three days and nights passed and the doors of the palace suddenly opened. All its inmates, devoured by the tigers came to life. Mālañcha took with her the king Dudhabaraṇ, the seven princes and the rest. She paid off the money she had borrowed for getting palanquins and couches. In the way the attendants of her father-in-law, destroyed by the tigers, were restored to life as she sprinkled over them the oil of the eight charmed lamps. What a great uproar of men arose there! When she was at a distance of seven days' journey from her father-in-law's palace, they could know that it was Mālañcha coming with her hosts.

She restores the dead to life.

As Mālañcha approached the palace-gate, the drums of the royal band announced her arrival triumphantly. It seemed as if the very waters of the tanks danced for joy; the lotuses bloomed; the armed soldiers, sentinels and guards, the ministers, the courtiers, in fact all the citizens, the king and the queen themselves cried out in exultation. For Mālañcha, the true bride, had come to her father-in-law's house.

She entered the palace, the *kotwal* and his wife also came there. Dhārā, Tārā, Bidhātā, and other gods appeared above to witness this happy event. Her parents, her father-in-law, mother-in-law and all kinsmen approached her. Some placed blades of grass over her head in order to bless her, others touched the dust of her feet with reverence. The whole palace was filled with joyous sounds. The *Pakṣirāj* came and said to the king, "Your Majesty, I have restored to life all whom I killed during the last twelve years."

The king passed the mandate, "Beat the royal drums in honour of Mālañchamālā." The order was instantly carried out.

Mālañcha came to Kānchī, the princess, and said, "Sister, weave a flower-garland to-day." Kānchī wove a garland. Mālañcha took that garland and hung it round the neck of Chandramānik. She held Kānchī to her bosom and kissed her. For seven days and nights the palace was lost

The garlanding and making the co-wife chief queen.

in joy. The poor people ate butter and other preparations of milk to their heart's content. The tigers devoured the armies of those monarchs who were enemies of our king, but they returned to his capital to satisfy their thirst with water. They were given golden couches to sleep on.

The king embraced the *kotwal* calling him a friend and brother, and made him a feudatory chief. He received the tigers kindly. They expressed high gratification at His Majesty's behaviour, while bidding adieu to him. The flower-woman did not go back to her home but lived in that city and made a garden there for herself. Dudhabaraṇ, the king, was immensely happy and after a stay of a few days there returned to his own capital.

Mālañcha made Kānchī chief queen, but the people installed Mālañcha in their hearts and called her the goddess of the palace. Heaven blessed them all. All men, birds and beasts and even insects were happy.

Then did the rays of the sun and the beams of the moon fall on the high towers of the palace causing them to glitter, as it were, with gold. The king, the prince Chandramānik and His Majesty's grand-children built a road decorated with gold and precious stones leading to the spot where stood the mango-tree and the *kotwal's* house. They lived for long years and flourished.

A REVIEW

We have given here a rather long story. As I have already said, the story as translated seems to be but a meagre reproduction of the original. The tenderness of the Bengali style, used by women, its exquisite grace and suggestiveness are lost in the translation, and reading it side by side with the original, I find it dull, uninteresting and even verging on the grotesque. But it will not be fair to judge the original story by this translation.

There are other stories which are replete with amusing events and romance of love-stories that will excite the curiosity of the young and catch their fancy, but this story is very singular from several points of view. It brings forward vividly the Indian conception of the ideal womanhood in a most striking manner.

Mālañchamālā is not to be classed with any other heroine of any other Indian tale or poem. Behulā alone in our vernacular literature approaches her in point of devotion to her lord and bears a family-likeness to her. But Mālañcha's virtues are of such high order and brought out in

Mālañcha's ideal character.

such a charming colour of rural simplicity and devotion that other heroines should be placed in more or less distance from this towering character. Like a diamond discovered in a Golconda coal-mine, she has been one of our richest finds, lying ignored in the unwritten and despised *patois* of this province. The heroines of our classics no doubt are glorious for their great sufferings and devotion, but where is one like Mālañcha who has taken the load of all possible sorrows on her head, silently—without a word? Like a rose or lotus—the sport of wind—the food of worms—the plaything of a child, exposed to all evils imaginable, she is Heaven's gift and the heavenly smile never fades from her lips, the heavenly forbearance never forsakes her. She is to be compared only to a flower; the petals are dried up, it smiles at death; it is worm-eaten, or torn off by a child, but nothing will make it divested of its loveliness and resigned spirit; it is a gift of Heaven to this vile earth of ours; you may destroy or maltreat it, but you cannot vitiate it by your own vices; you cannot teach it cruelty, however cruel you may be; you cannot make it give up its smile or change same into a grimace, by frowning at it in the most terrible manner; for it is not of this earth. Its purity and its beauty have come down from the land of immortal beauty, from the shore of eternal sacredness; like the stream of the Ganges, it cannot be soiled by earth's dust.

In the first place, an absolute indifference to body, its comforts and the ills to which it may be subjected, forms the main feature of Mālañcha's action. It is the spirit that needs be nourished; that which is destined to perish or decay need not be a matter of vital importance to us in deciding our course; body is the vehicle and instrument to our spirit, so far its value; but the good of the soul should be the primary object in view while deciding our course of action. Christ has commanded us to take off the unrighteous eye to save the soul. If necessary this body of ours may be sacrificed or allowed to be put to any torment for the sake of keeping our virtues intact. When Mālañchamālā is about to be married, she states certain conditions. These conditions are necessary for the preservation of her self-respect, for keeping up the dignity of her parents raised to a new status in life, for being able to do her duties as wife in the palace to the fullest extent. But if like the average woman she would feel elated and glorified simply because a prince happened to marry her, without caring for the honour and responsibility attached to her status, she would sink into a very common level indeed! The king chose her as bride for the prince; he must

She cares not for the body.

give her all the dignity, all the love and all the honour attached to this high place; she would not put up with any thing short of it. She claimed this not as a matter of favour or condescension but of right; she was conscious of the spirit of contempt prevailing in the court against her owing to her humble birth, for she was merely a *kotwal's* daughter; she would not brook that. And what a trial! Her eyes were taken out. She still insisted on the fulfilment of the conditions; her beautiful hands were cut off, but she insisted on, as if nothing had happened. This absolute indifference to body and heroic devotion to truth rank her as a martyr of the first order. This ideal womanhood is no unrealised dream in this country. Times without number instances have occurred in our history showing such firm rectitude and devotion in the fair sex. Sir F. Halliday, afterwards Lieutenant-Governor of this province, argued with a *sati* prepared for self-immolation on the funeral pyre of her husband, but failing in his attempts to dissuade her by arguments at last said, "You have no idea of what your sufferings will be." The woman who was young and beautiful smiled and ordered a lamp to be brought near her. To this she put her finger. Writes Sir F. Halliday, "The finger scorched, blistered and blackened and finally twisted up in a way which I can only compare to what I have seen happen to a quill in the name of a candle. During this time she never moved her hand, nor uttered a cry or altered the expression of her countenance." This happened quite in recent times. The heroine of a fiction in the Buddhistic period is verily a cousin of this historic woman who lived in our Gangetic valley in the 19th century.

The trial.

Then in the dark night when the very horses of the stall run mad and the goblins are at their wildest play and the city-gates are shut and the funeral pyres spread their smoke and gloom all around, she defies that spirit of evil—that great tempter who not only tried to lead astray and take a Buddha and a Christ to infernal regions, but in less pronounced forms appears to us in our little struggles for attaining a moral life every now and then. But see how she triumphantly sits with her baby husband surrounded by the invisible that had taken grim visible shapes, amidst all fears fearless,—amidst all horrors undaunted. The temptations and horrors that came to shake her resolve failed and passed away like gusts of wind dashing in vain against a lofty peak. The full beauty and blossom of the ideal of the Buddhistic renunciation, of undaunted heroism is here. The miraculous and the supernatural serve only to bring out and accentuate the triumphant conquest of the soul over material forces, however great these may be. It is like the *siddhi* or reaching of the final goal of a *yogī* as we find in Tāntrikism. In the north the funeral ground is still the resort of many an aspirant in the path of *siddhi*, of soul's strenuous struggling at any cost for a conquest over the flesh. The temptations, the appeals and the horrors are symbolical of the farewell-shot of animal passions on the eve of the soul rising above them. The attainment of the *nirvāṇa* of the Buddha is said to have been preceded by a visitation from the evil spirits, and since then it has been a common occurrence in the history of a Tāntrik's highest spiritual achievements. Mālañchamālā and Behulā are the two characters, described in our folk-literature, as facing such trials and triumphing over them.

What one longs for one gets.

This material form in which our soul is enshrined is but the result of our longings to come in contact with the outer world. Intense desire to attain a thing and unsparing labour bring the remotest, the highest thing within the hollow of our palms. The animal that wants to escape from its pursuers, who will give it no rest till they kill it, longing with whole soul to go beyond their reach, gets wings and flies up. The small fish gets the power to go against the tide which an elephant cannot. I say all this power grows by longings and will-force in quite a miraculous way. Mālañcha loses her eyes and her hands; but as she strongly wishes to have a sight of her husband, the eyes grow—ready to serve him, the hands grow. In the case of such a soul, to whom the body is the mere vehicle of a strong will, the workings of the unseen forces of nature are most strikingly observed. The esoteric law is here explained without a spirit of propagandism and though it is all but a fiction, it grapples with the problem of and illustrates the hidden strength of the soul in the most convincing manner.

Wife as mother.

Then the child is newly born. You have heard that Sanskrit *sloka* which says that a true wife is also a mother. She is a sister and a friend as well. Here as in nowhere else in the world's literature do we find wife in the capacity of mother. Yes the child is born to her, it was stone dead; it is motherly love that has given birth to it; it is reborn in the lap of Mālañchamālā, not born of the flesh, as an ordinary child is born, but born of love, of spirit; it is therefore a truer child than an ordinary one.

We pursue Mālàñcha in the capacity of mother; but she has the background of a love greater than that of a mother—it is wife's; gradually it comes to the front. With the growth of the feelings of the wife she retires from her habitual field of action and the flower-woman becomes the instrument through whom she renders her service,—herself remaining behind the screen satisfied like a devotee with "sight"—'*darśana*'—which is the highest bliss in the spiritual world.

Throughout this story there is no agency but the human, though in the beginning mention is made of some local gods. These are, however, mere recorders of fortune proving the inscrutable ways of Providence and seem to possess no independent power. The characters solve their own destinies by their *karma* and this is again a Buddhistic idea.

The Buddhist ideas.

Towards the end of the story Mālañcha would not enter the palace for a few days; she thus keeps in abeyance the realisation of the cherished dream of her life for one purpose. Not to taste any joy herself, until and unless the sorrows and wrongs of all the people with whom she came in contact or whom she knew, were fully remedied. This renunciation is again a purely Buddhistic idea; not to save oneself till the whole world is saved was the motto of the Mahāyāna Buddhists of those days.

The true wife in the Hindu society is one who is not only loyal to her husband, but is good to all the members of her husband's family, discharging her duties in the fullest manner to each. It is for this that we see Mālañcha so eager to have her due place in her father-in-law's home. There she wanted to bind all by ties of affection, to remove all jealousy and petty quarrels by her self-denial and to create an atmosphere of purity, peace and renunciation by her example. The true wife is to give herself away to all; the husband is of course the god whom she secretly worships in her soul, but she does not make a display of her devotion to him; it remains, however, as the secret spring of her love which makes the whole family her *own* in every sense of the word. The husband's house is thus her highest temple. In the attitude of one who comes to a shrine she approaches it as a bride; if she can discharge her duties in a way which will win for her a good name there, is she then and then only called a good wife, but not if she merely becomes her husband's darling. It is for this reason that Mālañcha prizes her father-in-law's home; it is the sanctuary in which she is to develop her virtues by service and self-dedication. This was the old idea. When all these are merely recited by the priests and blindly followed or imposed on by the mother-in-law or some other elderly woman with a rod in hand, it becomes devoid of all beauty. But when a spirit of self-dedication blooms forth of itself without any external agency to help an artificial growth, it shows itself beautiful as the lily in an Indian tank.

Why she prizes her father-in-law's home.

Self-dedication natural to Mālañcha.

Mālañcha's womanly virtues are thus shown in the most attractive manner. No priest ever told her what she should do, and what she should not do. The love she felt for her baby-husband was more than motherly at the outset but with this difference that she knew from the beginning that the child would grow in time and occupy his proper place in regard to her. When he grew to be five years old, she avoided his presence lest he called her *mother* which would be his first instinctive address—naturally opprobrious to wife. The fountain of all her action was of course profound love that pervaded her whole life. It was no animal passion. The mere sight of the beloved, to see him happy in all conditions even in the arms of her co-wife, was the highest recompense of this love; for she did not want reciprocation but merely the good of the object of his worship. The jealousies of an ordinary woman could not be in her. When the *Pakṣirāj* came back without her husband on its back, she was mad with grief; but when she learnt that he had married the princess,—that husband whom she had brought up as no mother could do, whom she had saved from the gaping mouths of the evil spirits and animals, for whom her eyes were taken out and hands cut off and her father beheaded, for whom in fact she had suffered as few martyrs ever did—that husband was

She wants no reciprocation.

happy in the palace in the arms of the princess, she stood silent for a time but did not weep. She told the tiger that she was "fortunate" for the mission of her life was fulfilled, her husband was made happy and there was no more any need of her existence; she said touchingly to herself, "How happy is the prince now with the princess! how happy shall I be to die in the blue waters of our beautiful tank!"

She does not resist evil.

She never resisted evil but bore all patiently. She gave love to those who were hostile towards her, like the tree that gives its flowers and fruits to one who cuts it with axe; by her nature she was good and could not be otherwise. When evil came she tried her very best to ward it off from her beloved by her own great sufferings and by all that she had in her power to do. She did not lament like an ordinary woman, nor vehemently protested against her oppressors however autocratic and cruel they might be, but Christ-like bore all ills without complaint, sparing no pains to protect her great trust—the life of her child-husband from all kinds of danger. Whenever an occasion came she was always up with her greatest resources of energy, never appealed to God whom she did not see, but depended to the fullest extent on her own *karma* which is a reality with every one. In doing what she thought to be her duty, she

Doing duty, heedless of the result.

was not to be daunted by any circumstances, for she cared not the ills to which body is subject. When the boy was five years old and required to be placed under a tutor, she did not care a bit as to what might happen to her, but left the protection of her "uncle and aunt" under which she was happy and above anxiety for a long time. A solitary wayfarer with the baby in her arm she wandered, without knowing where to go and would not rest till she found a suitable place from which she could give education to the child, for he was a prince and must have due training. Almost mute, brief in her speech when she cared to speak, she offers a striking contrast to some of the heroines of our modern romances, whose enthusiastic speeches, like the babbling ripples on the surface of shallow waters often indicate a lack of depth. Our

Mālañcha speaks but little.

Bengali writers of romances may take a lesson from these tales; the heroines here seldom speak out their love. The tree offers flowers and fruits without words, the sun its rays without words and He that is behind this nature and supplies rain, sunshine, moon-beams and a thousand other things to us out of His infinite love, speaks not except to the mystic soul. True love works and sacrifices, but does not spend itself in frothy words. The mother seldom speaks of her love for the child; Mālañcha speaks but little. But when for the first time in her life, her father-in-law speaks to her kind words in a spirit of repentance, she melts into tears and tells him, "Why should I go to the palace? This forest is far dearer, for have you not spoken here sweet words to me!" She is indifferent to material comforts so what is a palace or a mansion to her? Where her spirit finds a congenial thing she values that, and thus a piece of wood-land is elevated in her eyes to a shrine because she has got there what her soul wanted. The prayer she offers in her song in the nuptial chamber of her husband, sleeping in the arms of Kānchi, is a unique one, and shows her to be in a far higher plane than Enoch Arden of Tennyson. In these days all weaknesses of the body and all lower passions in men are sometimes valued in literature as giving human interest to it. But all human beings are not in the same level of existence. Here in this land women have always evinced a high spirit of sacrifice at the altar of domestic love, and their self-immolation on the funeral pyre of their husbands and practice of austere *Brahmacharya*, have evoked wonder of all unprejudiced minds. In this country Mālañchamālā is no day-dream of poets, no dealistic or unrealisable mental phantom "without human interest," simply because the human being in this case happens to possess a super-human strength of soul.

She prefers a wood-land to a palace.

The poetic situations.

Though Mālañchamālā, like many heroines in Indian literature lacks in professions of love, yet the romantic situations of the dawn of love are not wanting in this very interesting tale. She does not come before her child-husband but keeps gazing at him as he reads or sits to eat. When the flower-woman would by no means come to the fiery horse, and Mālañcha was obliged to come before him after long years, the delicacy of the situation makes her modest grace at this interview charmingly beautiful; large drops of sweat stood on her brow indicating her confusion, and she touched the feet of her husband on the pretext of dusting his shoes. I do not know if my foreign readers will realise the true import of this situation. To a Hindu wife nothing can be a more pleasing privilege than to touch the feet of her husband. In the present case she did it with a confused sense of delicacy and ardour of her warm soul, which is exceedingly woman-like according to oriental conception of modesty. Then for the first time after many years she glanced at his face and met him eye to eye; she could have avoided doing so, but her great control of self yielded a little for a moment, she had not the heart to give up this opportunity, for he was going to win a game and might not return; when he asked her who she was,—she could not say, "I am your wife"; feminine delicacy choked her voice and in half audible whispers she could merely say, "I am *kotwal's* daughter." On another occasion in the night she had entered the room of her husband and found him with his new consort. Both were sleeping; he suddenly awoke and asked Mālañcha, "Who are you to enter this room?" In great mental confusion she only briefly said, "One that can enter." This was her whole speech. The words were true for as wife she had every right to enter the room of her husband; then when the prince caught her by the edge of her *sari*, she bent down her head and said with down-cast eyes, "Prince, you do me wrong." The pictures are all delicately wrought, and nowhere is the veil of shyness which forms the true fascination of a woman's nature withdrawn. The fine shades of a true woman's heart, her mental psychology which silently offers service and devotion, and proves without words, that she can sacrifice every inch of herself for the beloved one, are traced in the most significant manner in this unassuming Bengali tale. Mālañcha's all-pervading love is ever employed in doing good to all, not merely those to whom she was personally indebted. When she was going to return to her husband's home, she restored the dead to life by the great esoteric power that had grown in her by her conquest over the flesh. So that none was miserable, none was unhappy. The wicked are not punished but reformed by love, proving its marvellous power of doing good in the human world, and surely this is a higher view of an esthetic situation in ethical planes.

The wicked are not punished but reformed.

She returns to the palace after many years, not to enjoy material comforts and what is strange not even to be in the arms of her husband. What other poets or dramatists would not make the husband and wife restored to each other's embrace after so much sufferings? Kānchi's career might have closed in the mouths of hungry tigers or in some other tragic way suggested by the fruitful brain of an author, in order to make the path clear for Mālañcha. But we find in this tale "Mālañcha made Kānchi chief queen." She willingly and gladly offered her own place to the co-wife. "But the people worshipped her as their goddess." Thus does indeed the heroine of the tale rise to the level of a true goddess that she was—a conqueror of the flesh; she who could break all her teeth in order to break a few links of the chain by which her husband was bound, was not a character to be won by the thought of the pleasures of the flesh. She was a thing dedicated and offered to love, from which

The "chief queen" and the "goddess."

all elements of the flesh were completely removed.

The story is like an epic poem in Bengali with many exquisite lyrical notes, and the language is so forcible, brief and colloquial, that it is not in the power of any Bengali writer to change a word, without marring its naive simplicity and effect. Unfortunately, as I have already stated, this story will have an exotic air in my translation; it will appear like a Bengali lady, who looked so lovely in her *sari*, putting on a gown and having an outlandish air; but this could not be helped.

The translator's apologies.

The weaving of the plot shows considerable art. Mālañcha is of course the central figure who connects the different episodes of the story and keeps up its continued interest. When the baby dies, the story might naturally end there, but we have a need of her for bringing it back to life. The natural end of the story is thus put off till the prince marries Kānchi. Here again the story would end, but he is put into the prison and there we have again a need of Mālañcha's help to set the prince free. Mālañcha does it and the king returns with the prince and the new bride to the palace and dismisses poor Mālañcha. The story would naturally end here. But now comes the moral need of showing that a devotee's labour has not gone for naught. Mālañcha is

The plot.

a true bride. She must enter the house to light the bridal lamp. After all that she has suffered and done, an ordinary reception will not do. The whole city, not to speak of the palace alone, should give the most cordial reception to the true bride by erecting triumphal arches and beating the royal drums in her honour. All the ceremonies that a devotee performs in the temples should be celebrated in honour of one who has proved by her action, too many to enumerate, that she is not an ordinary type of human being but a goddess. Any reception short of what was given her in the last part of the story would have been unworthy of her. Her reception has been late, but the author deferred it a long time, only to make it fitting in the fullest measure, in order to pave her path to the palace by repentant tears, and wreath the garland of welcome by the overflowing joy of all the citizens who rejoiced on the return of one who had brought the dead to life again.

The whole story is thus threaded by the episodes of sacrifices for love on Mālañcha's part and at the end takes us by surprise by the statement that she did not return to the palace to share the joys of nuptial life with her co-wife, but show her greatest renunciation by inaugurating the rival as chief queen in her place.

These tales different from Paurauic stories.

These tales have an old world charm which is irresistible to all of us. The revival of Paurānic religion has introduced a spirit of faith, and of devotion of a metaphysical type. But these tales disclose a beauty all of their own in which propagandism finds no place. Woman's fidelity is shown in its truest colour; men are righteous, good and amiable; but they have no stereotyped models put before them by the priests; the characters are rewarded or punished for their action, but there is scarcely any reference to the scriptures, nor are analogies sought to be established between them and those described in the Purānas. All these marks out the epoch of literature which produced the tales as a very unique one; it has some very distinctive features of its own, characterised by literary excellence of a quite different character than is to be found in the literature of the Renaissance. The lovers swear, not by any gods or goddesses, but by the earth, "Because it is sacred where the flowers bloom." When a princess takes the *kotwal's* son to task for making a proposal of marriage, and says, "How bold must you be to approach me in this way! I will bring this to the notice of the king. How could you be so daring?" "If the king takes me to task," replied the *kotwal's* son boldly,

Their simplicity as contrasted with the complicated model of Renaissance.

"here is my answer; my ancestors have shed their blood for generations to make Your Majesty's line of kings—this is my claim." No question of caste or social status which would have been inevitable in the days of the Renaissance was raised. When the princess was convinced that it was her duty to marry the *kotwal's* son because her parents had already pledged their words, the preceptor marked a change in her demeanour. On other days the cymbals sounded on her feet merrily as she entered the school room, to-day no sound of her steps was heard, so quietly did she enter the room with down-cast eyes, "and the sweet voice of hers in recitation did not charm everyone in the class room as was usual, but the voice trembled and its sweetness was gone, it sounded like a dry log." There is a rural method of expressing ordinary ideas which has also a special appeal for us "From a thousand eyes the gods stole sleep and put it in the eyes of the princess" is meant to show that the sleeping princess was absolutely unaware of the danger that awaited her. In order to indicate the resolute muteness of a woman, we have this metaphor "like the sleeping night she says nothing, nor moves."

The way of reckoning time.

The way in which these rural people used to reckon time, when there was no watch or clock to guide them is interesting. In one place we find the following " the day advanced, the peacock and her mate dropped feathers from their plumed tail; the birds *suka* and *sari* flung off the dust from their wings as they bathed in the muddy pools." By these little things the country people gave an exact idea of time; for the birds did as described, at particular and specified points of time recorded in the daily observations of the men who live in villages. In another place we find "before twilight had passed and the crows had crowed their last note indicating departure into the nests." These softly lift the veil from nature, disclosing to the observer how she gives response to each hour that passes, in a way far more interesting than by the dull hand of a clock.

Condemnation of wicked deeds.

The manner in which the rural people indicated their condemnation and honest disparagement of a wicked deed is sometimes very curiously expressed. The flowerwoman in the story of Kāñchanmālā wants to drive away the princess from her husband's home and get her own niece married to him. This wicked motive is frustrated in this way.

"If the flower-woman engages any house-wife to take part in the marriage of her niece, within three days the red mark of luck disappears from that wife's forehead (she becomes a widow). The

Brahmin whom she appoints to perform the marriage function finds his cowshed void of cows and his school void of pupils. So no Brahmin would open his almanac to fix the auspicious day and no house-wife take part in the ceremony. The flower-woman goes to the oil-man for oil and to the grocer for turmeric, the oil-man's bullock dies and the grocer loses his bargain. The flowers drop from the bride's crown and the lamps cease to burn on the sacred plate."

These are no doubt foolish, but imagine the glee and mirth with which children listened to this account of the wicked witch's disappointment. There may be many things said that are foolish; the child says many such things and listens to many such things from his grandmother, but is not the heart of true poetry there? Sometimes a situation is made romantically poetic by a mere touch; I do not know if the foreign readers of our folk-tales will appreciate the simple poetry in these few lines.

Romance.

"She came and bowed down before her husband. He saw this spot near his feet reddened with the vermilion of her forehead."

Index.

A

B

E

Page.

Page.

N

O

P

Q

R

S

Y

Z

OPINIONS

"HISTORY OF THE BENGALI LANGUAGE AND LITERATURE" (IN ENGLISH)

BY

RAI SAHIB DINESH CHANDRA SEN, B.A.

Published by

CALCUTTA UNIVERSITY

Price—Rs. 12. Demy 8vo. pp. 1030 with illustrations.

His Excellency Lord Hardinge of Penshurst in his Convocation Address, dated the 16th March, 1912 as Chancellor of the Calcutta University :—

"During the last four years also the University has, from time to time, appointed Readers on special subjects to foster investigation of important branches of learning amongst our advanced students. One of these Readers, Mr. Sen, has embodied his lectures on the History of Bengali Language and Literature from the earliest times tc the middle of the 19th century in a volume of considerable merit, which he is about to supplement by another original contribution to the history of one of the most important vernaculars in this country. May I express the hope that this example will be followed elsewhere, and that critical schools may be established for the vernacular languages of India which have not as yet received the attention that they deserve."

His Excellency Lord Carmichael, Governor of Bengal, in his address on the occasion of his laying the Foundation Stone of the Romesh Chandra Saraswat Bhawan, dated the 20th November, 1916 :—

"For long Romesh Chandra Dutt's History of the Literature of Bengal was the only work of its kind available to the general reader. The results of further study in this field have been made available to us by the publication of the learned and luminous lectures of Rai Sahib Dineschandra Sen. * * In the direction of the History of the Language and the Literature, Rai Sahib Dineschandra Sen has created the necessary interest by his Typical Selections. It remains for the members of the Parishad to follow this lead and to carry on the work in the same spirit of patient accurate research."

Sir Asutosh Mookerjee, in his Convocation Address, dated the 13th March, 1909, as Vice-Chancellor of the Calcutta University :—

"We have had a long series of luminous lectures from one of our own graduates, Babu Dineschandra Sen, on the fascinating subject of the History of the Bengali Language and Literature. These lectures take a comprehensive view of the development of our vernacular, and their publication will unquestionably facilitate the historical investigation of the origin of the vernacular literature of this country, the study of which is avowedly one of the foremost objects of the New Regulations to promote."

Sylvain Levi (*Paris*)—"I cannot give you praises enough—your work is a *Chintamani*—a *Ratnakara*. No book about India would I compare with yours......Never did I find such a realistic sense of literature... ..Pundit and Peasant, Yogi and Raja mix together in a Shakespearian way on the stage you have built up."

Extract from a review by the same scholar in the "**Revue Critique**" Jan. 1915 ;—(translated for the "Bengalee.")

"One cannot praise too highly the work of Mr. Sen. A profound and original erudition has been associated with vivid imagination. The historian though relying on his documents has the temperament of an epic poet. He has likewise inherited the lyric genius of his race."

. **Barth** (*Paris*)—"I can approach your book as a learner, not as a judge."

C. H. Tawney—"Your work shows vast research and much general culture."

Vincent Smith—"A work of profound learning and high value."

F. W. Thomas—"Characterised by extensive erudition and independent research."

E. J. Rapson—"I looked through it with great interest and great admiration for the knowledge and research to which it bears witness."

F. H. Skrine—"Monumental work—I have been revelling in the book which taught me much of which I was ignorant."

E. B. Havell—"Most valuable book which every Anglo-Indian should read. I congratulate you most heartily on your very admirable English and perfect lucidity of style."

D. C. Phillot—"I can well understand the enthusiasm with which the work was received by scholars, for even to men unacquainted with your language, it cannot fail to be a source of great interest and profit."

L. D. Barnett—"I congratulate you on having accomplished such an admirable work."

G. Hultzuh—"Mr. Sen's valuable work on Bengali literature, a subject hitherto unfamiliar to me, which I am now reading with great interest."

J. F. Blumhardt—"An extremely well-written and scholarly production, exhaustive in its wealth of materials and of immense value."

T. W. Rhys Davids—"It is a most interesting and important work and reflects great credit on your industry and research."

Jules Bloch (*Paris*)—"Your book I find an admirable one and which is the only one of its kind in the whole of India."

William Rothenstein—"I found the book surprisingly full of suggestive information. It held me bound from beginning to end, in spite of my absolute ignorance of the language of which you write with obviously profound scholarship."

Emile Senart (*Paris*)—"I have gone through your book with lively interest and it appears to me to do the highest credit to your learning and method of working."

Henry Van Dyke—(*U. S. A.*)—"Your instructive pages which are full of new suggestions in regard to the richness and interest of the Bengali Language and Literature."

C. T. Winchester—(*U. S. A.*)—"A work of profound learning on a theme which demands the attention of all Western scholars."

From a long review in the **Times Literary Supplement,** London, June 20, 1912—"In his narration, as becomes one who is the soul of scholarly candour, he tells those, who can read him with sympathy and imagination more about the Hindu mind and its attitude towards life than we can gather from 50 volumes of impressions of travel by Europeans. Loti's picturesque account of the rites practised in Travancore temples, and even M. Chevrillon's synthesis of much browsing in Hindu Scriptures, seem faint records by the side of this unassuming tale of Hindu literature—Mr. Sen may well be proud of the lasting monument he has erected to the literature of his native Bengal."

From a long review in the **Athenæum,** March, 16, 1912—"Mr. Sen may justly congratulate himself on the fact that in the middle age he has done more for the history of his national language and literature than any other writer of his own or indeed any time."

From a long review in the **Spectator,** June 12, 1912—"A book of extraordinary interest to those who would make an impartial study of the Bengali mentality and character—a work which reflects the utmost credit on the candour, industry and learning of its author. In its kind his book is a masterpiece—modest, learned, thorough and sympathetic. Perhaps no other man living has the learning and happy industry for the task he has successfully accomplished."

From a review by **Mr. H. Beveridge** in the Royal Asiatic Society's Journal, Jan. 1912.—" It is a very full and interesting account of the development of the Bengali Literature. He has a power of picturesque writing...his descriptions are often eloquent."

From a long review by **S. K. Ratcliffe** in " India," London, March 15, 1912—" There is no more competent authority on the subject than Mr. Dineschandra Sen. The great value of the book is in its full and fresh treatment of the pre-English era and for this it would be difficult to give its author too high praise."

From a long review by **H. Kern** in the *Bijdragen of the Royal Institute for Taal* (translated by Dr. Kern himself)—"Fruit of investigation carried through many years...highly interesting book...the reviewer has all to admire in the pages of the work, nothing to criticise, for his whole knowledge is derived from it."

From a review by **Dr. Oldenberg** in the *Frankfurter Zistung*, December 3, 1911 (Translated by the late Dr. Thibaut)..." It is an important supplementation of the history of modern Sanskrit Literature. The account of Chaitanya's influence on the poetical literature of Bengal contributes one of the most brilliant sections of the work."

From a review in **Deutsche Rundschan,** April, 1912—" The picture which this learned Bengali has painted for us with loving care of the literature of his native land deserves to be received with attentive and grateful respect."

From a review in **Luzac's Oriental List,** London, May-June, 1912—"A work of inestimable value, full of interesting information, containing complete account of the writings of Bengali authors from the earliest time...It will undoubtedly find a place in every Oriental library as being the most complete and reliable standard work on the Bengali Language and Literature"

From a review in the **Indian Magazine,** London, August, 1912—"For Mr. Sen's erudition, his sturdy patriotism, his instructive perception of the finer qualities in Bengali life and literature, the reader of his book must have a profound respect if he is to understand what modern Bengal is."

From a long review in the **Madras Mail,** May 9, 1912, "A survey of the evolution of the Bengali letters by a student so competent, so exceptionally learned can hardly fail to be an important event in the world of criticism."

From a long review in the **Pioneer,** May 5, 1912—"Mr. Sen is a typical student such as was common in mediæval Europe—a lover of learning for learning's sake...He must be a poor judge of characters who can rise from a perusal of Mr. Sen's pages without a real respect and liking for the writer, for his sincerity, his industry, his enthusiasm in the cause of learning."

From a review in **Englishman,** April 23, 1912—"Only one who has completely identified himself with the subject could have mastered it so well as the author of this imposing book."

From a review in the **Empire,** August 31, 1918—"As a book of reference Mr. Sen's work will be found invaluable and he is to be congratulated on the result of his labours. It may well be said that he has proved what an English enthusiast once said that 'Bengali unites the mellifluousness of Italian with the power possessed by German for rendering complex ideas."

From a review in the **Indian Antiquary,** December, 1912, by **F. G. Pargiter** :—" This book is the outcome of great research and study, on which the author deserves the warmest praise. He has explained the literature and the subjects treated in it with such fulness and in such detail as to make the whole plain to any reader. The folk-literature, the structure and style of the language, metre and rhyme, and many miscellaneous points are discussed in valuable notes. The tone is calm and the judgments appear to be generally fair."

BANGA SAHITYA PARICHAYA.

OR

TYPICAL SELECTIONS FROM OLD.
BENGALI LITERATURE

BY

Rai Sahib Dineschandra Sen, B.A,

2 vols. pp. 1914, Royal 8vo., with an Introduction in English running over 99 pages, published by the University of Calcutta.
(*With 10 coloured illustrations*) *Price Rs.* 12).

Sir George Grierson—"Invaluable work......That I have yet read through its 1900 pages I do not pretend, but what I have read has filled me with admiration for the industry and learning displayed It is a worthy sequel to your monumental History of Bengali Literature, and of it we may safely say "*finis coronat opus.*" How I wish that a similar work could be compiled for other Indian languages, specially for Hindi."

E. B. Havell—" Two monumental volumes from old Bengali Literature. As I am not a Bengali scholar, it is impossible for me to appreciate at their full value the splendid results of your scholarship and research, but I have enjoyed reading your luminous and most instructive introduction which gives a clear insight into the subject. I was also very much interested in the illustrations, the reproduction of which from original paintings is very successful and creditable to Swadeshi work."

H. Beveridge—" Two magnificent volumes of the Banga Sahitya Parichaya......I have read with interest Rasa Sundari's autobiography in your extracts."

F. H. Skrine—" The two splendid volumes of Banga Sahitya Parichaya I am reading with pleasure and profit. They are a credit to your profound learning and to the University which has given them to the world."

From a long review in **The Times Literary Supplement,** London, November 4, 1915—"In June, 1912, in commenting on Mr. Sen's History of Bengali Language and Literature, we suggested that that work might usefully be supplemented by an authology of Bengali prose and poetry. Mr. Sen has for many years been occupied with the aid of other patriotic students of the mediæval literature of Bengal in collecting manuscripts of forgotten or half-forgotten poems. In addition to these more or less valuable monuments of Bengali poetic art, the chief popular presses have published great masses on literary matter, chiefly religious verse. It can hardly be said that these piles of written and printed matter have ever been subjected to a critical or philological scrutiny. Their very existence was barely known to the Europeans, even to those who have studied the Bengali Language on the spot. Educated Bengalis themselves, until quite recent times, have been too busy with the arts and sciences of Europe to spare much time for indigenous treasures. That was the reason why we suggested the compiling of a critical chrestomathy for the benefit not only of European but of native scholars. The University of Calcutta prompted by the eminent scholar Sir Asutosh Mookerjee, then Vice-Chancallor, had already anticipated this need it seems. It had shrunk (rightly, we think) from the enormous and expensive task of printing the **MSS.** recovered by the diligence and generosity of Mr. Sen and other inquirers and employed Mr. Sen to prepare the two bulky volumes now before us. The Calcutta Senate is to be congratulated on its enterprise and generosity."

From a review in The **Athenæum**, January 16, 1915—" We have already reviewed Mr. Sen's History of Bengali Language and Literature and have rendered some account of his previous work in Bengali entitled *Bhanga Bhasa O Sahitya*. Mr. Sen now supplies the means of checking his historical and critical conclusions in a copious collection of Bengali verse......Here are the materials carefully arranged and annotated with a skill and learning such as probably no one else living can command."

From a review by **Mr. F. G. Pargiter**—in the Royal Asiatic Society's Journal—" These two portly volumes of some 2,100 pages are an anthology of Bengali poetry and prose from the 8th to the 19th century and are auxiliary to the same author's History of Bengali Language and Literature which was reviewed by Mr. Beveridge in this Journal for 1912......The Vice-Chancellor of the Calcutta University who was consulted, decided that the best preliminary measure would be to make and publish typical selections. The University then entrusted that duty to Babu Dinesh Chandra Sen; this work is the outcome of his researches....There can be no question that Dinesh Babu was the person most competent to undertake the task and in these two volumes we have without doubt a good presentment of typical specimens of old Bengali-literature....The style of the big book is excellent, its printing is fine, and it is embellished with well-executed reproductions in colour of some old painting. Is has also a copious index.

THE

VAISNAVA LITERATURE OF MEDIÆVAL BENGAL

[*Being lectures delivered as Reader to the University of Calcutta.*]

BY

RAI SAHIB DINESH CHANDRA SEN, B.A.

JUST PUBLISHED BY THE

CALCUTTA UNIVERSITY

Demy 8vo. 257 pages

WITH A PREFACE BY

J. D. ANDERSON, Esq., I,C.S., (*Retired*)

Price Rs. 2 only.

Sir George Grierson :—Very valuable book......I am reading it with the greatest interest and am learning much from it.

William Rothenstein.—I was delighted with your book, I cannot tell you how touched I am to be reminded of that side of your beloved country which appeals to me most—a side of which I was able to perceive something during my own too short visit to India. In the faces of the best of your countrymen I was able to see that spirit of which you write so charmingly in your book. I am able to recall these faces and figures as if they were before me. I hear the tinkle of the temple-bells along the ghats of Benares, the voices of the women as they sing their sacred songs crossing the noble river in the boats at sunset and I sit once more with the austere Sanyasin friends I shall never, I fear, see more. But though I shall not look upon the face of India again, the vision I had of it will fill my eyes through life, and the love I feel for your country will remain to enrich my own vision of life, so long as I am capable of using it. Though I can only read you in English, the spirit in which you write is to me so true an Indian spirit, that it shines through our own idiom, and carries me, I said before, straight to the banks of your sacred rivers, to the bathing tanks and white shrine and temples of your well remembered villages and tanks. So once more I send you y thanks for the magic carpet you sent me, upon which my soul can return to your dear land. May the songs of which you write to me remain to fill this land with their fragrance ; you will have need of them, in the years before you, as we have need of all that is best in the songs of our own seers in the dark waters through which we are steering.

From a long review in the Times Literary Supplement, 2nd August, 1917

The Vaisnava Literature of Mediæval Bengal. By Rai Sahib Dineschandra Sen. (Calcutta :—The University.)

Though the generalisation that all Hindus not belonging to modern reform movements are Saivas or Vaisnavas is much too wide, there are the two main divisions in the bewildering mass of sects which make up the 217,000,000 of Hindus, and at many points they overlap each other. The attempts made in the 1901 Census to collect information regarding sects led to such unsatisfactory and partial results that they were not repeated in the last decennial enumeration. But it is unquestionable that the Vaisnavas—the worshippers of Krishna—are dominant in Bengal, owing to the great success of the reformed cult established by Chaitanya, a contemporary of Martin Luther. The doctrine of Bhakti or religious devotion, which he taught still flourishes in Bengal, and the four lectures of the Reader to the University of Calcutta in Bengali here reproduced provide an instructive guide to its expression in the literature of the country during the sixteenth and seventeenth centuries. The first part of the book is devoted to the early period of Vaisnava literature, dating from the eleventh century.

The Rai Sahib is filled wiih a most patriotic love of his nation and its literature, and has done more than any contemporary countryman to widen our knowledge of them. His bulky volume recording the history of Bengali Language and Literature from the earliest times to the middle of the nineteenth century is accepted by Orientalists as the most complete and authoritative work on the subject. The industry and learning displayed therein and in his thought is still dominant in modern Bengali literature not directly Vaisnava in import.

There is refreshing ingenuousness in his claim, "my industry has been great," and the "forbearing indulgence" for which he asks if he has failed from any lack of powers, will readily be granted in view of the enthusiasm for his subject which somewhat narrows the strictly critical value of his estimates, but does not impair the sustained human interest of the book.

Chaitanya clearly taught, as these pages show, that the Krishna of the Mahabharata, the great chieftain and ally of the Pandava brother, was not the Krishna of Brindaban. The latter, said the reformer, to Rupa, the author of those masterpieces of Sanskrit drama, the Vidagdha Madhava and the Lalita Madhava, was love's very self and an embodiment of sweetness : and the more material glories of Mathura should not be confused with the spiritual conquests of Brindabon. The amours of Krishna with Radha and the milkmaids of Brindabon are staple themes of the literature associated with the worship of the God of the seductive flute. But Mr. Sen repeatedly insists that the love discussed in the literature he has so closely studied is spiritual and mystic, although usually presented in sensuous garb. Chaitanya who had frequent ecstasies of spiritual joy ; Rupa, who classified the emotions of love in 360 groups and the other authors whose careers are here traced were hermits of unspotted life and religious devotion. The old passionate desire for union which they taught is still dominant in modern Bengali literature not directly Vaisnava in import. As Mr. J. D. Anderson points out in his preface, the influence of Chaitanya's teaching may be detected in the mystical verses of Tagore.

Chaitanya and His Companions

From a long review in the Times Literary supplement 25th April, 1918:—

"This delightful and interesting little book is the outcome of a series of lectures supplementing the learned discourses which Mr. Sen made the material of his "Baisnava Literature of Mediæval Bengal" reviewed by us on August 2, 1917.

It is an authentic record of the religious emotion and thought of that wonderful province of Bengal which few of its Western rulers, we suspect, have rightly comprehended, not from lack of friendly sympathy but simply from want of precisely what Mr. Sen, better than any one living, better than Sir Rabindranath Tagore himself, can supply.

It is indeed, no easy matter for a Western Protestant to comprehend, save by friendship and sympathy with just such a pious Hindu as Mr. Sen, what is the doctrine of an *istadevata*, a "favourite deity" of Hindu pious adoration. In his native tongue Mr. Sen has written charming little books, based on ancient legends, which bring us very near the heart of this simple mystery, akin, we suppose, to the cult of particular saints in Catholic countries. Such for instance, is his charming tale of "Sati," the Aryan spouse cf the rough Himalayan ascetic god Siva. The tale is dedicated, in words of delightfully candid respect and affection, to the devoted and loving wives of Bengal, whose virtues as wives and mothers are the admiration of all who know their country. Your pious Vaisnava can, without any hesitation or difficulty, transfer his thoughts from the symbolical amorism of Krisna to that other strange creation-legend of Him of the Blue Throat who, to save God's creatures, swallowed the poison cast up at the Churning of the Ocean and bears the mystic stigma to this day. Well, we have our traditions, legends, mysteries, and as Miss Underhill and others tell us, our own ecstatic mystics, who find such ineffable joy in loving God as, our Hindu friends tell us, the divine Radha experienced in her sweet surrender to the inspired wooing of Krisna. The important thing for us, as students of life and literature is to note how these old communal beliefs influence and develop that wonderful record of human thought and emotion wrought for us by the imaginative writers of verse and prose, the patient artists of the pen.

When all is said, there remains the odd indefinable charm which attaches to all that Dinesh Chandra Sen writes, whether in English or his native Bengali. In his book breathe a native candour and piety which somehow remind us of the classical writers familiar to our boyhood. In truth, he is a belated contemporary of, say, Plutarch, and attacks his biographical task in much the same spirit. We hope his latest book will be widely (and sympathetically) read."

The Vaisnava Literature of Mediaeval Bengal

J. D. Anderson, Esq.—retired I. C. S., Professor, Cambridge University;—I have read more than half of it I propose to send with it, if circumstances leave me the courage to write it, a short Preface (which I hope you will read with pleasure even if you do not think it worth publication) explaining why, in the judgment of a very old student of all your works, your book should be read not only in Calcutta, but in London and Paris, and Oxford and Cambridge, I have read it and am reading it with great delight and profit and very real sympathy. Think how great must be the charm of your topic and your treatment when in this awful year of anxiety and sorrow, the reading of your delightful MS. has given me rest and refreshment in a time when every post, every knock at the door may bring us sorrow.

I write this in a frantic hurry—the mail goes to-day—in order to go back to your most interseting and fascinating pages.

History of the Bengali Language and Literature

Extract from a long review by Sylvain Levi (Paris) in the "Revue Critique" Jan. 1915;— translated for the Bengalee).

'One cannot praise too highly the work of Mr. Sen. A profound and original erudition has been associated with a vivid imagination. The works which he analyses are brought back to life with the consciousness of the original authors, with the movement of the multitudes who patronised them and with the landscape which encircled them. The historian, though relying on his documents, has the temperament of an epic poet. He has likewise inherited the lyrical genius of his race. His enthusiastic sympathy vibrates through all his descriptions. Convinced as every Hindu is of the superiority of the Brahmanic civilization, he exalts its glories and palliates its shortcomings, if he does not approve of them he would excuse them. He tries to be just to Buddhism and Islam; in the main he is grateful to them for their contribution to the making of India. He praises with eloquent ardour the early English missionaries of Christianity.

The appreciation of life so rare in our book-knowledge, runs throughout the work; one reads these thousand pages with a sustained interest; and one loses sight of the enormous labour which it presupposes; one easily slips into the treasure ef information which it presents. The individual extracts quoted at the bottom of the pages offers a unique anthology of Bengali. The linguistic remarks scattered in the extracts abound in new and precious materials. Mr. Sen has given to his country a model which it would be difficult to surpass; we only wish that it may provoke in other parts of India emulations to follow it."
